FROM THE WOMB TO THE BODY POLITIC

From the Womb
TO THE BODY POLITIC

Raising the Nation in Enlightenment Russia

Anna Kuxhausen

To Marc ~
With eternal
gratitude for your
generosity and
humanitarian spirit.
Without you & Irina
I never would have
made it!
Much love,
Anna

THE UNIVERSITY OF WISCONSIN PRESS

Publication of this volume has been made possible, in part, through support from the Andrew W. Mellon Foundation.

The University of Wisconsin Press
1930 Monroe Street, 3rd Floor
Madison, Wisconsin 53711-059
uwpress.wisc.edu

3 Henrietta Street
London WC2E 8LU, England
eurospanbookstore.com

Library of Congress Cataloging-in-Publication Data

Kuxhausen, Anna.
From the womb to the body politic : raising the nation in
Enlightenment Russia / Anna Kuxhausen.
    p.   cm.
Includes bibliographical references and index.
ISBN 978-0-299-28994-2 (pbk. : alk. paper) — ISBN 978-0-299-28993-5
(e-book)
    1. Child rearing—Russia—History—18th century. 2. Children—
Russia—Social conditions—18th century. 3. Russia—Social
conditions—18th century. I. Title.
HQ792.R9K89   2013
649′.1094709033—dc23
2012013016

A version of chapter 3 was originally published as "The Modern Miracles of Mother's Milk: The New Science of Maternity in Enlightenment Russia," *Ab Imperio*, no. 3 (Fall 2009): 94–118.

TO MY DAUGHTER *Nadia*

Contents

Illustrations

Acknowledgments

It is a satisfying and humbling pleasure to thank the people who have helped to make this book a reality. I am grateful to William G. Rosenberg, who believed in and helped to shape this project from its very beginning and through every stage. For their help during the research process, I am indebted to the directors and staff at the State Historical Archive of the City of Saint Petersburg and the Russian State Historical Archive, and to the librarians of the rare book collections of the Library of the Academy of Sciences and the Russian National Library. For help with research questions while in Russia, I thank Viktor Cherniaev, Natalia Pushkareva, and Olga Shnyrova. I am grateful to the following institutions and organizations for supporting my research and writing with generous fellowships and grants: the US Department of State Fulbright Program; the Woodrow Wilson Foundation Charlotte W. Newcombe Fellowship Program; the University of Michigan's Institute for Research on Women and Gender, Department of History, and Center for Russian, East European, and Eurasian Studies; the Ford Foundation; and St. Olaf College. I thank the Andrew W. Mellon Foundation for supporting the publication of this book through its Slavic Studies Initiative.

For their help in conceptualizing various aspects of this project and for critical reactions to early drafts, I thank Bill Rosenberg, Andreas Schönle, Dena Goodman, Christine Ruane, and Jochen Hellbeck. I am grateful to the three anonymous reviewers at *Ab Imperio* for their useful suggestions for improving an earlier version of chapter 3. For reading numerous drafts and providing helpful feedback, I am indebted to Rebecca Friedman, Gregory Vitarbo, Kate Thomas, and Peggy Lin. Bill Rosenberg and Adele Lindenmeyr deserve special recognition for reading the manuscript more than once, and for their generous assistance in helping me to clarify, refine, and reorganize many parts of this book. At the University of Wisconsin Press, I am grateful for the patient dedication of

Gwen Walker, Sheila McMahon, and Matthew Cosby. For the reproduction of illustrations, I thank Stephen Greenberg and the National Library of Medicine as well as the New York Public Library and its staff. For permission to reproduce paintings by Jean-Baptiste Le Prince and by D. G. Levitskii, I thank the J. Paul Getty Museum and the State Tretyakov Gallery in Russia, respectively.

A number of colleagues and friends have helped me in practical ways to bring this book into being. I thank my colleagues at St. Olaf for useful advice and encouragement, especially Marc Robinson, Irina Walter, and Judy Kutulas. For entertaining my daughter in Russia while I worked in the archives, I am grateful to Eranui Gabrielyan and to Naomi Cleghorn and her family. In Minnesota, many people provided loving care and enrichment for my child while I labored on this manuscript; I thank especially Kate Thomas, Natalie Ojala, the teachers and staff at Prairie Creek Community School, and my mother, Marlene Kuxhausen. For logistical help during the final months of manuscript preparation, I would like to thank my mother and Kate Thomas, who have both put many miles on their cars in this respect, and Abdulai Iddirisu. I thank Rich Young for his heartfelt encouragement. I thank all of my dearest friends and sisters (you know who you are) for their boundless support. For inspiring and delighting me in endless ways, I thank my daughter Nadia Kuxhausen Ralph, to whom I dedicate this book.

Note on Transliteration and Translation

The transliteration of Russian terms follows a modified version of the Library of Congress system. Following the convention of other historians, I have omitted diacritical marks and have allowed exceptions to the rules for readability (e.g., "Alexander" instead of "Aleksandr"). Unless otherwise noted, all translations are my own.

FROM THE WOMB TO THE BODY POLITIC

INTRODUCTION

From the Womb to the Body Politic aims to recover eighteenth-century Russian notions of the child, from the beginning of life to the threshold of adulthood, and to reveal the prescriptions and plans of different stakeholders in the new endeavor of saving infants and raising healthy children. Based on the arguments of eighteenth-century Russian Enlighteners concerning the importance of the early years of a child's life, this book seeks to enlarge our notion of eighteenth-century upbringing to include infancy and early childhood. Catherine II's associate Princess Ekaterina Dashkova, director of the Academy of Sciences and president of the Russian Academy, joined other Russian Enlighteners when she argued that parents and society needed to give more attention and care to the raising of children; *vospitanie* (upbringing), she argued, "starts earlier and ends later than is generally believed."[1] To date, little scholarship has treated the eighteenth-century interest in expanding the notion of upbringing. With the exception of David Ransel's work on Catherine's creation of foundling homes, most work on the topic of upbringing or education has focused on the years of childhood corresponding to the age of formal education.[2] Works that treat domesticity and family life during this era provide rich insight into marital relationships, sexuality, and bonds of attachment between older children and their parents, but shed little light on ideas and practices concerning pregnancy, childbirth, infant care, and early childhood.[3] Historians have researched some of these topics for the nineteenth and twentieth centuries in Russia, but for the eighteenth century general works on women's history, edited collections on women and gender, and sourcebooks continue to suffer from gaps on these topics.[4] While this book is not a social history of these issues, it aims to open the field of inquiry into childhood to include them. Its purpose is to begin to recover the cultural meanings of childhood and of the processes and events attached to it—pregnancy, childbirth, infant care, child rearing, and schooling.

In addition to expanding the inquiry into childhood to include the early stages of a child's life, this book also restores another aspect of the original discourse: the construction of the child's body as a critical site for shaping a future member of society. Russian Enlighteners interested in upbringing invariably referenced three components of child rearing: physical, moral, and intellectual. Following the dictum made popular by John Locke, "a sound mind in a sound body," writers sought to persuade their readers that developing a child's body was equal in importance to other components—indeed, that it was the necessary foundation for the others. While historians of childhood in the West have shown the ways in which children's bodies came to be regarded in the early modern era as needing special environments, clothing, and sustenance, and historians of later periods in Russian history have drawn attention to a fuller range of experiences of children, including the material world and the bodily experiences of children, historians of the eighteenth century have yet to undertake studies on these aspects of childhood in the Russian context.[5] While much scholarship exists on educational projects and policies under Catherine's aegis, it tends to focus on the political, intellectual, and moral goals of schools, and physical upbringing receives little attention beyond brief references.[6] This book remedies this by investigating Russian ideas about the child's body and the physical aspects of upbringing in the eighteenth century.

Upbringing is an interesting topic for the historian because it is infrequently studied, yet related to many lines of inquiry in historical scholarship. Philippe Ariès first argued that attention to the vulnerability of the child marked an entirely new conception of childhood in early modern Europe, establishing the field of the history of childhood.[7] As is often the case with pioneering works, some of Ariès's conclusions have been discredited by subsequent research, yet his primary premise that the meaning of childhood changes over time holds true. Fifty years after the publication of his work, sociologists, anthropologists, and historians have produced a rich and deep scholarship on the changing conceptions of childhood, the place of the child in society, and the expression of parental love and care, to name a few topics within this broad field.[8] Historians of Europe have debated when childhood in the modern sense—understood as a special, vulnerable period in the human life-span, one that requires special care, feeding, nurturing, and instruction designed for children's non-adult bodies and minds—really began. Ariès also sparked intense debate among historians over when parents began to love their children from infancy as precious, irreplaceable family members. Some historians argued that perhaps a correlation existed between high infant mortality and low parental affection in the medieval and the early modern eras. These two debates in the historiography have been largely settled in favor of nuanced, contextual interpretations of love and care over rigid periodizations and general claims, and the search for a master narrative that might hold true for all of Europe has been retired.[9] Scholarship in the European context has shifted toward the study of the material culture of childhood, the childhoods of less economically fortunate children, and the political meanings of the child and childhood.[10]

Historian Margaret King notes that the history of childhood remains underresearched for the periphery of Europe, including the vast region of the Russian empire.[11] King is right in suggesting that the scholarship related to childhood in medieval and early modern Russia is quite thin compared to that for England, France, and the German lands. Max Okenfuss has analyzed the first primers for Russian children, from the early eighteenth century, and argued for dating the discovery of childhood in Russia to coincide with their appearance.[12] David Ransel has produced the first study of the history of foundling homes in Russia, demonstrating that attitudes toward illegitimate children became more humanitarian during the eighteenth century.[13] Research by Olga Glagoleva and Natalia Pushkareva on domesticity and the family in Russia during this era has focused on familial relationships. Their work shows that children loved their mothers and, as adults, used words in their memoirs to express their gratitude, reverence, and sense of indebtedness.[14] Beyond these tantalizing glimpses of the domestic life of children, and the historical treatments of institutions created for the care and education of children in Catherine's Russia, there is much fertile ground to be explored concerning how members of state and society were beginning to develop opinions on childhood and children during this era.

As children began to be recognized as a national resource and their welfare seen a measure of Russia's socioeconomic and cultural status, the stakeholders in their development multiplied. Interested parties worked from within a range of social, political, and intellectual contexts; thus, to gain a rich picture of how Russian Enlighteners imagined the child, I draw upon a variety of source material, including advice manuals for parents, midwifery treatises, plays, memoirs, primers to teach literacy to children, and documentation from state projects to establish midwifery institutes and public schools. In seeking works that addressed upbringing, I found lesser-known publications by well-known personalities, including Nikolai Novikov, Catherine II, and Ekaterina Dashkova. I also encountered and have chosen to include the endeavors of Russian Enlighteners who are less renowned, such as the physicians Semyon Zybelin and Nestor Maksimovich-Ambodik.

I am emboldened to gather this range and variety of materials by other cultural historians. In *The Family Romance of the French Revolution*, Lynn Hunt mines nontraditional sources for political representations and narratives employing family metaphors. Along with political sources, Hunt incorporates novels, erotic texts, and paintings to argue that imagining familial relationships became a means of reconceptualizing political and social relationships in revolutionary France.[15] Cultural historians working on other eras and topics in the Russian context similarly incorporate varied source material in striving to recover meaning. In her magisterial work on childhood in twentieth-century Russia, Catriona Kelly uses advice manuals, propaganda, literary representations, and legal codes to achieve a lush study of Soviet childhood. For the eighteenth century, Hans Rogger, Richard Wortman, and Iurii Lotman in particular have produced scholarship that integrates a wide range of sources, including belles lettres, paintings, engravings, plays, and legal codes. Seeking the cultural meanings of representations of national identity, political power, and everyday behavior (including, sometimes, gendered behavior), these scholars challenge us to think of noble culture, the Russian Enlightenment, and eighteenth-century politics as dynamic, contested categories.[16] Other scholars, such as Cynthia Whittaker, Elise Wirtschafter, Andreas Schönle, and Michelle Marrese, pursue interpretive paradigms that serve as heuristic tools inviting creative and daring approaches to exploring Russia's past.[17]

One issue with the varied nature of source material in these types of studies is that historians are limited in how much we can know about the reception and use of the sources. We know that medical texts and handbooks sold very well in bookshops, had large print runs, and were the most successful items commissioned by the Free Economic Society. Advice literature and primers for children also enjoyed multiple printings, often at the behest of the autocrat. We do not know, however, how most eighteenth-century texts were used; that is, we do not know very much about who read them or whether the instruction offered was heeded or discarded. Some memoirs mention actual book titles, allowing us to guess at their popularity. Issues of reception and use plague historians of other early modern topics, too. For example, Helen King notes the possible range of uses of midwifery treatises in England; illiterate midwives and inexperienced male practitioners might have relied upon the pictures with potentially disastrous results, while curious laypeople may have consulted the manuals, with their illustrations of reproductive organs, for completely different ends.[18]

Similar problems of reception adhere to Alexander Radishchev's *Journey from Saint Petersburg to Moscow*, which I also mine for the mentalities of the era. While this semi-fictional work managed to slip past the censors and went into publication in 1790, Catherine banned it not long after and sentenced Radishchev to ten years of exile in Siberia,[19] but Radishchev's work survived to inspire the nineteenth-century radical intelligentsia. Like other historians of the eighteenth century, I treat this work and other cultural materials as sources for attitudes, anxieties, and preoccupations of the era.[20] In the absence of evidence on reception, I try to avoid assuming that discourse influenced social reality. However, I do accept as the premise of the aforementioned scholars that some sort of perceived social, material, intellectual, or political reality influenced discourse.

In my approach to conceptualizing Russian society and the state during this era, I am inspired by work that challenges us to think beyond established interpretive frameworks. Andre Wakefield's work on the seventeenth- and eighteenth-century Prussian bureaucracy shows how ambitious state servitors used the language and the discursive aims of cameralism to further their own careers.[21] By revealing the corruption and chaos behind the facade of the "well-ordered state," Wakefield introduces greater dynamism into the historical perception of Prussian bureaucrats and their relationships to hierarchies of power and the crown. This upending of the usual assumptions about politics in an autocratic state is useful for thinking about other autocratic contexts. Illuminating how dialogue and consensus between autocrat and servitors were represented in many different iterations of political power during Catherine's reign, Jan Kusber and Cynthia Whittaker offer complex understandings of the operation and representation of power within politics.[22] Colum Leckey's work on the Free Economic Society and Thomas Newlin's research on Andrei Bolotov both demonstrate the possibilities and the constraints of the emerging and ambiguous public sphere in Russia. Bolotov eschewed participation in politics, but very much viewed himself as an Enlightener, engaged in service to Russia through his intellectual work, including his contributions to the journal of the Free Economic Society. This organization, as Leckey shows, functioned as an entirely voluntary society, yet it existed somewhat uncomfortably within the state's influence.[23] In a similar vein, John T. Alexander's depiction of the medical bureaucracy's response to a crisis portrays this unit of the state as a particularly activist arena.[24] Interpretations of Eastern Europe and Russia as entirely dominated by powerful autocrats and their growing, obedient bureaucracies are challenged by this recent work, which draws attention to the creative agency employed by individuals within the state and to the value placed in Prussia and in Russia on the appearance of particular values, whether consensus or order. To this nuanced, dynamic view of activity within the Russian autocratic state, I hope to add a degree of gender

analysis. In my interpretations of the works and projects designed and promoted by men within the Russian state, I am inspired to consider how masculinity was constructed through statesmen ostensibly focused on feminine
behavior.[25] In this respect, I follow contemporary scholars of gender who insist
that challenges or revisions to what is considered feminine usually inform the
opposing category.[26]

As for the quantity of source material, prior to the eighteenth century,
Russia had almost no reading public or literary world. The Russian Orthodox
Church controlled all printing presses until the reign of Peter the Great, imped-
ing the publication of secular literature, newspapers, and scientific literature
until the eighteenth century.[27] The first Russian universities were founded in
this same century, necessitating foreign recruitment of the first generations
of academics. Russians were required to travel to Europe to acquire advanced
degrees, and few had the intellectual and linguistic preparation to do so.[28] In the
1760s, for example, only ninety-four degree-holding physicians were practicing
in the Russian Empire. Of these, only twenty-one were of Russian or Ukrainian
descent.[29] Moscow University did not grant medical degrees until nearly the end
of the eighteenth century. Given its precedents, the eighteenth century saw a
flowering of intellectual life in Russia—but it was a far cry from the publishing
and academic worlds of European nations. There were fewer published advice
manuals, health aides, and journals in Russia because there were fewer intellectuals, writers, professors, and physicians. During the last quarter of the eighteenth century, Russia's reading public and publishing world began to blossom,
and higher education experienced significant growth. The autocratic state sometimes boosted the expansion of education and learning, as under the reform-
minded Peter I and Catherine II.[30] The same sovereigns (not to mention their
less progressive progeny) just as handily undermined development by restricting the intellectual public sphere either by design (controlling access) or as a
consequence of underfunding and neglecting educational projects.[31] As a result,
twenty-first-century scholars who study eighteenth-century Russia must make
creative use of the sources available to them (while envying the thicker source
base of other European countries).

A few words on terms used in this book are in order. Throughout, I use the
term "Russian Enlightener" to refer to the individuals in this study who considered themselves as such. These Enlighteners shared in common only the
self-perception that they had a duty or purpose to serve humanity and their
homeland by spreading enlightenment, defined in various ways. By "Russian" I
mean individuals who by birth or by choice were subjects of the Russian empire

and who could communicate in the lingua franca of their local peers and associates. I have in mind the term used in the eighteenth century to indicate subject status rather than ethnicity, that is, "Rossiiskii" rather than "Russkii."[32] I include within this category foreign-born members who immigrated to Russia permanently, made careers in service to the Russian state, and acquired competency in speaking and writing in Russian. One might think of these personalities as not dissimilar from Catherine herself; they adopted Russia as their country and identified their "Russianness" through various means of assimilation. I exclude from the category "Russian Enlightener" those foreigners in service to the Russian state who never intended to reside permanently in Russia and stayed only for a limited time, as well as those who made no attempt to adopt the local language.[33]

Finally, a note on the term "subject-citizen." Most of the authors of the eighteenth-century texts considered here used the term *grazhdanin* to indicate a member of the body politic. The English translation of this term is "citizen," but this translation is problematic because of its political meanings in other contexts. Clearly, when Catherine the Great imagined raising new "citizens," she did not have in mind instructing children to understand themselves as part of a republic or a constitutional monarchy. The autocratic context was assumed; Catherine's choice of *grazhdanin* instead of "subject" signals, I think, her interest in encouraging, up to a point, a degree of individual initiative and civic activity, provided that these actions were in accordance with her wishes. Whether Catherine's contemporaries and the authors included here had the same understanding in mind when, like Novikov, they wrote of future "citizens" is another matter. To signal the inherent linguistic tension of this Russian term in its Catherinian context, I use the phrase "subject-citizen." The ambiguity is intentional, in much the way Elise Wirtschafter adopts the term "civic society" instead of "civil society" when describing some public-minded values of this era, and Colum Leckey makes a similar move to highlight the "ambiguity" of the "public sphere" in which the Free Economic Society operated.[34]

To lend some structure to a work that is not a narrative history, I have organized the chapters to follow the trajectory of human development throughout childhood, from conception through adolescence. I do not treat every aspect of child development, but focus on areas that provide, in my assessment, the greatest opportunity for filling gaps in the historical scholarship. The first chapter illuminates the germination of the discourse on upbringing by introducing some of its chief architects and by revisiting the eighteenth-century notions of the concept of *vospitanie* itself. Chapters 2 and 3 treat discourses and projects focused on midwifery, childbirth, and the earliest years of life. Chapter 4 addresses the discursive construction of the child's body and the growing attention to the physical care of children. Chapter 5 explores the means of teaching children to discipline their bodies in preparation for participation in society as good Russian subject-citizens, defined according to gender and social status. Chapter 6 argues for the emergence of an idea of girlhood for the elite, and considers the tension between protecting girlhood and raising girls to be women. The final chapter reviews the main actors of the preceding chapters and their contributions while reflecting upon the interpretive issues that these Russian Enlighteners ask us to consider.

I

THE MEANINGS OF *Vospitanie*

One of the luminaries of the Russian Enlightenment, Nikolai Novikov, chose the metaphor of an intricate contraption to represent the complexity involved in raising a child. He wrote in his prescriptive work on child rearing: "Upbringing is like a complicated machine, consisting of many different springs and gears, each of which must bring another into motion if the proper operation is to be brought about."[1] Such a metaphor for upbringing—*vospitanie* in Russian—was inherently masculine in its eighteenth-century context. The construction and maintenance of a machine implied knowledge of mathematics, engineering, and science, all realms that men monopolized to the exclusion of women. For Novikov, the proper upbringing of children demanded explicitly masculine attention; it was too important to be left to tradition or to nature, which were both coded as feminine within his Enlightenment field of reference.[2] Novikov is not known for his thinking on *vospitanie*; rather, he is better known for the ink he spilled needling Catherine the Great in his journals, testing the limits of expression within an autocracy. Yet this political thinker and leader of the Masonic movement also took up his pen to persuade his readers of the urgent need to reform the flabby manner in which they were raising their children. In this respect, Novikov serves as an archetype for the writers and advocates of *vospitanie* who populate this book; they put quill to paper to argue about the quotidian tasks of child rearing—and to intervene in the perceived feminine status quo—because they believed in the power of upbringing to change the identity of Russia itself.

This book argues that a polemical, varied discourse on upbringing began to emerge among the reading public and in the Russian halls of political power during the eighteenth century. Through these discussions and the projects they produced, the notion of the child underwent a fundamental revision in Russian public life. Statesmen, public intellectuals, and physicians began to focus attention on children as future members of the body politic. As such, they argued, the welfare of infants and children should be recognized as a primary interest of the state and society. Novikov's rival in political matters, Empress Catherine II, concurred that the time had come for a radical intervention in upbringing. In the words of the plan Catherine commissioned from Ivan Betskoi, "On the Upbringing of Both Sexes," the goal of reforms was nothing less than to raise "a new breed" of Russians.[3] As this book shows, voices from all perspectives on Russia's political continuum advocated for greater attention to, resources for, and deliberation about how children were shaped into adults. The idea of the child as a resource to be maximized for the good of the state, in true cameralist fashion, carried heavy political freight in an era of Westernizing reform driven by an ambitious autocrat. If children could be rescued from early mortality and ignorance alike, then the future of Russia as a European power would be bright indeed.

This discourse was polemical because so much was at stake; at its heart one finds the contested issue of Russian national identity itself. The assessment by some Russian authors, statesmen, and physicians that their country lagged behind as a latecomer to the benefits of European education, science, and culture is reflected in their ambitious plans and prescriptions for reforming upbringing in Russia. The allure of the concept of *vospitanie* lay in its optimistic promises; raw material (infants or even fetuses) could be transformed into strong, healthy, hardworking, morally upright Russians. All of Russia's perceived shortcomings—however they were defined—could be reversed if the proper upbringing were applied to all of the empire's children.

To return to Novikov's metaphor for *vospitanie*, a machine is not a natural phenomenon; it is fabricated by humans and requires intentional and deliberate planning to create and to maintain. If *vospitanie* was to become a well-oiled, complex machine, as Novikov hoped, producing perfectly formed Russians for generations to come, it would require the exacting attention of many learned men. These men, with their precisely detailed plans, would design and direct the overall architecture of the machine, the imbrication of the gears. Midwives, medics, mothers, wet nurses, nannies, and teachers were to function as the system of gears, in harmony and under the direction of the machine-makers. Crucial to this project of vast social engineering was the essential premise that brain, body, and character were malleable and could be shaped profoundly in childhood through appropriate intervention and education. Novikov argued that the time had arrived in Russia to abandon "the delusion that parents can bring up their children well without special knowledge, without reflection, and without

D. G. Levitskii, *Portrait of Catherine the Great as Legislatress in the Temple Devoted to the Goddess of Justice*. Early 1780s. Oil on canvas.

(© Copyright The Tretyakov Gallery, Moscow, Russia. Used with permission.)

great care"; a project as important as building the new Russia could not be left to amateurs.[4]

In seventeenth- and eighteenth-century Europe, the idea of childhood as a privileged and critical period of a human being's development began to emerge in medical, pedagogical, and philosophical discourses. This interest in shaping children's bodies and minds stimulated the production of advice literature and polemics on child rearing and encouraged experimentation by parents and tutors in child rearing and education. Eventually, this interest in childhood spawned the field of pediatric medicine and created new markets for specialized clothing, books, and toys for the children of the middle and upper classes.[5] A similar phenomenon developed more slowly in Russia, where a significant reading public emerged only in the second half of the century. Before the eighteenth century, very few works included the topic of upbringing, and little is known about circulation of manuscript copies. The sixteenth-century handbook of household rules, *Domostroi* (*Domestic Order*), is one of the only known texts to have addressed Muscovite family life and child rearing.[6] Concerned especially with the maintenance of social hierarchy, this guidebook instructed the patriarch in regulating the behavior of all members of his household in accordance with Orthodox Christian teaching and Muscovite traditions. In 1717, Tsar Peter the Great initiated the publication of the first prescriptive work to include advice for children and youth borrowed from Western, secular sources. In keeping with Peter's efforts to reform the manners of his subjects toward European norms, *The Honorable Mirror of Youth, or A Guide to Social Conduct* offered a compendium of advice drawn from unnamed European sources along with some lessons in Orthodox virtues included as a primer.[7] This type of unattributed borrowing was a common feature of advice literature in Russia until the Soviet era.[8] *The Honorable Mirror of Youth* prescribed Western rules of etiquette for social settings, such as not blowing one's nose at the dinner table, and advocated learning foreign languages and European dances in order to improve one's suitability for advancement at court.[9] Reissued seven times in small print runs of 100 to 1,200 copies, Peter's handbook was the only one of its kind until the market for child-rearing manuals began to expand in the mid-eighteenth century. As Lindsey Hughes puts it, *The Honorable Mirror of Youth* qualified as a bestseller by contemporary standards.[10]

The issuing of a Russian translation of Jean-Baptiste Morvan de Bellegarde's *L'Éducation parfait* signaled an approaching surge in domestic publishing related to upbringing and moral instruction.[11] In Russian bookshops during the middle of the century, French works were popular, including François Fénelon's treatise on the long-neglected issue of education for girls, *Traité de l'éducation des filles*.[12] From 1755 to 1764, the journal founded by the Russian scholar and Enlightenment luminary Mikhail Lomonosov, *Monthly Essays*, frequently published translations of works addressing child-rearing precepts in the ancient worlds of Greece and Rome, thus uniting interest in upbringing with efforts to make the intellectual fruits of the classical world available in Russian.[13] A Russian translation of John Locke's *On Education* first appeared in 1759—translated not directly from English, but from a French version. This type of indirect appropriation of European works was fairly typical of the Russian Enlightenment.[14] In the 1760s, the market for advice manuals on upbringing and for books meant to teach morals directly to children continued to blossom.[15] This increase in publication of foreign works reflects a developing reading public and changes in the realm of publishing. During Elizabeth's reign in the 1740s and '50s, private patronage began to be a source of funding for translations and printings, while the primary publishing house, the Academy of Sciences, developed a "new commercial consciousness" born of the need to increase its revenues from nongovernmental sources.[16] The uptick in publishing of titles related to upbringing reflects the growing interest in the private sector and an expanding market for such literature.

From the beginning of Catherine the Great's reign, in 1762, the empress expressed her interest in *vospitanie* through a variety of projects, plans, and texts, all of which had the moral reform of Russian society as their chief goal. In 1764, she and her educational adviser at the time, Ivan Betskoi, issued "On the Upbringing of Both Sexes."[17] This legislation led to the establishment of two boarding schools for noble children and two orphanages for abandoned children. The school for noble girls, or Smolny Institute, was officially titled the Society for the Upbringing (*Vospitanie*) of Well-Born Maidens. The orphanages were called Houses of Upbringing (*Vospitatel'nye Domy*). The names of these institutions, with their emphasis on upbringing rather than education (*obrazovanie*), instruction (*obuchenie*), or enlightenment (*prosveshchenie*), underscored Catherine's primary interest in character formation. Catherine's compendium of Enlightenment thought, *The Instruction to the Deputies of the Legislative Commission* (1767), provided specific rules for child rearing in a chapter devoted entirely to *vospitanie*.[18] Indeed, the topic received lengthier treatment than her chapter on developing the "middle estate." Given Catherine's interest in the economy and state revenues, one might have expected her to devote more space to ways of stimulating this tax-paying estate than to ways of stimulating childhood moral development.

During Catherine's reign (1762–96), interest in *vospitanie* continued to grow among the Russian literati and the nobility. The topic was addressed at the meetings of the Legislative Commission, convened by Catherine in 1767 for the purpose of drafting a new code of laws. Representatives of the state medical college, an administrative body invited to participate, and deputies representing rural and urban nobility presented their perspectives on how upbringing ought to be altered or preserved in Russia. Physicians began publishing works that addressed child raising. The Free Economic Society, a volunteer organization that had the empress's blessing, commissioned a home health manual aimed at a rural audience that also addressed issues related to children's health and child rearing.[19] In addition, belles lettres began to reflect the widespread interest in children and upbringing. In satirical journals, operas, and plays, writers criticized contemporary practices and provided prescriptions for the reform of child rearing.

Many of the great writers and publishers of the era also began producing works explicitly for children. Professors at Moscow University created new alphabet primers and grammars aimed at teaching literacy and morality to children; these books included many moral tales and anecdotes along with grammar lessons. Two examples were Nikolai Kurganov's *The Letter Writer* (first published in 1769) and Anton Barsov's *Civil and Church Alphabets* (1768).[20] The famous satirist and poet Alexander Sumarokov wrote *Instruction for Children: Morals, History, and Geography* (1774).[21] Novikov created *Children's Reading for the Heart and the Mind*, a compendium of tales meant to amuse and instruct children. Published between 1785 and 1789, this journal became a favorite text of children, beloved and treasured well into the nineteenth century. Memoirists fondly recall family evenings spent reading these tales many times over.[22] The dramatist P. A. Plavil'shchikov promoted theater as a means of fostering patriotic feelings in children.[23] Andrei Bolotov created the first children's theater, with children performing as actors. The scholar Berdyshev reported that as many as two hundred people would come to see performances at Bolotov's children's theater, the first of its kind in Russia.[24] In 1776, Bolotov wrote *Children's Philosophy* to assist mothers in teaching morals to their children.[25] Between 1781 and 1783, Catherine published a number of works that she had written for children, including *Tale of Tsarevich Fevee, Tale of Tsarevich Khlor, Selected Russian Sayings, The Russian Alphabet, Beginning Civics Lessons, Continuing Civics Lessons, Beginning Notes* (lessons in geography, history, and virtue), and *Dialogues and Stories*. Catherine ostensibly drafted some of these works for her grandsons; the multiple printings, large print runs, use in primary schools, and sale to the reading public suggest that the empress had larger audiences in mind.[26]

Depiction of a Russian midwife by the French painter Jean-Baptiste Le Prince. A guest of Catherine II, Le Prince created a study of the Russian peoples. Jean-Baptiste Le Prince, *Habit of a Russian Midwife in 1764. Sage femme Russe.* From *A collection of the dresses of different nations, antient [sic] and modern.* 1764. Hand-colored engraving.

Other eighteenth-century writers and activists began to approach the issues of childhood and *vospitanie* from allegedly medical and scientific perspectives. The physician Nestor Maksimovich-Ambodik, sometimes credited as the founder of obstetrical and pediatric medicine in Russia, published a five-volume manual for midwives and medical students over three years in the 1780s. His opus, *The Art of Midwifery or the Science of Midwives' Affairs*, instructed the reader on pregnancy, birth, child rearing, and childhood health.[27] His decision to write in Russian and to include many illustrations signals his ambition to make available knowledge on these subjects to a wide audience. Maksimovich-Ambodik also developed the first Russian lexicon for Latin medical terms, which facilitated the study of medicine in a country without a tradition of studying Latin. Khristian Peken authored one of the most popular home health manuals, *The Home Healer*, published in 1765. His son, Matvei Peken, also became a doctor and published a revision, aptly titled *The New Home Healer*, with added chapters on women's health and the raising of children.[28] Andrei Bakherakht, a prominent Russian-born physician who spent most of his career with the navy and focused on issues of public health, published *On Immoderation of the Passions in Both Sexes* in 1779.[29] Bakherakht thought upbringing must be reformed to curb the epidemic of venereal disease in Russia. Semyon Zybelin, the first Russian physician on the medical faculty at Moscow University, published, in addition to journal articles, two works addressing issues of child rearing, *On the Correct Upbringing from Infancy* (1775) and *On a Method for Preventing the Chief Cause of Slow Population Growth* (1780).[30] In 1793, Khristian Ivanovich Rost, a medic in service to the Russian army, published *The Village Doctor*, which included sections related to pregnancy, breast-feeding, and children's health.[31] Ioann Kreizel', an assimilated Russian citizen, became a member of the Medical Collegium and an instructor of midwifery.[32] In 1792, he wrote, in Russian, *Instructions to Beginners in the Art of Midwifery*.[33]

All of these authors studied medicine at European universities, a necessity for those seeking advanced medical training at the time, as the medical faculty at Moscow University was not established until 1764–65. Zybelin and Maksimovich-Ambodik both earned medical degrees abroad after beginning their educations as seminary students, a biographical fact they shared with other Russian-born physicians of the era.[34] Peken and Bakherakht also defended medical dissertations abroad and then returned to Russia to practice.[35] Rost and Kreizel' both had some degree of higher education in medicine, but neither had earned the title of "doctor" in Russia, although Kreizel' claimed to have a medical degree. Written by men with advanced education in medicine, the

ИСКУССТВО ПОВИВАНІЯ

ИЛИ

НАУКА
О БАБИЧЬЕМЪ ДѢЛѢ.

НА ПЯТЪ ЧАСТЕЙ РАЗДѢЛЕННАЯ

и

МНОГИМИ РИСУНКАМИ СНАБДѢННАЯ.

ВЪ КОЕЙ

Кратко но ясно толкуется : какое дѣтородныя женскія
части имѣютъ строеніе ; коимъ образомъ надлежитъ
пособлять Беремѣннымъ при родахъ , роженицамъ
послѣ родовъ, и новорожденнымъ ихъ младен-
цамъ во время младолѣтства ; и какія именно
болѣзни , какъ Беремѣннымъ чрезъ все
время ихъ беремѣнности, и природахъ :
такъ и роженицамъ послѣ родовъ, и
новорожденнымъ ихъ младен-
цамъ обыкновенно при-
ключаются.

Для пользы повивальныхъ Россійскихъ Ба-
бокъ и Лѣкарей.

СОЧИНИЛЪ

ВРАЧЕБНОЙ НАУКИ ДОКТОРЪ , и ПОВИВАЛЬНАГО
ИСКУССТВА ПРОФЕССОРЪ

НЕСТОРЪ МАКСИМОВИЧЬ - АМБОДИКЪ.

Печатано во Градѣ С. Петра 1784. года.

Title page to *The Art of Midwifery*, the first midwifery manual written by a Russian physician for a Russian audience. Maksimovich-Ambodik, *Iskusstvo povivaniia*, vol. 1. (Courtesy of the National Library of Medicine, Washington, DC) publications by this group express a *mentalité* that was unique in eighteenth-century Russia. The authors saw themselves as experts and enlighteners, working to achieve the goals of the state through their influence on society and the population. Like other Russian Enlighteners, they appealed directly to an educated public, framing their purpose in grand terms of service to humanity and the fatherland. Most of them did not belong to the nobility, and owed their status to education and to their positions as medical personnel. Rather than birth or patronage, education and ambition secured their livelihoods. Access to and promotion within their proto-profession was controlled by the Medical Collegium, a committee of physicians that acted as gatekeeper to positions within the medical bureaucracy of the state. Catherine herself refused to adjudicate in disputes over medical credentials and insisted that the Medical Collegium act as the governing body.[36] The men who worked within the medical bureaucracy, especially in its upper ranks, served in a context that valued educational expertise and service to humanity, while also drawing salaries from the state. A general commitment to civic virtues among high-ranking Russian physicians is evident in the choice of many to become members of the Free Economic Society. To name a few, Nestor Maksimovich-Ambodik, Georg fon Ash, Khristian Peken, and Andrei Bakherakht were physicians who joined this voluntary society together with other significant Enlightenment figures including Novikov, Denis Fonvizin, and Andrei Bolotov. All of these men became interested in and committed to issues concerning child welfare and upbringing.[37]

Medical writers claimed the authority of knowledge, academically acquired and certified by degrees and licenses. "Knowledge" was positioned against sources of women's authority for bringing children into the world and raising them: "custom" or "fashion." In this way, medical writers' conception of what constituted "knowledge" was gendered masculine, whereas "custom" and "fashion" were gendered feminine. They presented the type of child rearing informed by custom and fashion as inferior to the knowledge-based type that they promoted and as a threat to the health of society and the state. Maksimovich-Ambodik explicitly presented the customary, informal knowledge of lay midwives as dangerous to infant life and thus an impediment to the population goals of the state: "Such fatal occurrences, which take place solely because of the extreme obstinacy, superstition, stupidity, and abuse of ignorant midwives, are the reason for the deterioration of the people, so that rarely do a quarter of newborns reach majority age."[38]

Whether children survived to become healthy, useful members of society or grew into adults who were afflicted with moral or physical disease depended

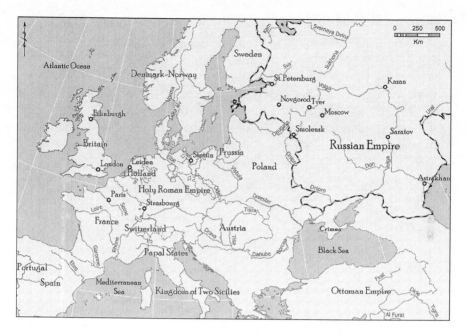

Russia and Europe in 1762
(Boundary Cartography)

upon the environment in which they were raised, according to the Russian medical experts. They assumed collectively a number of premises that were not a priori assumptions a century earlier anywhere in Europe, let alone on its periphery in Russia. These premises included, first and foremost, the assumption that human nature and perhaps even intelligence could be shaped by the environment. This premise warrants attention because it began to appear in so many places and informed the dreams of many a reformer. A passion for critiquing and reforming upbringing practices appeared during this era in a variety of contexts, including that of the theater, the literature and journals consumed and discussed by an ever-growing reading public, the emerging medical and scientific fields among statesmen, and at court. While the methods and content of reforms proposed in these contexts varied dramatically, the premise and overriding goal remained constant: *vospitanie* had the power to dramatically reshape the population (the premise), and *vospitanie* could produce a strong Russia, prepared to rival or surpass European countries (the goal).

In Russia, some architects of new schemes of upbringing went even further than the boldest adherents in Europe to advocate for very rigid control of children's environments in order to ensure the desired outcome. Russian society might rightly be seen as a latecomer to the party (or late adopter of the new technologies of upbringing), but members of Russian society proved their allegiance to Enlightenment ideals by advocating reforms and schemes that matched or exceeded the grandest or most extreme European versions in scope. What is of particular interest is not only the extent to which these schemes were successfully realized (although these are important and interesting stories that will be conveyed), but also the daring scope of these schemes and the sparkling imagination of their advocates. They dared to dream that reform in the realms of pregnancy, childbirth, infant care, and the general rearing of children was possible on a grand scale, and they would not be deterred by low salaries, high infant mortality, and daunting geographical spaces.

From imagined depopulation to the abuses of serfdom, no problem seemed beyond the reach of the transformative power of *vospitanie*. Yet, precisely because of the perceived scope and potential of the power of *vospitanie*, it is essential to define exactly what contemporaries meant by this term within the context of the eighteenth century. The term has been rendered in English in various ways, ranging from "education" to "childhood."[39] Close readings of eighteenth-century texts show that contemporaries made distinctions between *vospitanie* (upbringing) and *obrazovanie* (education) or *obuchenie* (instruction). *Vospitanie* in its eighteenth-century usage included "education" as a component, but it also could refer to the feeding of an infant, to a set of rules for behavior and social interaction, or to the inculcation of moral virtues in a child.[40] The German *Bildung* is an example of word that would lose much of its meaning if a one-word translation were sought and one that invokes a spiritual dimension like *vospitanie*.

Vospitanie involved every aspect of a child's development, from birth to adulthood. The state institutions of *vospitanie*—midwifery teaching and licensing, lying-in hospitals, orphanages, schools—extended "upbringing" from infancy to adulthood. Some authors even argued that *vospitanie* began at conception and prescribed advice for prenatal care. In Dashkova's words, "a complete *vospitanie* consists of physical upbringing, moral upbringing, and finally of schooling or classical upbringing."[41] Novikov similarly stressed the breadth of the correct *vospitanie*: "All other definitions, being imperfect, will fail to encompass the full scope of upbringing."[42] Catherine incorporated Dashkova's three aspects in her detailed *Instructions to Prince Nikolai Ivanovich Saltykov on the Upbringing of the Grand Princes* (1784) and in the child-rearing practices at the state institutions of upbringing, such as the Smolny Institute.[43] Catherine's decision to publish this handbook as a guide for parents was in keeping with the genre in European literature. Locke and Fénelon wrote guides for child rearing for a specific high-born noble child, which were then published as handbooks that parents might use in rearing their own children. Rousseau's *Emile* was unique in providing principles for child rearing by discussing the upbringing of an imaginary pupil. By publishing her own guide, Catherine clearly meant to place herself among the other leading Enlightenment figures writing on child rearing.

In addition to traditional education, spirituality, and morality, the Russian focus on physical upbringing—encompassing nourishment, clothing, hygiene, and exercise—was equally bound up in *vospitanie*. Novikov wrote, "in childhood the foundation is laid for the health and strength, and also the weakness and ailments, of the body . . . the first important component of upbringing: it is the care of the body." The physical aspect of raising children received so much attention because the care of the body was understood to influence the evolution of the soul that resided in that body. Locke perhaps most famously promoted the notion of a sound mind in a sound body; Catherine, Dashkova, Novikov, and other Russians subscribed to this idea as well. Mothers and other women caring for children needed to train children's bodies so that they would become accustomed to hard work, simple food, and physical discomfort.[44] Moral upbringing was very much related to the physical component, Novikov explained: if one cannot control one's passions, the body suffers along with the soul. In the Russian texts under consideration here, the material and spiritual bled into each other; material substances could transmit spiritual qualities and vice versa. Thus, a mother's "sin" could be passed on to an unborn child, or unsavory characteristics of a wet nurse could be communicated through her breast milk. Contagion could also carry positive attributes; a good mother transmitted her purity and virtue through her milk to her nursling.[45]

It is also important to understand what *vospitanie* was not. *Vospitanie* was not vocational. Novikov wrote that training "for a particular calling in no way constitutes the principal aim of upbringing."[46] Dashkova similarly wrote that "*Vospitanie* does not consist in developing outer talents." Second, *vospitanie* was not only (or even mostly) about learning academic subjects: "*Vospitanie* does not consist in acquiring foreign languages nor only in learning the sciences." At the heart of *vospitanie* was the development of a whole human being. Finally, for many reformers, like Dashkova, *vospitanie* relied upon persuasion, not force: "*Vospitanie* is taught more by example than by command."[47] This aspect of *vospitanie* is particularly significant in view of the fact that the zenith of concern with *vospitanie* coincided with a period of female rule. The preference for the gentle guidance of example over the punitive aspects of traditional pedagogy captured in the Old Testament dictum "spare the rod, spoil the child" was echoed in Catherine's political image. Catherine desired, at least until the final years of her reign, to appear benevolent and enlightened, as a monarch seeking consensus in her relationship with the nobility. Her masking of coercion in imperial contexts as maternal love or compassion also traded on Enlightenment notions of gentle parenting. Despite having declined, ceremonially at least, the appellation "Mother of the Fatherland," Catherine's decrees often invoked the image of her as such, referencing her "maternal care" and her "compassion" for all of her subjects.[48]

Vospitanie also contained a social status or *soslovie* (estate) dimension. For Dashkova, intellectual development (or schooling beyond simple literacy) was essential only for certain "titled people"; she stressed that a classical education "adorns the highest rank."[49] Novikov's prescriptions, though flexible according to one's station, clearly were intended for a well-to-do audience, not the *chern'*, or rabble.[50] Catherine and Betskoi similarly designed educational curricula based on notions about what was appropriate for each social echelon of the population. Pupils at the noble institutions, the Corps of Cadets and Smolny Institute, received what would be characterized in the West as a liberal arts education, while girls of the *meshchanstvo* (townspeople) and abandoned children at other state institutions of upbringing received a more practical program.[51] At the Legislative Commission, instruction in arithmetic, basic literacy, and trade skills was thought to be sufficient for non-noble *sosloviia* (estates).[52] Yet, it is important to note, in all of the projects and literature under review here, Russian reformers tended toward the humanitarian: all children, regardless of sex or social status, were deemed worthy of life itself and, ideally, would receive good nutrition, proper physical care, exercise out-of-doors, and an upbringing that instilled dignity and love of the fatherland. While disdain for lower orders is perceptible in the comments of Novikov, and rare were the noblemen who wished to endow non-noble children with a privileged upbringing, one finds no heartless attitudes toward the poor.[53] Thomas Malthus, the author of *An Essay on the Principle of Population* (1798), criticized projects aimed at improving the welfare of the poor, which, in his eyes, would lead only to a dangerous surplus population without an accompanying increase in food production. When Malthus visited one of the Russian foundling homes, he commented that, given the high infant mortality common to all such institutions, they might serve as an effective check on population growth.[54] Russian Enlighteners showed no such cynicism and continued to seek ways of saving infants and children, even when initial projects and plans failed. The thinkers and intellectuals who were excited about the power of *vospitanie* to transform Russia were also excited about the possibilities of harnessing the power of the state to achieve these goals, and they continued to press forward for the good of the state and society.

Whether the ideal Russian was imagined as a peasant or a noble, gender also informed the discourse on upbringing. Not surprisingly, given the thinness of the sources left to posterity by women and nonliterate people, the majority of voices that can be heard through the historical records belong to men of middling and higher ranks.[55] These self-appointed male "experts" constructed their own masculine expertise through their discussions of upbringing. While critiquing the behavior of women who were engaged in child-rearing practices—midwives, nannies, mothers, and other women—they also promoted their own judgment as superior because of its masculine attributes. These masculine qualities derived from an Enlightenment-era set of gender dichotomies.[56] In this respect, these Russian Enlighteners joined the English and French philosophers, physicians, and social critics who inspired them, including Locke, Rousseau, and the "man-midwives" William Hunter and William Smellie.[57] Masculine reason, represented in Novikov's machine, thus trumped feminine ignorance in the prescriptions and plans of many male reformers.

Issues of social estate complicated both the assessment of existing child-rearing practices and the construction of the ideal feminine caregiver. Sounding very much like Rousseau's *Emile*, treatises written by Russian men tended to attribute women's insufficiencies in the realm of upbringing to nature (an essentializing argument that could apply to women of any social echelon) or to an excess of vanity and artifice (a critique reserved for women of the nobility). In the discourse on upbringing, the ideal womb and breast for nurturing Russian life were most often found in the countryside, rather than among the nobility. In a sense, the female peasant body became a site for critique of the aristocracy.[58] Medical men, in particular, constructed a new masculine identity through the critique of female midwives, wet nurses, and mothers. Significantly, on the basis of their claims to scientific expertise, these men promoted a new kind of masculine identity that existed outside peasant, merchant, or noble society and assumed for itself the omnipotent gaze and authority to critique the child-rearing practices found at all social echelons of Russian society. This gendered discourse thus served not only to construct feminine archetypes like the good peasant mother or the ignorant midwife, but also to validate and promote a new masculine identity and status based not on social estate, proximity to the crown, or wealth but on academic achievement, scientific expertise, and a privileged ability to diagnose society's ills.

The discourse on upbringing constructed ideas of the preciousness of infant life and childhood while providing new conceptual avenues for thinking about the political meanings around the concepts of pregnancy, birth, and upbringing. The metaphors derived from this discourse provided new political paradigms through which to conceptualize Russia's opportunity for rapid progress. Catherine and her contemporaries, all of whom subscribed to an Enlightenment scale of civilization, embraced metaphors of *vospitanie* as a means of imagining and reinterpreting Russia's status vis-à-vis Europe. Rather than focusing exclusively on the perceived deficiencies in the empire's social, cultural, and economic development, Russia became, through this lens, Locke's proverbial blank slate. In the new discourse on upbringing, infants were not inherently bad or good; they were simply ruled by their passions because of their immaturity. The playwright Denis Fonvizin, after visiting France, reinterpreted Russia's lack of culture as evidence of the country's youth and subsequent opportunity to be shaped and raised into a better form, which he juxtaposed with France's decline in its old age.[59] Rather than a weakness, immaturity read through the paradigm of *vospitanie* became Russia's greatest opportunity. With time and proper care, an infant or country would learn to manage its appetites, suppress self-interest when necessary for the greater good, and grow into its nearly limitless potential.

Birth metaphors also suited Catherine's political representation of her reign—her "scenario of power," in Richard Wortman's useful phrase.[60] The emphasis on a new beginning after a struggle suited her self-perception as a benevolent, maternal monarch. After Catherine composed a primer for school-age children—itself a very interesting choice for an empress also engaged in waging war and expansion in all directions—she optimistically predicted: "This primer will be the midwife of all of our future bright minds."[61] Her choice of a birth metaphor is significant. It emphasizes the role of the midwife in delivering a healthy new life; indeed, it emphasizes the new birth—or rebirth—of Russia itself. These projections of meaning could work in the other direction, as well. Physicians and public intellectuals sought to convince their readers that the loss of a child was a loss for society and the entire nation; in turn, birth itself took on another discursive meaning. Pregnancy, labor, and delivery became not only a physical and emotional event belonging to a woman and her family, but one that also held meaning for a civic society anticipating a new member.[62] Thus, the intimacies of the birthing chamber and the outcome of labor—a healthy infant or a tragic loss—figured in the treatises of physicians as private matters that demanded public attention.

THE STATE AND MIDWIFERY

Most of the Russian Enlighteners who were concerned with pregnancy, child-birth, and child care were not private doctors seeking a living among the well-to-do in Moscow or Saint Petersburg; they were servitors in the Russian state medical bureaucracy. This made them different in identity and perspective from the English man-midwife and the French accoucheur, who typically sought careers outside state service and who continually attempted to encroach on the territory of midwives. In the urban areas of England especially, this made for a fierce rivalry among male and female childbirth attendants. As Monica Green emphasizes for the Anglo-American case, the masculinization of midwifery (defined as male doctors replacing midwives) has often served as the unacknowledged standard story, creeping into master narrative territory.[1] This chapter argues that the story of Russian obstetrical medicine and its relationship to childbirth and midwifery is one of negotiation and manipulation but rarely replacement.

The story of midwives and medical men in the Russian context is particularly ripe for consideration. While articles of varying length have been published during the past 150 years, the history of midwifery in Russia is still waiting for its very first monograph to be written.[2] Even areas of Europe considered less studied than France and England, such as Prussia and other German lands, have received much more attention than the Russian case. Mary Lindemann cites fourteen prominent historiographical works on early modern German midwifery alone.[3] As a consequence of the thinness of scholarship for the early modern period in Russia, historians of later periods have no general works or narrative histories upon which to rely for context or comparison. Eve Levin's research on the medieval period in Russia demonstrates that birth was "an exclusively female event," protected from the influence of outsiders by strict rituals regarding purity. No men were admitted to the birthing chamber. Samuel Ramer researched late nineteenth-century childbirth practices among the peasantry, finding that women relied on trained female midwives when available or local women who had attended births, known as *povituhki*.[4] As a consequence of the lack of scholarship, general European narratives must stand in as background or reference where Russia-specific scholarship is lacking, even when that results in the less-than-ideal importation of the Anglo-American standard to an entirely foreign territory.[5] As Green underscores, this type of substitution elides the regional differences in the history of midwifery and obstetrical medicine and perpetuates the Anglo-American master narrative. This chapter aims to begin to bridge the gap in literature on midwifery in the Russian context.

In the Russian case, male physicians aspired to license, educate, and manage female midwives—but sought to replace them only in emergency situations when life was endangered. Doctors in Russia were few, often rare, with only ninety-four doctors in all of Russia in the 1760s. By the end of the century, this number had grown to only 236. With a population of about 26 million in 1782, the ratio of physicians to civilians was roughly one to twenty-six thousand.[6] Given the vast size of the Russian empire and the uneven distribution of the population, rural residents would have experienced an even greater shortage of physicians than these numbers suggest. Doctors in Russia relied heavily upon lower-level medical personnel (e.g., medics, barber-surgeons, and midwives) and had no desire to replace them. Nonetheless, Russian Enlighteners, doctors and a few medics included, did want to train and control rural practitioners, especially midwives. Enlightenment goals proved more difficult to attain than the leading physicians had imagined, owing in large measure to their assumptions about feminine preferences and behavior—and even birth itself. These physicians and medical men worked to construct an institutionalized medical hierarchy in which midwives' local and traditional practices and experiential knowledge were dismissed as inferior. Rural medical practitioners tended to be raised and trained in Russia while physicians, the majority of whom were foreign born, without exception received their medical degrees abroad. No medical degrees were even granted within Russia until the last decade of the eighteenth century.[7] Russian Enlightener advice manuals constructed a gendered hierarchy based on medical training so that those without formal medical education and training were viewed as assistants to or pupils of physicians and public intellectuals. The frustration expressed by physicians at women's reluctance to seek the help of a male doctor reveals that women were dismissive of the superiority physicians bestowed upon their own profession.

A note on language is in order. While the modern translation of *akusherstvo* is "obstetrics," this term is usually regarded by historians of eighteenth-century midwifery as anachronistic, necessitating awkward-sounding translations. When midwifery education was directed at female students, it was referred to as *povivaniia*, *povival'noe iskusstvo*, or *iskusstvo povivanii*. When the students were male, the term *akusherstvo* was used. I translate the former as "midwifery" and the latter as "man-midwifery" to reflect this gendered distinction in usage.

STATE INTEREST IN BIRTH

Peter the Great, like many of his European contemporaries, had a passion for collecting rarities and oddities of nature, which he displayed in his cabinet of curiosities.[8] His interest in the wonders of nature extended to human beings born with anatomical differences, some of whom were kept as live exhibits in his *Kunstkamera* as "freaks" and "monsters," to use the common terms of his era. Many philosophers and scientists of the seventeenth and eighteenth centuries perceived in infants born with deformities an opportunity to discern the natural laws governing fetal development. From Francis Bacon to Jean le Rond d'Alembert, fascination with unusual progeny stimulated observation, study, and speculation about fetal development.[9] Before the theory of epigenesis became fully accepted in the nineteenth century, philosophers and academicians debated the role of the mother in fetal development. Did conditions in the womb, the mother's diet, and her moods influence the health of the infant? Or, according to preformation, had the ultimate outcome been predetermined? A desire to learn what happened in utero and an impulse to disregard superstitious beliefs as explanation for all manner of "unnatural" and tragic outcomes of pregnancy, including premature birth, deformity, stillbirth, and maternal death, led to greater interest and research on the part of naturalists and medical men in the realm of pregnancy and birth during the Enlightenment.

Peter's interest in these topics first became evident in 1704, when he issued a decree instructing midwives on the appropriate response to a "monstrous" birth. On threat of punishment by execution, Peter warned that midwives must not "kill or hide infants who were born as monsters."[10] Shortly thereafter, in 1705, in a local decree, he directed clergy to remand the corpses of mothers and infants who died in childbirth to the recently established anatomical theater in Moscow.[11] By 1718, Peter was seeking data from around the entire empire on strange births and on maternal mortality. Offering monetary rewards for living or deceased children born with deformities, Peter also lectured his subjects a bit on the fragile nature of pregnancy in this same decree. While there is little to support claims that Peter was interested in the debate over theories of epigenesis and preformation, it is clear that he sought to collect information from around the empire about births. He was willing to invest resources in this endeavor, not only through rewards for those who reported on rarities, but also in establishing the Academy of Sciences and staffing it with learned men, including physicians who began to study fetal development in humans and animals from midcentury.[12] Peter's interest in rescuing illegitimate children has also been documented. However, Peter's interest in saving healthy infants from untimely death rested entirely on the opportunity to supply more troops to the army; his agencies would support male children only until the age of ten and then remand them to garrisons.[13] While civilian life was not yet the focus of the crown's initiatives related to pregnancy and infancy, Peter's reign marks the beginning of the state's interest in pregnancy and early life, as well as the beginning of the state medical bureaucracy.

In the decades following Peter's death, his successors showed little concern for continuing his interests in these arenas. In 1740, however, Empress Anna pursued a reliable midwife for entirely personal and dynastic reasons. Wanting to ensure the healthy delivery of the niece or nephew she intended to name her heir, she wrote to the physician Lavrentii Blumentrost, a member of the Academy of Sciences and the director of the *Kunstkamera*, asking that he send a "learned midwife" to court, as her services would "be needed soon." Blumentrost replied with a recommendation for an experienced midwife in Moscow who not only had delivered at least five hundred babies but also had the additional advantage of being literate—as he put it simply: "she is able to read books." As he explained to the empress: *Other midwives in Moscow have no foundation in science*; and consequently in serious situations they are unreliable for they cannot express directly the condition of the parturient to doctors because they have no knowledge of Anatomy."[14] Blumentrost refers here to the case of a midwife calling a physician during a difficult delivery. In practical terms, if both physician and midwife had an education in anatomy, it would be easier for them to communicate.

The fact that Anna thought to contact a physician employed by the state for help in procuring a skilled midwife indicates that she or someone near to her recognized physicians' potential roles as evaluators of midwives' competency. Across Europe in the eighteenth century, the preoccupation with perceived depopulation and infant mortality, the increased awareness of infancy as a period of delicate health, and the rise of medicine as a profession all worked to focus attention on existing practices of midwifery. The challenges posed to female midwives differed by national contexts, as noted, but the messages issuing from male physicians and statesmen were quite similar: female midwives lacked the formal, scientific education of male physicians and medics and, because of their "ignorance," were likely responsible for many infant deaths. Within the discourse on populationism and from the view of the modernizing state, midwives needed scientific training in order to advance the needs of a modernizing society; in the words of one scholar, "modernity meant science."[15] Within this semiotic field, "science" signified abundant, healthy, robust infants safely delivered from the womb. The extent to which physicians really had more to offer than midwives in terms of safety is a matter for consideration. Roy Porter warns against swallowing whole the claims of eighteenth-century physicians; their promises often exceeded what medicine was capable of before the discoveries of anesthesia, germ theory, sterilization, and antibiotics.[16] That said, physicians did have access to formal education in anatomy and to medical instruments, including forceps, which were denied to midwives and may have assisted some physicians in difficult births, although any conclusions in this direction must be taken as theoretical in the absence of more research.[17] In Russia, early modern physicians promised that replacing "ignorance" among midwives with formal training and instruction in hygiene and female anatomy would work to save infant life for the good of the state.

In the English context, the gendering of science and modernity as masculine and urban had an impact on the demand for male midwives.[18] David Harley has shown that changes in taste among the English middle and upper classes also contributed to the demand for men-midwives and surgeons as attendants for normal deliveries, as they "represented metropolitan modernity and scientific progress."[19] Historians have shown that medical men like the surgeon William Hunter, the physician William Smellie, and "man-midwives," as they were called, sought to replace female midwives as regular childbirth attendants and marketed their services as superior and safer—not only in difficult deliveries but for uncomplicated childbirth as well.[20] Although the English narrative itself has been complicated by recent scholarship, it nonetheless remains a story of the decline of female midwives in the eighteenth century. As demand for male physicians grew, midwives were increasingly driven out of business. This became a recognizable, widespread phenomenon to such a degree that Mary Wollstonecraft despaired of the extinction of female midwives in England altogether by the end of the eighteenth century.[21]

The "tyranny of an Anglo-Saxon model," as Lindemann noted, has in the past created the impression that all of Europe experienced a similar decline in the status and number of midwives during the eighteenth century. New research has shown, however, that, in many parts of continental Europe, midwives continued to be the first choice for uncomplicated deliveries throughout the eighteenth century.[22] Hilary Marland explains one way in which the Dutch context differed dramatically from the English: "Though rhetoric was used against midwives throughout the eighteenth century—they were criticized for everything from a lack of skill to an absence of social graces—no determined effort was made to put them out of business."[23] In France, men began to offer midwifery services as accoucheurs, but the state also reinforced the practice of female midwifery, as Nina Gelbart's work on Madame du Coudray has shown. Madame du Coudray, an experienced midwife, traveled the country at the state's expense, providing both anatomical and practical instruction to other midwives for thirty years. She also devised a model of a womb made of leather, fabric, and sponges for use in instructing midwives in the actual birth process. Du Coudray called her anatomical model a "machine," indicative of its moving components, including a newborn-sized doll and placenta.[24] Records from the Saint Petersburg midwifery institute (discussed below) show that an order was placed for one of du Coudray's "leather female machine[s] [zhenskaia mashina] with infant and reproductive moving parts," indicating that male professors knew of her invention.[25] While du Coudray received much support for her ambitions, it should also be noted that the French context was not entirely collaborative with respect to the relationship between physicians and midwives. In 1755, the Parisian Parlement made it illegal for midwives to use forceps, thus restricting the use of this technology to men with medical training.[26] In Holland and southern German states, male physicians succeeded in establishing professional hierarchies that recognized male doctors as superior in cases of emergency or difficult deliveries, but they also assumed that female midwives would continue to be the first choice for normal, uncomplicated deliveries.[27] In all contexts, however, from England to Spain to Italy, a new emphasis on scientific training for birth attendants—whether female or male—issued from male physicians, the state, or both.[28]

In Russia, one eighteenth-century statesman and physician in particular took an interest in childbirth. Pavel Zakharovich Kondoidi, a Russian of Greek extraction, began to pursue state intervention into the realm of midwifery soon after he became the head of the Medical Chancellery (Medical Department) in 1754, during Empress Elizabeth's reign.[29] Before then, the Russian state had little to do with civilian medicine, especially as it concerned women and children. The court always employed a private physician, of course, usually a foreigner.[30] In the early part of the century, Peter the Great established medical training schools for medics and surgeons who would serve the military but not the civilian population, except in cases of epidemics.[31] The lack of activity might be explained in part by the development of academic medicine, which arrived only in the mid-eighteenth century and took several decades to make an impact. Moscow's only university, founded under Elizabeth in 1755, as mentioned previously, had no medical faculty until 1764.[32] All physicians who practiced in Russia earned their degrees at European universities, then returned to Russia. The absence of a domestic context in which to produce Russian physicians no doubt encumbered the development of medicine.[33] The rather underdeveloped school system also contributed; there were not yet established paths to becoming a doctor in the Russian context. The seminaries became the "feeder" schools for the "professions" because these were the only institutions that produced students who had some facility with Latin, yet the overall preparation was often insufficient for the demands of university-level study.[34] The Academy of Sciences faced a similar challenge in seeking to develop Russian-born scientists. Before the schools and universities were fully established in Russia, professors and physicians continued to be either Europeans or those few Russians who had completed graduate study abroad.[35]

Empress Elizabeth, recognizing the need for more Russian-born physicians, agreed to fund Kondoidi's proposal to send ten "native" or "*prirodnye*" Russians to Holland to study medicine in 1761.[36] The Medical Chancellery (reorganized as the Medical Collegium in 1763) had the authority to grant medical licenses.[37] Women, infants, and children were not the regular beneficiaries or targets of state medicine at this time, but their importance to population growth was becoming more apparent as the century progressed. As director of the Medical Chancellery, Kondoidi pursued an entirely new strategy that reflected the accelerating interest at midcentury among statesmen, writers, and readers in child rearing and the health of the nation's population. Just two weeks after assuming leadership of the Medical Collegium, Kondoidi presented a plan to the Russian Senate for a new government institution.[38] Arguing that the Russian state urgently needed to intervene in childbirth practices around the empire due to a perceived population decline, he proposed addressing the problem of infant mortality in childbirth in two ways. First, he suggested establishing training schools for women at which physicians would teach anatomy and other aspects of medical science. Second, Kondoidi proposed a licensing program for midwives that would ensure some level of skill attainment and some level of supervision by the state. The language of his plan reveals how he constructed the problem. Like his counterparts in Europe, with whom he had studied medicine, Kondoidi blamed the "ignorance" of midwives for high maternal and infant mortality. An unfathomable loss was thus projected: "it is not known how many evil consequences occur every day to mothers in childbirth owing to midwives who lack education and skill." He called for his contemporaries in the Senate to pity the victims of "ignorance," reflecting his own Enlightenment ethos, like that which motivated the founders of the *Encyclopédie*. He wrote of the urgent need to train midwives to prevent suffering and needless death: "Because of these unskilled midwives, it often happens that poor, miserable women in labor and their innocent infants are left with one or another permanent injury [and] even prematurely lose their lives." Referring to the dire situation of "the folk [*narod*]" suffering from a dearth of learned midwives, Kondoidi argued that the state had a moral duty to take action to promote public good: "Consequently, this extreme need, the good of society, and the example of other states necessarily demands . . . the fulfillment and establishment, on good and solid foundations, of institutions and order for midwives."[39] Ignorant midwives were to blame, but supervision and education—organized and implemented by the state—would remedy the situation, he argued.

In his statist solution, Kondoidi reflected trends beginning to emerge in the eighteenth century. Like the other physicians and statesmen who would follow him and continue to pursue reforms in *vospitanie*, he sought to rescue infant life not only as a private good but also as a good for the state. As George Sussman notes with respect to infant welfare reformers in France, the "Enlightened humanitarianism" of eighteenth-century physicians was often in tension with a viewpoint that sought to manipulate populations for the benefit of the state's military and economic strength.[40] So, too, with Russian physicians like Kondoidi and, later, Semyon Zybelin, Nestor Maksimovich-Ambodik, and Ioann Kreizel'.[41] It is worth noting that Kondoidi referenced the example of other European nations in a direct play for national sentiment among his colleagues. Russia's status as a strong European power thus depended on acting like other European states, which were already investing in institutions to improve the nation's population, an idea we will return to later.

Kondoidi also intended that licensed midwives literally become the eyes of the state and report all births to medical regulators. To ensure that tax records were kept up-to-date and that payments were made, Kondoidi provided that every midwife would be required to make a monthly written report to the Medical Chancellery. These reports were to contain detailed information about all the births attended by the midwife during the previous month, including details of the mother's and father's rank and financial condition (*sostoianie*). Kondoidi was well aware that what he was asking for might violate contemporary practices in terms of privacy. He insisted, in explicit language, that midwives report all of the asked-for personal information about their clients "without concealing the name and dignity of the mothers who were served." Kondoidi aspired to a degree of management that ambitiously sought to hold fathers of illegitimate children responsible for the costs of childbirth. The midwife, in Kondoidi's plan, would be required by law to submit the name of the father to the medical bureaucracy even if the mother and father were not married. The father of the illegitimate child would be forced to pay the costs of the delivery and the birth tax. Under Kondoidi's plan, midwives who failed to submit the required reports or who attempted to protect the identities of their clients would be fined and could face other punishments.[42] It is not much of a stretch to see Kondoidi as the archetype of a Foucauldian bureaucrat, who is visionary in his aspirations to collect information about the population for the benefit of the state. The Russian case undermines the hegemony of a Foucauldian interpretation, however, as we will see later.

Kondoidi added another argument that might have held sway with Russian statesmen at midcentury with his reference to the "example of other states." He informed his colleagues that other European nations were *already* instructing and licensing midwives:

> [Mistakes] in midwifery are of the most extreme magnitude, as frequently the very life of the birthing mother and infant depend on the skill of the midwife, and because of this, in almost all states and significant cities in Europe, special schools have been established [to teach midwifery], which is why it is also necessary to establish such schools in Russia.[43]

By invoking competition with other nations, Kondoidi elevated tragedies that occurred during childbirth to a level of national importance and national identity. In the post-Petrine era, many elite Russians were cognizant of and anxious about Russia's degree of "civilization" relative to that of Europe.[44] The perceived need to compete in terms of population with other European nations and concerns about the degree of Russia's Westernization may have helped Kondoidi's plan achieve ratification in 1754. Kondoidi's sense of competition with other European nations is also evidenced in his intention to retain the midwives trained at the expense of the Russian state. He stipulated that graduates of the midwifery courses would "be forbidden to take positions in other states for a period of six years."[45] In fact, Kondoidi's plan closely resembled the state licensing procedures followed in certain southern German states.[46]

Under Kondoidi's system, male physicians would not replace midwives as attendants at "normal" deliveries but would act as superiors to midwives in several ways. First, male physicians and their male assistants (surgeons or medics) would provide instruction to female midwives. This formal instruction was to include both theory and practice, as Kondoidi argued that both were necessary to train competent midwives. This meant that midwives would receive instruction in anatomy, as well as in birthing procedures and hygiene. Second, Kondoidi wanted male physicians to administer exams to midwives who had completed the course of instruction, thereby ensuring that the midwives had mastered certain knowledge and skills. Third, members of the Medical Collegium would determine whether or not a midwife should receive a license from the state. If a license was granted by a committee of physicians, the midwife would take an oath to the state. She would thus be certified as understanding her duties as a Russian licensed midwife. Finally, male physicians would have the legal authority to perform certain surgeries and to administer certain therapies to parturients. These included surgical procedures to save the lives of infants whose mothers had died during labor, blood-letting, and the administration of certain medicinal substances. Midwives were thus excluded from these aspects of maternal and infant health care.

Kondoidi also instructed midwives that they were to immediately call for a doctor in the case of a prolonged labor or "unnatural" delivery.[47] This represents an effort to further establish the medical hierarchy referenced by Blumentrost. Of course, this goal was also aspirational; in Russia at midcentury there were few men who had the training to treat such cases successfully. Midwifery had not yet been added to the training at surgical schools, nor had a medical faculty been added to Moscow University. Male physicians or medics trained in midwifery were few.[48] Women, as clients of midwives, would not have been accustomed to the possibility of a male birth attendant, even in emergencies. Even decades later, in 1792, the physician Kreizel' complained that women were too modest to allow a man to attend their birth and would submit themselves to the "tortures" of an "unskilled and ignorant midwife" rather than accept a male physician, even if the physician might save their lives.[49]

Kondoidi's system rested on a particular assumption about female midwives; Kondoidi believed that they would obey his directives and accept the new procedures, including the new licensing process. In other words, they would be good subjects—and good women. Under Kondoidi's plan, practicing midwives in Saint Petersburg and Moscow, the two major metropoles, would voluntarily appear before the Medical Chancellery to take exams. (Students who completed the midwifery courses would also be eligible to sit for the exam.) Those who passed would swear an oath and then receive a license certifying their knowledge and skill in midwifery. These midwives would be known as "sworn midwives," or *prisiazhnye babki*. Those who failed the exam, his plan implies, would not be able to legally practice midwifery. But what if women who practiced midwifery (or intended to) did not show up for the examinations or for the courses? How did Kondoidi intend to enforce his new regulations?

Kondoidi imagined an autocratic state operating in tandem with willing subject-citizens, eager to respond to and to obey state directives. Within his vision, the names of licensed midwives would be published "for the people's information" to enable clients to engage a state-licensed midwife for deliveries. These names were also communicated to the police, so that the police might verify whether a midwife had the proper license. Midwives caught practicing without this license would be fined, and these fines in turn would be used to support midwifery education.[50] If a midwife's actions were judged by the Medical Chancellery as "dangerous to others," she would be "publicly punished with lashes to the body."[51] Except in cases that came to the attention of the courts because of tragic outcomes and accusations of negligence, Kondoidi did not explain how the police would identify unlicensed midwives. According to his directives, in the case of "normal" deliveries there was no stated mechanism for ensuring that a licensed midwife attended the birth, other than voluntary compliance by both midwives and their clients. In other words, Kondoidi's system left normal deliveries, in practical terms, as a "private" matter that would require self-policing by participants. Only abnormal outcomes would come to the attention of the state.

Kondoidi anticipated that his initial announcement of the new licensing procedure would produce fifteen sworn midwives in Moscow and ten in Saint Petersburg, with each midwife taking on two apprentices who would eventually become licensed midwives, as well. In time, there would be at least one sworn midwife in every town throughout the empire, reporting back to the Medical Chancellery.[52] In order to motivate these women to appear for licensing, Kondoidi intended to improve the pay for licensed midwives. He drafted a table of fees for licensed midwives that amounted to a sliding scale according to the civilian or military rank of the father. He explained to the Senate:

> According to the opinion of the Medical Chancellery, it is necessary to improve the awards to midwives for their labor in the delivery of the parturient; for the consideration of all a schedule is presented, which was written according to

ranks, so that each and every would be without burden . . . and midwives would
be satisfied with their sustenance and pay . . . and so that each and every would be
paid without excuses.[53]

As with the threat of fines for noncompliance, there was no mechanism for
enforcement in Kondoidi's fee scale. Private, licensed midwives were to receive
their fees from their private clients, not from the state. In other contexts, a
supplemental salary issued directly from the state to licensed midwives would
provide a material incentive to midwives to endure the licensing procedure.[54]
For example, in some German contexts, midwives received a salary "paid by
the city treasury" in addition to the fees paid by their clients.[55] Kondoidi also
stipulated that all sworn midwives would be required to take charity cases as a
matter of course, without payment, and that they were to view these as opportunities to serve humanity while also improving their skills.[56] In Holland, by
way of contrast, municipal midwives "were paid by local councils to deliver
poor women."[57] While Kondoidi gave some thought to the material side of the
midwifery business, he expected the issue of midwives' livelihood to be of little importance.

On the other hand, Kondoidi devoted considerable time to the moral character and behavior he expected of midwives. In fact, he spilled more ink on his
moral directives to midwives than on actual obstetrical and medical issues. In his
Oath for Midwives, the midwife swore to go quickly when called to assist a woman
in labor, whether that woman was "rich or poor," and to treat her with respect.
She pledged "to completely restrain from swear words, curses, drunkenness,
obscene jokes, impolite speech and so forth."[58] In his *Instructions to Midwives*,
Kondoidi also added "superstitious speech" to his list of forbidden behaviors for
midwives.[59] While drunkenness in a midwife is easy to recognize as medically
unwise, it is difficult to see impolite speech as posing an actual medical hazard.
Kondoidi is more concerned about respectability and status in such directives
and about socializing midwives into a proto-professional hierarchy.

Kondoidi was also concerned with establishing a medical hierarchy that
placed men above women. In this respect, academic credentials (and thus masculinity) trumped actual knowledge or experience in midwifery. In the *Oath*, the
midwife promised not to rush a long labor and to call a surgeon or doctor if a
birth became "difficult."[60] Surgery and medicine were professions open only
to men, but, at the time of Kondoidi's writing, midwifery was not part of the
curriculum at surgical schools, nor was there anywhere in Russia for physicians
to receive either theoretical or practical training in midwifery.[61] Thus, calling a

male surgeon or physician to a birth was no guarantee of improving the outcome of a difficult birth, as there were few medical men with midwifery experience or knowledge. Merry Wiesner claims that German city councils wrote
similar directives about calling a male professional because of considerations
based on gender rather than on medicine:

> In this instance, gender was also an issue, for, though councils could not exclude
> women from the practice of midwifery as they could from other areas of medi-
> cine, they could place them under the control of male authorities and so con-
> vince themselves that the women were not practicing independently. In reality,
> of course, the women were, for it was not until the mid-eighteenth century that
> a man was recorded as practicing midwifery in these cities.[62]

These observations also pertain to eighteenth-century Russia.

The medical hierarchy that Kondoidi hoped to institute with his plan, and
for which other physicians would argue, corresponded not to actual experience or knowledge but to gender. Midwives occupied the lowest position in the
hierarchy because they were women and not because they lacked midwifery
experience or knowledge. They lacked the titles available exclusively to men,
titles that, until later in Catherine's reign, bore little relationship to the holder's
knowledge of midwifery or ability to deliver babies. Even at the Romanov court,
midwives—not doctors—attended births.[63] Insisting that midwives call men for
"difficult" births would have had little impact, in most cases, on birth outcomes.
As Porter writes of early modern physicians, their claims reflected their optimism about science, rather than reality.[64] Thus, the stated purpose of saving
infant lives was an aspirational goal undermined by Kondoidi's emphasis in his
Oath and Instructions on the moral character of midwives and by the imposition
of a gendered professional hierarchy that took precedence over actual medical
concerns.

Kondoidi also provided detailed guidelines on the type of woman who would
be the best candidate for the midwifery courses. He hoped to attract women
who were already practicing midwifery or who were apprenticed to midwives.
He specified that midwifery students should be between eighteen and twenty-
five years of age but imposed no restrictions on marital or social status (although
serfs would need their lord's permission).[65] These requirements are interesting
when we compare them to what we know of midwifery elsewhere in continental Europe. Elsewhere, midwives were usually older women, married or wid-
owed, who had already raised families.[66] A woman of eighteen to twenty-five

years of age would not have had very much experience attending births. Perhaps Kondoidi wished to avoid the kind of midwife that his colleagues complained about elsewhere: the experienced lay midwife who did not hesitate to tell a male doctor what to do. As the physician Andrei Bakherakht complained of midwives in an article in a Saint Petersburg newspaper in 1779, "in the cities and villages you won't find a single stupid midwife who doesn't consider it her duty to curse at and correct a doctor whom she doesn't completely like."[67] Given the lack of hands-on opportunities for men to practice medicine on women in labor, it is not unreasonable to imagine that in some cases midwives did give directions to physicians.

Kondoidi considered a prospective student's moral character to be the most important consideration. In order to apply to the midwifery courses, a woman needed a character reference from a senior licensed midwife.[68] This senior midwife was expected to attest that the prospective student was, in Kondoidi's words, "hard-working," "obedient," "sober," of "honest virtue," and "quiet in worldly behavior."[69] The moral character of midwives was sometimes an issue in other contexts because midwives were called upon to testify in cases of rape or suspected prenuptial pregnancy. This was certainly a consideration for Kondoidi, as well; he created salaried positions for municipal midwives who would serve in such a capacity for the police and the judicial system.[70] In the case of a suspicious infant death, for example, a municipal midwife would be called upon to examine an accused woman to determine whether she had recently given birth. In other cases, women convicted of crimes sometimes claimed pregnancy to avoid harsher physical treatment. Midwives on the city payroll were expected to make a determination of veracity in these situations as well.[71] These positions were few, however, and Kondoidi wished to direct the behavior and morals of all midwives. The characteristics he hoped midwives would possess were not only practical but political. Kondoidi wanted not only ideal midwives but also ideal Enlightened subject-citizens, "obedience" and "honesty" being their chief qualities. These ideals and the emphasis on "industry" have much in common with Catherine the Great's objective of raising "ideal" citizens, who would serve the autocracy through industriousness and obedience, while also reforming society through their honesty and virtue. Such "citizens" are indeed ideal—and perhaps essential—for the functioning of a weak autocracy ruling over a vast land.

IDEALS AND OUTCOMES

Kondoidi had hoped to begin by licensing fifteen midwives in Saint Peter burg and ten in Moscow. In December 1754, Kondoidi ran announcements in newspapers in Russian and in German, requesting that practicing midwives appear for examinations in the two capitals.[72] A total of fourteen midwives appeared in Saint Petersburg and five in Moscow. During the next year, nine midwives passed the licensing exam in Saint Petersburg and four in Moscow, becoming the first sworn midwives in Russia.[73] Research on German municipalities suggests similar numbers. For example, Lindemann reports that between 1750 and 1799 in Braunschweig, "the number of licensed midwives, that is, midwives who had been examined by the duchy's *Collegium medicum* (board of health) and sworn-in by the city magistrates, rose from five to eight."[74]

The reasons these midwives responded is difficult to ascertain since women of the early modern period rarely left much behind in the way of written records. What little can be learned about these women is noted in the following table. While we cannot draw any general conclusions about midwives in Russia from this small pool, we can and should make a few observations about the first sworn midwives in Saint Petersburg and Moscow. Nearly all of the candidates were widows of craftsmen or artisans, which suggests a trend similar to that found in other continental European contexts with regard to the types of women who became midwives. It also suggests that midwifery practice may have been a necessary

THE FIRST LICENSED OR "SWORN" MIDWIVES IN RUSSIA, 1754–55

Name	Rank	City
Sharlota Beata Diuval	Wife of a sail craftsman	Saint Petersburg
Anna Gertruda Gausman	Widow of an industrialist	Saint Petersburg
Anna Margarita Kristin'iak	Unknown	Saint Petersburg
Nenila Mikhailova	Widow of an industrialist	Moscow
Anna Maria Morgenstern	Widow of a firearm craftsman	Saint Petersburg
Yelisaveta Otto	Widow of a cook	Saint Petersburg
Sof'ia Khristoforova Rant	Widow of a sword craftsman; relative of a surgeon	Moscow
Mariia Rotger	Widow of a tool craftsman	Saint Petersburg
Malan'ia Afanas'eva Shcherbakova	Widow of a soldier	Moscow
Eva Stroben	Widow of a cook	Saint Petersburg
Yelisaveta Ivanova Tapteva	Widow of a dragoon quartermaster	Moscow
Doroteia Elisaveta Vedel'	Wife of a carpenter	Saint Petersburg
Anna Vil'brekht	Wife of a button craftsman	Saint Petersburg

Source: Chistovich, *Ocherki iz istorii*, 155–56.

means of earning a living for these women, who as widows would likely have been living in poverty.[75] Also, a number of the first licensed midwives were of German descent, a fact not lost on Kondoidi, who later appealed directly to German pastors to help in recruiting midwives from their Lutheran congregations. It is interesting to note that religious confession was not an issue for the licensing body at this time in Russia, unlike in some other European contexts.[76] Both Orthodox and Lutheran midwives were licensed by the Russian state.

However, after the initial positive showing from midwives in Saint Petersburg and Moscow, the licensing program stalled. Kondoidi had planned to pay for the midwifery courses through a new birth tax. Licensed midwives were meant to be the conduit for the collection of this tax. Kondoidi drafted a tax schedule according to social rank: poor families would be excluded from the tax, merchants would pay three to ten rubles depending upon their profession, and the nobility would pay from five to twenty-five rubles depending upon their military or civilian rank.[77] Judging by Kondoidi's next appeal to the Senate, the licensed midwives saw their business diminish as a consequence of the birth tax and the reporting policy. In 1757, Kondoidi asked the Senate to end the birth tax and the requirement that licensed midwives report tax information to the Medical Chancellery. In his letter asking for state funds to run the midwifery courses, he explained that the situation was temporary: "It is the opinion of the Medical Chancellery that it is necessary to cease the levy on births until the time when this young institution becomes customary as in other European states."[78] In this instance, Kondoidi imagined that the problem was partly one of taste and preference—what was considered "customary." Eventually, he suggested, the tastes of Russians would become similar to those of Europeans, who preferred a licensed midwife over an unlicensed one. Eliminating deterrents like the tax would, of course, assist in bringing about this change of cultural attitudes. The tax was lifted on February 11, 1757.[79]

Having eliminated one obstacle—an unpopular tax—Kondoidi faced another problem. His midwifery courses were failing to attract students. Kondoidi ascribed the problem to the "timidity" and "poverty" of female midwives in Russia. To address these issues, in 1759 he eliminated the requirement that midwives appear for courses at the Medical Chancellery or its Moscow office. Instead, a midwife could report directly to a professor if she possessed a "clean" Russian passport or, for immigrant midwives, a certificate from a clergyman.[80] This measure eliminated the cost of procuring a notarized document attesting to one's identity and was meant to make it less intimidating to enroll in midwifery courses. But, a few years later, the Medical Collegium was again exhorting the professors of midwifery to recruit more female students. Decades later, as the new director of the midwifery courses, Maksimovich-Ambodik was still confronting the problem of low enrollment.

The wilting of Kondoidi's licensing and education program suggests that assumptions about women might have influenced Kondoidi's expectations and responses to problems. Kondoidi had expected lay midwives and midwifery students to be "obedient" and to voluntarily obey his directives. When they did not show up, Kondoidi blamed, in part, the "timidity" of midwives. When guessing why clients preferred to avoid licensed midwives, Kondoidi reasoned that the new birth tax created a monetary disincentive for clients and their families. Why, when thinking about the motivations of midwives or would-be midwives, did Kondoidi fail to consider how to attract or entice midwives to his program? While we cannot reconstruct Kondoidi's thoughts, we can consider his construction of midwives. While he imagined that midwives were too timid to appear at the state office of the Medical Collegium, one might also conclude that they were brave enough not to appear for licensing; the threat of fines was not sufficient motivation to cause them to do so. The evidence suggests that unlicensed lay midwives continued to practice with impunity; they were neither obedient nor timid. Also, some women who did appear for the midwifery courses actually had the temerity to complain to the Medical Collegium about male professors who routinely canceled class and treated them rudely.[81] When the women who were the targets of Kondoidi's system behaved in ways that defeated his expectations, Kondoidi was unable to think beyond his assumptions to seek other solutions.

Additional insight into why Kondoidi's system failed can be gathered by comparing it to similar, successful institutions in other contexts. Merry Wiesner and Mary Lindemann write about midwifery licensing in German states during the early modern period. Wiesner shows that in Nuremberg, Frankfurt, Munich, and Stuttgart, city councils had been taking "great care to license, regulate, and oversee midwives" since the fifteenth century.[82] These municipalities and other southern German municipalities continued this tradition until the end of the eighteenth century or later. Lindemann is interested in "the careers of that relatively small number of women who comprised the corps of licensed midwives and their assistants" in eighteenth-century Braunschweig.[83] She documents how these licensed midwives reinforced the boundaries of their "profession" against unlicensed midwives and assistants waiting for licensed positions. These German cases offer a glimpse of successful licensing programs in the eighteenth century and raise important questions about the relationship between state and society in eighteenth-century Russia. It is perhaps interesting that the first "learned" midwife in Russia was an immigrant from Braunschweig who accompanied Princess Kristina Sophia, the future wife of Tsarevich Alexei Petrovich, to Petersburg in 1711.[84]

What enabled the midwifery licensing systems in these German towns and cities to work? Most German city councils studied by Wiesner appointed women who were members of high-status families to supervise the licensed midwives. These women "examined those wishing to become midwives, assigned midwives to indigent mothers . . . , [and] disciplined midwives who they believed were not living up to their oath."[85] As upper-class women, they were literally able to straddle two worlds: they negotiated between the upper-class male world of local government and the middle- and lower-class female world of midwives.[86] Kondoidi's licensing system might have made more inroads if officials had been able to find such "go-between" women to bridge the world of government and the communities of midwives. This strategy had analogies in Russian society and culture: consider the historical importance of women to kinship politics in pre-Petrine Russia, the "public" personas of the tsaritsas and the empresses, and the role of noblewomen in public charity work.[87]

Lindemann's work on Braunschweig shows that licensed midwives in the German context worked to reinforce the licensing system themselves. Perceiving unlicensed midwives as poachers on their territory and as a threat to their livelihoods, the licensed midwives named them in written grievances to the authorities.[88] The system "worked" in part because midwives who became licensed adopted a policing role, relieving the state of the nearly impossible task of learning who was practicing midwifery without a license. This self-policing is an aspect missing in the Russian context. Absent subject-citizens who would or could bridge the public world of government licensing and the private world of the midwifery market, there was little chance of enforcing or encouraging the new licensing directives.

When we compare these examples from German midwifery licensing programs to the Russian failed program, we find that a "well-ordered police state" needs more than autocratic decrees, *Instructions*, and *Oaths* in order to function.[89] It needs integration with the society it means to govern and control. Were the midwives in Germany more "obedient" to governmental authority than those in Russia? Or did the local German governments work more effectively to communicate with midwives through "honorable women" and to reward midwives for their voluntary participation in the licensing program? The Russian state in its effort to supervise midwives resembled not a well-ordered police state but rather an ineffective autocracy, short on local ties to the communities it wished to police (the midwives) and unable to direct its subjects toward the behavior most in keeping with the state's interests. While the German licensing programs issued from local city councils and were reinforced through local channels, the Russian program issued from a centralized bureaucracy. In other words, the German programs were local; Kondoidi's plan was imperial in scope, with broad goals meant to eventually put Enlightened, state-licensed midwives in every town of the Russian empire. Kondoidi was thinking like a large state, but the reach of that state proved short of his goals.

In the end, Kondoidi's top-down thinking, along with the noncompliance of both midwives and their clients, led to an apparent abandonment of the licensing effort. The spottiness of the Medical Collegium archive itself is further evidence that, in some areas, the Russian bureaucracy was far from well ordered until the beginning of the nineteenth century. An anonymous critic complained to Catherine that the Medical Collegium lacked a library and an archive and was in need of more space.[90] As for supervising midwives, under Maksimovich-Ambodik's directorship, a few midwives sent in reports on births they attended, but there is little to suggest that the licensing of midwives continued to be a goal of the state. In 1798, a report was filed regarding the establishment of "learned midwifery" in certain villages of the empire. While the Medical Collegium members gave up on supervising midwives, however, they did not surrender the goal of educating lay midwives. [91]

EDUCATING MIDWIVES

Kondoidi's greater legacy concerns his establishment of midwifery courses for lay midwives in Moscow and in Saint Petersburg. He appointed Johann Friedrich Erasmus, a German who had studied in Strassburg and who had passed the Russian medical exam in 1756, "professor of midwifery" in Moscow at a salary of six hundred rubles per year.[92] In addition, he named Ivan (Johann) Pagenkampf, who had entered Russian service in 1721, to the post of "accoucheur" in Moscow. Kondoidi cited Pagenkampf's native fluency in Russian as an important asset, as Erasmus did not have even a basic familiarity with the Russian language. Pagenkampf's salary was four hundred rubles per annum. A word about salaries is in order: instructors of midwifery were not compensated as well as instructors of other subjects. For example, at the Moscow general hospital, a professor of pathology in 1793 earned one thousand rubles per year. However, at three hundred rubles per year, a senior female municipal midwife earned nearly as much as her male counterpart, a municipal accoucheur.[93]

In Saint Petersburg, Kondoidi encountered a similar problem in finding a professor to teach midwifery: there were no local, Russian-speaking candidates. Kondoidi appointed a Baltic German, the Lithuanian-born Andrei (Andreas) Lindeman, who had earned his medical diploma at Goettingen University and won the right to practice medicine in Russia in 1756.[94] Like Erasmus, his salary was six hundred rubles per year, and, like his Moscow counterpart, he never acquired a command of the Russian language. His assistant was Khristof Yakov Fonmellen (Christopher Jacob von Mellen), who had been in service to the Russian state since 1735 as a medic.[95] Kondoidi appointed him accoucheur with a salary of three hundred rubles per year.[96]

The professors in both cities began giving lectures to female students during the following year, but in both cases certain problems created obstacles to the development of consistent courses. Primary among these seems to have been the problem of language. Erasmus and Lindeman did not speak Russian, so their assistants were directed to translate their lectures. In Saint Petersburg, Fonmellen became so tired of this duty that he petitioned the Medical Collegium in 1763 to release him from this responsibility.[97] His request was denied, because, without his translation services, the courses would have been accessible only to those who spoke German. Another problem concerned the professors' commitment to their female students. In both cases, the professors took on additional posts that diminished the time available for teaching. Lindeman became a member of the Medical Collegium in 1763, and Erasmus became a professor of anatomy at Moscow University.[98] Yet both continued to collect their salaries as professors of midwifery. Lindeman and Erasmus also managed to be absent from Russia for long stretches while still holding their teaching posts and collecting their salaries. After a two-year absence, from 1778 to 1780, Lindeman was relieved of his teaching duties and reassigned as physician at a home for victims of smallpox.[99] Maksimovich-Ambodik, a native Russian who would prove much more devoted to developing midwifery education, was named to replace him.

In Moscow, Erasmus escaped termination from his midwifery teaching position, despite many altercations with the Medical Collegium.[100] He continued to collect his salary as professor of midwifery until his death, in 1777. Communications between Erasmus and the Medical Collegium indicate that, in addition to being absent from Moscow for long periods, attempting to hold more than one teaching post, and spending time on his private practice, Erasmus also apparently had a personality conflict with his female students. The midwifery students complained that the professor was inclined to frequently cancel lectures, which he gave at his apartment. Kondoidi asked Erasmus for a progress report in March

1758, but instead received a letter from him complaining about how often the midwives skipped class.[101] Erasmus also had a reputation for treating his female students in a rude and condescending manner.[102] Despite his short-comings as a teacher, Erasmus deserves recognition for writing one of the first pregnancy-related texts for a Russian audience. His handbook on diet and regime, published in 1762, explicitly addressed the nutritional needs of pregnant and post-partum women.[103] Erasmus was also the first physician known to perform caesarean surgeries in Russia. The success of these surgeries is not known, but we might surmise, on the basis of data from Europe, that they were performed on women who were close to death or had already died during childbirth in order to save their infants. Until the advent of anesthesia and antiseptic surgery, both at the end of the nineteenth century, few women survived such surgeries.[104]

In 1763, the second year of Catherine's reign, training in *akusherstvo* (man-midwifery) was added to the curriculum at training hospitals. In February, the Medical Collegium, now under the directorship of Baron Alexander Cherkassov, ordered that six medics (*podlekary*) from the Saint Petersburg and Moscow general hospitals report to the professors of midwifery to hear lectures on childbirth and learn midwifery procedures. Lindeman and Erasmus both demanded an increase in pay for assuming these additional duties. In return for granting Lindeman an additional two hundred rubles and Erasmus an extra one hundred rubles per year, the Medical Collegium made a number of counterdemands. They asked the professors to start giving their lectures at the hospital schools, rather than at home, to try to recruit more female students, and also to train the male medics in "women's and children's diseases."[105]

The Medical Collegium also sought to improve the quality of education and to make more midwifery textbooks accessible to Russian-only speakers. In 1764, the Collegium commissioned the translation of a Swedish handbook by Dr. Johan von Hoorn from the Moscow surgeon and accoucheur Ivan Pagenkampf.[106] The Russian text was titled *Povival'naia babka* (*The Midwife*).[107] The term *povival'naia babka* ("granny midwife" or simply "midwife") indicates that female students, rather than male ones, were the intended audience. The book was a sensible choice. If it found its way to literate midwives, the book offered practical advice on delivery presented in a question and answer format. The Medical Collegium also wished to establish a program at the university level that would lead to a medical doctorate. By eliminating the need to study medicine at a European university, such a program would make the medical profession much more accessible to Russians. In 1764, the medical faculty was founded at Moscow University.[108] In the same year, the first anatomical theater was opened.[109]

In the 1780s, the Medical Collegium became interested in reorganizing medical education. It received permission to send two Russian professors abroad, at the state's expense, to investigate foreign universities. Professors Terekhovskii and Shumlianskii returned to Russia in the second half of 1786 and made recommendations to the Medical Collegium. The members of the Collegium created a plan for establishing a faculty to teach at all of the capital city hospitals. Shumlianskii, who also had a private "obstetrical" practice, protested the absence of a specific midwifery department in the plans and insisted that the Collegium submit a report on this issue to the empress.[110] This incident is worth noting for two reasons. First, it is more evidence that Russian physicians consciously sought to improve medicine in Russia according to European standards. Second, it provides an example of a Russian physician advocating for professional training in midwifery, seeking to increase the number of male practitioners of midwifery, and appealing to the highest authority (the empress herself) to help achieve these ends.

CATHERINE AND MIDWIFERY

As empress, Catherine proved to be much more interested in issues related to childbirth than any previous rulers had been. She became quite dedicated to the cause of midwifery education, perhaps because of her own experience. Catherine remembered the birth of her son as both physically and emotionally painful. She recalled in her memoirs: "I woke up Mme Vladislov; she sent to fetch the midwife, who declared that labour had started. . . . I had a very hard time; at last towards noon the following day, September 20th, I gave birth to a son." She remained on her *"lit de misère,"* as she put it, for several hours unattended after the birth: "I had been in tears ever since the birth had taken place, particularly because I had been so cruelly abandoned, lying in discomfort after a long and painful labor . . . I was half-dead with fatigue and thirst."[111] While Catherine never makes explicit the connection between her own experience and her commitment to improving midwifery in Russia, she did not keep private her feelings about the lack of adequate care in her case. This episode clearly influenced her subjectivity, earning bitter comment in her memoirs, which was far from standard in her era.

During Catherine's reign, Maksimovich-Ambodik rose through the Russian civil service to become a member of the Medical Collegium and a prominent professor of midwifery. His captivating lectures attracted men and women to his courses and became extremely popular; some were opened to the public and advertised in newspapers. His native Russian fluency made his courses far

more accessible (and therefore more successful) than those of the first professors of midwifery under Kondoidi. Records show that Maksimovich-Ambodik's
courses for women were well attended.[112] Like Kondoidi, Maksimovich-Ambodik
thought on a large scale, but he focused on practical, accessible education in
Russian, rather than on licensing. The goal of increasing the Russian population "would not be difficult to bring into being with the sound establishment of
Russian obstetrical schools."[113] He imagined a time when "learned" midwives
would be found "everywhere in the Russian empire."[114] His optimism contrasts
sharply with the despair expressed by one of his compatriots. At a committee
meeting convened as part of Catherine's Legislative Commission, one deputy
spoke on the need to train midwives to serve in rural communities: "What kind
of cruel heart isn't touched, whose blood doesn't boil, upon seeing women giving birth without any kind of help and without even anyone who would take
upon themselves the task of explaining all the dangers [. . .] that these women
subject themselves and their innocent babes to without any cause?"[115] In an
essay contest sponsored by the Free Economic Society, Alexei Polenov offered
this bleak assessment: "As regards the establishment of skillful and trained midwives, although this would be extremely useful, one ought not think of it, when
it's still impossible to find them not only in the villages, but even in the towns."[116]

Maksimovich-Ambodik advocated the creation of permanent midwifery institutes to replace the intermittent midwifery courses offered in Saint Petersburg
and Moscow. Denigrating midwives who had only "read books" or been "present at several births," he insisted that "theory, reading, and practical experience"
should be the standard for midwifery education.[117] This represented a change
in custom for lay midwives, who, Maksimovich-Ambodik and other male physicians pointed out, were usually experienced but short on actual anatomical
knowledge or instruction. Acting as an "anonymous donor," in 1781 Catherine
gave thousands of rubles for the construction of permanent midwifery institutes,
which continued to operate into the twentieth century.[118]

At the midwifery institutes, students received instruction in female reproductive anatomy, learned how to assist during routine deliveries, and were introduced to the use of surgical instruments and aids during obstructed deliveries.
The instructional texts written by physicians and the new technologies of medicalized birth helped to create and promote the idea of an ignorant, untrained
midwife, who lacked access to textual knowledge and to surgical instruments.
Maksimovich-Ambodik's Russian text for midwifery instruction includes engravings of the technologies used by physicians and man-midwives. Midwives
used different aids than male midwives and physicians; for example, midwives

administered a special brew meant to give the laboring woman sustenance and to ease her discomfort. Each midwife had her own recipe of medicinal herbs, elixirs, and sometimes wine or spirits. Physicians were suspicious of these drinks. Birthing chairs were sometimes part of a midwife's kit. These were made in different dimensions, but typically consisted of a stool with a curved or u-shaped seat and a back meant to support the mother's back, hips, and thighs during delivery. Physicians introduced birthing tables and birthing beds, which were expensive and less portable than midwives' stools.[119] Physicians and man-midwives also were trained to use various surgical devices designed to assist with the extraction of infants from the womb. Thus, physicians had access to technologies that midwives could not afford. Some Russian physicians advertised these technologies as superior to the stools and comfort items used by midwives. The volume of engravings in Maksimovich-Ambodik's multivolume midwifery treatise includes a title page whose illustration depicts a uterus and fallopian tubes as objects pinned for dissection and anatomical instruction.[120] The hand of a fetus extends from the uterus. Surrounding and embedded in the circulatory system of the reproductive organs are the surgical instruments used by physicians to extract matter from the womb, including various types of hooks, scalpels, clysters, and tools designed to aid in dismembering and removing the remains of a miscarriage or of an infant that had died during an unsuccessful birth.[121] Maksimovich-Ambodik's decision to include these instruments and this graphic image on the title page of his work underscores his faith in the technologies of obstetrical medicine. While we cannot know how the women who enrolled in his courses perceived these images, it is likely that they had few reference points at this historical moment in Russia to help them read the anatomical image or recognize the purpose of the instruments. It is impossible to know whether other women had access to Maksimovich-Ambodik's book, although some evidence suggests that midwifery treatises were purchased by laypeople. The Empress Maria Fedorovna, second wife of Paul I (Catherine's son and heir) had a copy of Maksimovich-Ambodik's multivolume set printed and bound for her library.[122]

We do not know, however, how many women chose to have male midwives, trained female midwives, or physicians at their births at home during this era. Kreizel' had hoped that, over time, girls in Russia could be raised to accept a male medic or doctor—in effect, to be less modest by contemporary standards.[123] Maksimovich-Ambodik, for his part, continued to seek ways of increasing the number of trained midwives, especially in rural areas. Students taking courses in midwifery gained a site for instruction during actual births with the establishment of lying-in hospitals attached to orphanages, which are discussed in

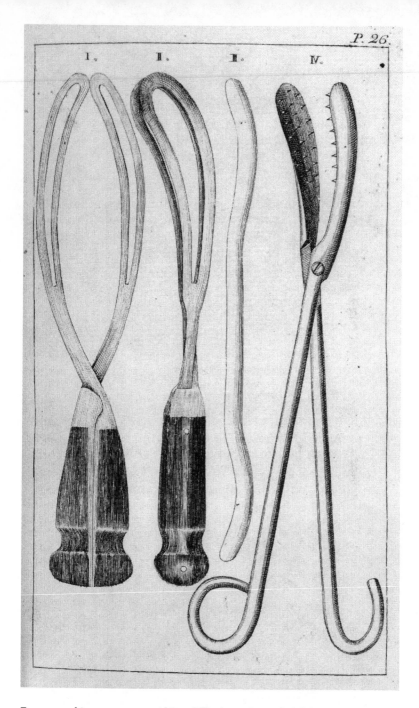

Forceps and instruments to aid in a difficult or obstructed delivery. Doctor Maksimovich-Ambodik taught techniques using these aids to female midwives. Maksimovich-Ambodik, *Iskusstvo povivaniia*, vol. 6.

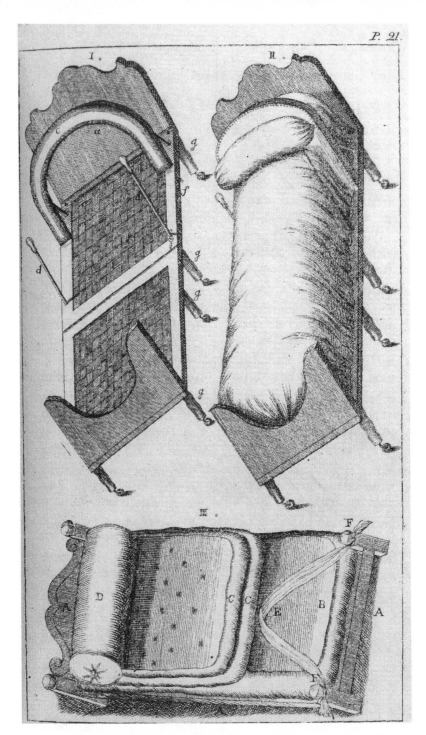

Examples of birthing beds. Maksimovich-Ambodik, *Iskusstvo povivaniia*, vol. 6. (Courtesy of the National Library of Medicine, Washington, DC)

Frontispiece depicting or suggesting female reproductive body parts as though displayed for dissection and instruments used by physicians in the practice of midwifery. Maksimovich-Ambodik, *Iskusstvo povivaniia*, vol. 6.

the next chapter. The lying-in hospitals provided the missing component of instruction for male students especially, because they had almost no chance of being admitted to a birth in any non-hospital context. It is estimated that, during the first seven years of the Moscow lying-in hospital's existence, more than seven thousand babies were born there.[124] Thus, from this era on, some women in Russia did have dramatically different experiences of labor and delivery than those whose home deliveries were attended by lay midwives.

3

MOTHER'S MILK

This chapter focuses on one contentious aspect of the new campaign to reform maternal practices for the greater good: the issue of maternal breast-feeding. This issue is particularly rich for the historian; its discourse reveals the connections among modernity, empire, and the construction of motherhood in the age of Enlightenment. By deploying the languages of state interests and of *nauka* (knowledge, learning, and science), physicians and men of letters posited themselves as qualified to assess mothering practices and argued that reforming the care and feeding of infants was a matter of imperial importance. In this discourse, mothers were identified as potential agents of the state; their choices regarding infant care would either further or impede the growth of the empire. Thus, the campaign to reform the domestic, feminine tasks of caring for infants functioned to connect the private world of the home and the family (and the previously all-female world of midwifery, wet nursing, and child care) to the public, masculine sphere of statecraft and empire building.

MOTHERS AND WET NURSES: AN INTRODUCTION

In the contemporary Western world, a new mother must decide whether to feed her infant from a bottle or from her breasts, or some combination thereof. Before the advent of infant formula and glass bottles, for most women in the world there was no choice to be made. For women of wealth, however, there existed the option of engaging a woman from a lower echelon in society to perform the task of breast-feeding one's infant. A wet nurse, or *kormilitsa* in Russian, essentially sold her breast milk to women of means (usually noble in origin) in an arrangement that provided income to women who needed it and freedom to women who could afford it. A wet nurse had duties beyond breast-feeding a newborn every few hours; she also provided all infant care during the period of her employment, including diapering, swaddling, bathing, and, the birth mother hoped, a degree of supervision. In some wealthy households, a wet nurse would be engaged to live with the family. In other cases, the infant would be sent to live with the wet nurse for a period of one to three years. This meant that it was not unusual for infants and toddlers to live away from their families and to see their birth mothers only occasionally during their early years.[1]

Few historical studies of medieval or early modern Russia have investigated breast-feeding and wet-nursing practices.[2] Eve Levin's research suggests that wet nursing was a common practice in the pre-Petrine era. Because a woman who had given birth was considered impure for forty days, a wet nurse was often engaged to nurse her infant until the mother had undergone purification rites at the end of the forty-day period.[3] Given the biological fact that a birth mother's lactation would have ended without an infant to nurse, it seems likely that many mothers came to rely on wet nurses by the end of the forty-day period. Frequent references to wet nurses in medical and advice literature in the second half of the eighteenth century seem to confirm that engaging wet nurses was common practice among noblewomen in early modern Russia. Memoirs and literature from the eighteenth and nineteenth centuries indicate that peasant wet nurses and nannies were standard figures in many noble families.[4]

While it is clear that the practice of wet nursing was not unusual, not many sources exist from which to reconstruct attitudes about wet nursing and breast-feeding in medieval Russia. *Domostroi*, an anonymously written sixteenth-century household manual, prescribed many rules about familial relations, domesticity, and home economics.[5] It is silent on infant feeding, which indicates at the very least that how infants were fed was not judged an important or appropriate topic for this well-known domestic handbook from the pre-Petrine era. During the medieval period, the Church approved of wet nurses as necessary in the observation of purity rituals.[6] Only one Russian source that expressed an opinion on the dangers of wet nursing prior to the mid-eighteenth century has been located.[7] Dmitrii, the archbishop of Rostov and a leading light among prominent clergy of the late seventeenth and early eighteenth centuries, admonished noble mothers to nurse their own infants rather than hire wet nurses. In a sermon about the biblical story of Sarah, who was barren and childless and granted a pregnancy by God, Dmitrii suggested that God also gave Sarah abundant milk to nurse her offspring. Dmitrii argued that this miracle showed that God wanted all mothers to nurse their infants. He invoked both religious and natural laws: "mothers must feed [*pitat'*] their infants with their own breasts, and not give them to other women [wet nurses]; this duty is laid upon them by both God and nature, who gave them breasts to feed their offspring."[8] Dmitrii also argued that maternal breast-feeding had both material and metaphysical justifications. Citing Pliny, Dmitrii argued that "drinking the milk of his own mother, a newborn is healthy and when he grows up, is of strong body and sharp mind."[9] An infant "who is fed the milk of another woman, and not of his own mother, is not healthy and soon dies; if he survives, he will not be strong[.]"[10] Dmitrii's goals—to promote health and to please God—were ends in themselves. Nowhere does he suggest that his goals had a political function.

THE NEW RUSSIAN EXPERTS

In sharp contrast, the Russian Enlighteners publishing on infant feeding later in the eighteenth century reference explicitly the benefits they predict will accrue to society, the public, and the state. The writers under consideration here were motivated by secular aims. To the extent that moral or spiritual qualities were addressed, they were referenced as important to the vibrancy of the population from the perspective of the reforming state. Although their arguments vary in content, these Russian men of the Enlightenment shared in common a view of Russia's population that reflected and buttressed state ambitions and imperatives. This evidences the European impulse toward state building in the eighteenth century and also registers the impact of Peter I's reforms and Catherine II's ambitions.[11] These Enlightened Russian reformers thought like moderns and Europeans—but also like Russians. Such men include Nestor Maksimovich-Ambodik, whom we met in the previous chapter; Semyon Zybelin, also a prominent physician in Catherine's era; Nikolai Novikov, author of a prescriptive essay on child rearing; Ivan Betskoi, who published work on child rearing; and Khristian Rost and Matvei Peken, authors of two medical handbooks for domestic use. The first part of this analysis explores their interest in maternal breast-feeding; the second part considers the social and political implications of their arguments and places them in a broader European context.

The physician Nestor Maksimovich-Ambodik addressed the topic of breast-feeding in two volumes of his five volume work *The Art of Midwifery*: volume 1 (1784), on women's anatomy, pregnancy, and birth, and volume 5 (1786), on child rearing. Writing of birth in general, he said that it ought to be a happy event not only for the family but also for "society," which grows in numbers with each new member. Birth is not only a private issue but a societal, public concern.[12] To prove his point, Maksimovich-Ambodik cited at length a contemporary Russian authority: Empress Catherine. It is interesting to note that he deployed her *Instruction* as though it were already law, mistakenly referring to it as the "Code of New Laws [*Ulozhenie novykh zakonov*]," rather than as Catherine's guide for the drafting of future legislation.[13] He quoted directly from Catherine's *Instruction*, citing chapter 22, section 226, on increasing the population of Russia: "What a flourishing situation there would be for this world power [*derzhava*] if this destruction [of infants] could be averted or prevented through wise institutions."[14] He also constructed infant death as an "overt harm" done to "the entire state."[15] This is the context that Maksimovich-Ambodik established for his entire oeuvre; the goal of his advice was to save infant lives not only for their own sake but also to increase the population of Russia and thus the economic strength and political power of the Russian state.

To this end, Maksimovich-Ambodik had much to say about the importance of maternal breast-feeding in preventing infant death. The reasoning he provided goes beyond simply promoting infant welfare. Like Dmitrii, Maksimovich-Ambodik argued that women's anatomy was designed explicitly for feeding offspring. Maksimovich-Ambodik agreed with Dmitrii that hiring wet nurses to breast-feed infants was a bad practice that could lead to illness and death. But, unlike the clergyman, Maksimovich-Ambodik also argued that it was a woman's "civic duty" to nurse her own children; maternal breast-feeding was political.[16] In the chapter "On the Duty of the Mother Concerning Suckling," he wrote that "civil, natural, and moral law" compel mothers to breast-feed their own infants.[17] More than once, he posited the idea that breast-feeding is a "civic" duty, perhaps one that should be enforced by state law. He wrote: "Every mother is required, by natural and *civil* laws, to feed her own offspring from her own breasts."[18] Maksimovich-Ambodik's references to civil law suggest that he viewed the issue of who nurses an infant as a concern worthy not only of the state's attention but even of legislation.

Like Maksimovich-Ambodik, the physician Zybelin also constructed maternal infant care as a matter important to the state, in particular to the goal of increasing the population. A professor on the medical faculty at Moscow University, Zybelin gave a public lecture on maternal breast-feeding that was later published as a short book, *On a Method for Preventing the Chief Cause of the Slow Population Growth of the People*.[19] The title itself shows very clearly that Zybelin understood the issue not as a personal, moral, or private familial matter but as an issue so vital to state interests that it warranted a campaign to correct bad practices. Like Maksimovich-Ambodik, he explicitly cited Catherine's *Instruction* to establish the political importance of his work. Even more forcefully than Maksimovich-Ambodik, Zybelin argued that the issue of who fed infants and what they were fed was central to increasing the Russian population and therefore a political and imperial issue.

The size and health of the population, Zybelin argued, directly affect all of the goals of Catherine's *Instruction*; the success of Catherine's reforms depended on having a large enough population to carry them out. Referring to the empress's plans, he wrote: "for all of this, without sufficient numbers of people as the main instrument toward each undertaking, is not easily achieved." He also credited Catherine with leading the way toward reforms in *vospitanie* by including in the *Instruction* suggestions "on how to increase and strengthen the fatherland by increasing the population."[20] Zybelin provided a scientific comparison of the number of births, the number of deaths, and age at death, determining that "it is now possible to conclude that the slowness of the increase of the *narod*, or its great decrease, begins from infancy, and more in the first year from birth than in the second or third."[21]

Zybelin argued that infectious diseases and illnesses claimed the lives of many infants, and he laid the blame primarily on mothers. The introduction of solid food, usually chewed by the mother or grandmother before being fed to the infant, was identified as a serious threat to infant health: "for usually among the *narod* on the second or third day after birth they start to give heavy, thick, and indigestible foods to infants."[22] Women were identified as the custom-keepers who mistakenly, "out of ignorance or simplicity," believed that infants were not satisfied by human milk alone. He made an argument based on the laws of nature: "But I am asked what infants should be fed so that they will be contented, will be strengthened, and will grow? The answer is so well known to all, that it would seem unnecessary to demand an explanation from me: for nothing other than nature prepares a special juice [*sok*] in the mother's body for this [purpose]."[23] Zybelin arrived at the same prescription as Maksimovich-Ambodik: in keeping with natural law—and for the good of the Russian state—all mothers should breast-feed their infants.

In addition to physicians like Maksimovich-Ambodik and Zybelin, other writers and statesmen engaged the issue of infant care and feeding. Nikolai Novikov, the publisher and essayist, and Ivan Betskoi, Catherine's elder statesmen, were two non-physicians who also published advice on this issue. Like their physician peers, Novikov and Betskoi understood this issue as an imperial and societal concern. Novikov, writing for an educated, noble audience, sought to draw parents' attention to the importance of the earliest months of child rearing and to convince them to follow the advice of physicians, rather than custom or fashion: "Our readers should believe us and the skillful doctors, according to whose words we are writing."[24] He placed all of his advice within the frame of improving "the state," arguing in the first sentence of his work that child rearing was more than a family matter: "it is recognized that the upbringing of children is as highly important for the state as it is for every particular family."[25] On the issue of who should feed the newborn infant, he acknowledged that "mother's milk should always be preferred." Nonetheless, he recognized that many in his audience would hire wet nurses, rather than nurse their own infants. He wrote that, if a mother was unable to breast-feed "or does not want to feed her infant herself," then a suitable wet nurse, someone physically and morally healthy, should be hired to ensure that the infant would receive "good" milk.[26]

Ivan Betskoi, the architect of Catherine's early pedagogical institutions, addressed the issue of infant feeding in two different contexts. He published advice on child rearing and also addressed the issue in practice at the Moscow Foundling Home. In 1766, he published *A Brief Instruction, Chosen from the Best Authors with a Few Notes on the Upbringing of Children from Birth to Youth*.[27] Intended for a noble audience, the very first set of rules gives advice on selecting the proper wet nurse for a newborn infant. Betskoi recommended that parents consider a wet nurse's physical and moral qualities: "Select a wet nurse, to the extent possible, who is healthy, virtuous, without silly pretenses, with scarlet red gums and white teeth, who is neat, tidy, and agile; and exclude all redheads."[28] Most Russian physicians believed that there was a moral component to breast milk, although this view was being challenged by some medical voices in the eighteenth century. For example, the English physician Henry Bracken preached against such a viewpoint, writing in 1737:

> Former authors were much of a belief, that the child sucks in the temperament and disposition of its nurse; that is, the vices both of the nurse's body and mind are impress'd upon her milk, insomuch that the child shall become alike unto her. . . . But for a physician to argue that there is so much to be attributed to the milk, as most of them pretend, is much folly and mere quackery . . . I say then, that a creature does not with the milk suck in the vices either of body or mind.[29]

This was certainly a minority opinion for much of the eighteenth century, however. The French campaign against wet nursing often cited the moral contamination of wet nurses' milk as a reason for maternal breast-feeding.[30] For example, in 1750, the French author and defender of noble women's intelligence, Madeleine de Puisieux, warned that the milk of evil wet nurses caused "their vices and stupidity . . . [to flow] into the veins of children."[31] Pavel Kondoidi, the first state physician to try to reform midwifery, instructed midwives to find wet nurses for their clients who were "of clean body" and "virtuous."[32]

In recommending "extreme circumspection" in choosing a wet nurse, he explained that "not only our health, but also our spiritual qualities depend on our nourishment and our upbringing."[33] This very much reflected the dual conception of *vospitanie* that entwined the moral and the physiological. Zybelin believed that strong passions like fear, anger, and lust spoiled a woman's milk. He instructed mothers and wet nurses, in the event that they experienced strong emotions, to avoid breast-feeding for at least an hour and to express by hand their morally contaminated milk. He warned: "If these instructions are not followed, then of course one should expect soon afterward some kind of great change in [the infant's] health and sometimes even death itself." Novikov also warned his readers that strong passions "spoil the milk."[34]

POPULATION ISSUES, MOTHER'S MILK, AND THE RUSSIAN EMPIRE

These men had in common a view of "mother's milk" as central to the population goals of the state. In this respect, these men reflect pan-European concerns about depopulation. Montesquieu contributed significantly to this phenomenon by promoting the notion that the population in France was in danger of declining.[35] The eighteenth-century physiocrats believed that agricultural surplus alone produced a nation's wealth, and thus, a nation's wealth could be sustained and increased only through population growth. This idea, in turn, contributed to natalist viewpoints and worked to focus attention on reproduction. Both Zybelin and Maksimovich-Ambodik cited Catherine's goal of "increasing the population" of Russia, as articulated explicitly in her *Instruction*, as the inspiration for their works. In this respect, it was Catherine, the "Mother of the Fatherland," as she was called by all of our medical authors in the usual mode of address and flattery, who established and promoted the *Russian* goal of population growth. Maksimovich-Ambodik and Zybelin, as enterprising physicians and statesmen, referred explicitly and repeatedly to her text, adopting the terms and goals of the *Instruction*. In this way, their rhetorical strategies allied their goals with those of the crown.

Here we might also pause to consider how all of the men writing on the importance of improving Russia's population were beginning to adopt a perspective that reflected cameralist and mercantilist philosophies of how best to manage the state's resources.[36] Their concern reflected the populationism of these philosophies, but it is also worth noting that these writers began to adopt the viewpoint of an abstraction, presented as "the state," "society," or "the nation." They also departed in their perspectives from Walter Gleason's conception of "moral idealists."[37] While morality was certainly an important category for them, they explained the motivation to improve the population in terms of the perceived benefits to the state. In other words, they were pragmatists seeking simple solutions to the perceived problem of slow population growth. The eighteenth-century European anxiety about declining population had less to do with reality (population was, in fact, increasing) than it did with an expanding awareness of the world and a reinterpretation of power. The intellectual historian Eric Voegelin cites the new tendency in the eighteenth century to evaluate the power and influence of a country not by its cultural contribution (e.g., ancient Rome) but by its size. Thus, it was believed that Russia, as the largest empire in terms of geography, could come to dominate if the land became populated.[38]

Zybelin, more than any other Russian writer on upbringing, explicitly developed the theme of population management and state power. He grounded his treatise in the mercantilist idea that Russia was competing with other European nations. To bolster his claims of urgency, he cited Catherine's *Instruction* as proof that the empress would be grieved "if some other nation on the earth were to prosper more than ours."[39] He imagined a future in which Russia, led by Catherine, was first among all nations, leading other nations to a brighter future: "Bring peace and give your wise counsel, which flows from the mouth of your Sovereign, to the universe, Russia! . . . Succeed under HER wise reign, open prosperity to all, give charity to all, for your own glorification and for the perfection of well-being for all of Humanity!"[40] This spirit of national or imperial pride informs all of Zybelin's work.

In another fine example of Enlightenment governmentality, Zybelin assembled a great number of statistics to propel his arguments about the urgency of addressing population growth and reforming infant care. Drawing extensively on both European and Russian data, he concluded that the vast majority of deaths occur before the age of four, most of these during the first year of life:

> If we now compare these foreign notes and observations to Russia, then we will see similarly that death steals incomparably more infants than those already in adulthood: for example in the Ukrainian province of Slobodskaia in 1774 out of 13,688 deceased 1,519 infants of a year old died, 2 years 941, 3 years 592, 4 years 328, 10 years 104, 20 years 102, 30 years 116.[41]

Zybelin used his data to conclude that Russia was actually competing quite effectively with European nations in terms of population growth. He writes in an extended footnote: "It is worthy of comment that compared to foreign States, fewer infants die in Russia, and everywhere many more are born [than in other states]. . . . Our Fatherland, in fertility and long life and in many other advantages, is therefore superior." Zybelin argued that the first months of life deserve greater attention, as they claim the greatest proportion of lives. In Russia, he wrote, the first months of infants' lives were particularly hazardous because they often coincided with "cold months [and] damp times of year."[42] Thus, Zybelin posited that Russia was superior to other European nations in the rate of population growth, but added that this advantage must be safeguarded and improved upon, with methods specific to Russia's context. Enter the idealized "natural mother," with the responsibility (and power) to raise Russia to new heights.

THE NATURAL MOTHER

In Western Europe, the Enlightenment campaign for maternal breast-feeding by physicians, philosophers, and statesmen dates from the mid-eighteenth century. While some physicians argued against wet nursing before the second half of the eighteenth century, the plethora of texts on the topic appearing at this time constituted a broad campaign.[43] Most important, according to scholar Christine Theré, was Rousseau's *Emile*, published in 1762, which argued for breast-feeding as an "essential" maternal duty.[44] George Sussman sees *Emile* not so much as the primary influence in a movement but, rather, as a text that found wide acceptance precisely because it captured the zeitgeist of the era. Sussman argues that none of Rousseau's recommendations regarding maternal breast-feeding were original to him and makes a case for viewing *Emile* as part of a general "polemical campaign" against wet nursing.[45]

Historians have analyzed European arguments in favor of maternal breast-feeding as part of a larger critique of elite women and their relationship to luxury.[46] French women of the aristocracy were less likely to have healthy infants in part because their love of fashion led to overly tight corseting, which Madame de Puisieux argued caused "the noble parts, which are too confined, [to] spoil and dry up."[47] William Cadogan suggested that mothers of the aristocracy irreparably weakened their children by keeping them in excessive heat and luxury for their first month of life; then they doomed them by sending them away to live with a wet nurse in a radically different environment: "this Hot-bed Plant is sent out into the Country, to be rear'd in a leaky House, that lets in Wind and Rain from every Quarter. Is it any wonder the Child never thrives afterwards?"[48] In his *Essay on Women*, Antoine-Léonard Thomas argued that, because of immoral salon sociability, "the two sexes were denatured." Women avoided maternal duty altogether: "Among a people in whom the spirit of society is carried so far, domestic life is no longer known. Thus all the sentiments of Nature that are born in retreat, and which grow in silence, are necessarily weakened. Women are less often wives and mothers."[49] Rousseau, perhaps most infamously of all, associated elite women with luxury, frivolity, and corrupt society.[50]

Read against this critique of aristocratic women, the campaign for maternal breast-feeding seems to have been as much about prescribing women's gender roles as it was about infant welfare. The scholar Steinbrügge writes that, through the eighteenth-century reconsideration of "female identity," one viewpoint became dominant:

> It was precisely the great significance attributed to women's physical nature that, in conjunction with physiocratic discourse, led to an unprecedented reduction of woman to the creatural. . . . [T]he woman who emerged from reflexions about female nature was not a full individual but a being viewed solely in terms of her sex.[51]

Steinbrügge argues that this reduction of "woman" to a biological definition led to the identification of women with the emotional, moral realm of the private sphere and to women's segregation from the realm of public action, rationality, and masculinity.[52] It is a short step from here to the full flowering in the late eighteenth and early nineteenth centuries of an ideology of "Republican Motherhood" and the "Cult of Domesticity," as historians have termed the rise of the maternal image that linked women's civic duty to childbearing and rearing in republican contexts.[53] Convincing the public that mothers should be at home, breast-feeding their infants every few hours, rather than out in mixed-gender social contexts seems one part of a larger movement by male intellectuals, physicians, and statesmen toward ascribing (or re-ascribing) women to the domestic realm.

Viewed in the broader European context, the Russian writers who promoted breast-feeding were shoulder to shoulder with their contemporary European counterparts in the campaign against wet nurses and in favor of maternal breast-feeding. Russian texts on the topic were appearing in print during the same era as the leading French and English publications. This is worth noting in part because some eighteenth-century Europeans held the impression that Russia was barbaric, uncivilized, inhospitable, and worse.[54] The *Encyclopédie* entry on Russia, while praising the Westernizing advances of Peter the Great, also warned that his reforms "have not yet sunk such profound roots, that some interval of barbarism might not be able to ruin this beautiful edifice, undertaken in an empire depopulated and despotic, where nature never spreads its benign influences."[55] When Mary Wollstonecraft sought a comparison that represented the most egregious example of patriarchy reinforced by violence, she referred to Russia. She wrote that if women, once emancipated, were shown to be undeserving of their freedom, "it will be expedient to open a fresh trade with Russia for whips: a present which a father should always make to his son-in-law on his wedding day, that a husband may keep his whole family in order by the same means."[56] While Russian writers were formulating arguments similar to those of their Western counterparts, however, it would be incorrect to conclude that these Russians were simply transferring European ideas to a Russian audience. The men who were writing on upbringing in Russia were very conscious of the social and political context in which they were writing. With this in mind, we turn to a discussion of the "good" or "natural" mother trope, which reveals some of the tensions and issues specific to the Russian social and political context.

The trope of the natural mother emerges from these Russian texts as an ideal type. Immediately after giving birth, she puts her baby to her breast. She is "content" to breast-feed her own child, staying at home and breast-feeding "every 3 to 4 hours."[57] Through her milk, she provides the perfect "medicine" for her newborn infant, eliminating the need for harsh purgatives.[58] She gives her infant no other food until the child has plenty of teeth; she decides to wean only when a nearly full set allows for the chewing of solid food.[59] She has beautiful breasts, which makes her quite "pleasing" to the male sex.[60] She loves her child, but always within reason, avoiding an indulgent love and a suffocating "endless tenderness."[61] She "is the example of a true mother and the example of motherly affection! . . . How rare are such examples of motherly love in our own age!"[62] This romantic, yet enlightened ideal mother, who followed both natural law and the dictates of medical writers, was definitely not the typical noble mother, but to what extent, if at all, did these writers imagine her as a peasant?

Khristian Rost, a Russia Enlightener and author of domestic medical texts, and the doctors Peken and Zybelin, all acknowledged that peasant women were doing something that noblewomen generally were not (at least in the writers' conception): they were breast-feeding their own children. The physician Rost painted a rather lovely picture of the peasant mother and left it to his reader to perceive the difference between a natural mother and her opposite, the noblewoman:

Beginning from birth, the upbringing and manner of life of every person is different: the newborn infant of well-to-do families is fed by a wet nurse, but among the simple folk [*prostoi narod*] a mother is content to feed her own child with milk from her own breast, whose strength is so effective and perfect for drawing off and cleansing the pungent phlegm from the stomach of the newborn, for which the well-to-do usually use small, polished millstones, English magnesium, rhubarb syrup or other similar substance.[63]

Rost also wrote that peasant women were healthier and stronger, gave birth more easily, and had fewer problems breast-feeding. He reasoned that "women of the simple folk have stronger builds because of almost continual movement during work and because they always take the same foods with great moderation and abstinence."[64] Rost was alone, however, in offering such an overtly positive portrayal of the peasant mother.

While Zybelin saw the Russian countryside as fertile and, in general, a healthier environment for child rearing, he did not trust peasant mothers to know how best to care for their infants. None of the childhood diseases were as dangerous to infants as the ill-informed practices of their peasant mothers, he wrote. He explained that young infants needed only their mother's milk and "not what is usually given, especially among the simple folk, the raw oats boiled with milk under the name of kasha." This folk tradition, based on the mistaken belief that babies are hungry for solid food, "kills, in a manner similar to a slow poison, a great number of infants."[65] For Zybelin, the problem with the peasant mother was that she needed instruction and supervision to understand what is "natural" and therefore good for her infant.

Maksimovich-Ambodik's ideal mother was more of a romantic creation than an example drawn from observation of the Russian countryside. The degree of romanticization in Maksimovich-Ambodik's conception of maternal breast-feeding is revealed in the following excerpt:

> A true mother, having successfully given birth, quickly puts her child to her own breast. Holding him in her embrace, with motherly love, she continually admires him. The child cannot speak, cannot express his needs with words; but a true mother already guesses and knows all of his desires through secret, tender warmth of feeling. Before she became a mother, nature planted this feeling in her heart.[66]

The natural mother understands her child completely. A wet nurse cannot supply this love, Maksimovich-Ambodik wrote. When in need of a positive example of an actual living mother, Maksimovich-Ambodik referred to the animal kingdom or to indigenous people living far away on other continents. In the following example, he clearly meant to shame noblewomen by suggesting that even animals are better mothers: "All animals, which willingly nurse their own offspring from their own bodies, could serve as examples to every expectant mother."[67] Elsewhere, like Zybelin and Rousseau, Maksimovich-Ambodik noted the healthy children produced by indigenous mothers in North America who nursed their children for at least a year and sometimes up to age five. Maksimovich-Ambodik suggested that Russian mothers look to such women for models of good mothering: "Wild, unenlightened people always nurse their own children and in general do not know the diseases from which many of our newborns suffer."[68] The Russian peasantry did not figure in Maksimovich-Ambodik's mind as an example of unenlightened people worthy of emulation. Rather, the Russian countryside was often represented as barbaric and superstitious, with child rearing left to the influence of ignorant women.

SOCIAL COMMENTARY IN AN AUTOCRATIC CONTEXT

It is interesting that Russian peasant mothers did not figure as positive examples of natural mothers in Maksimovich-Ambodik's or Zybelin's texts but rather were seen as negative, ignorant mothers. The chief English and French proponents of breast-feeding, Cadogan and Rousseau, praised the lower orders of women who nursed their own infants. Were it not for peasant women, Rousseau argued, the urban centers of Europe would become depopulated: "And what would become of your cities if women living more simply and more chastely far away in the country did not make up for the sterility of the city ladies?" In his comparison of peasant and aristocratic mothers, Rousseau attributed virtue to the former while suggesting that the latter engaged in vice during the time they did not spend nursing their children: "Prudent husbands, . . . you are fortunate that women more continent than yours can be found in the country, more fortunate yet if the time your wives save [by not breast-feeding] is not destined for others than you!"[69]

Other than Rost, who gently and implicitly suggested that peasant mothers do better for their children, the Russian medical authors did not come close to the social commentary of Rousseau and Cadogan. The reasons for this are not entirely clear. Rousseau and others who attacked wet nursing as an explicitly aristocratic practice were also keen to criticize the aristocracy and the social system that produced inequality, artifice, and all of the other sins against nature that belong to feudalism. We might speculate about why the Russian Enlighteners stopped short of extending criticism of noble mothers to the nobility in general. Most of the Russian writers were dependent on the state for their positions, but they were not born into the nobility. The medical bureaucracy offered the opportunity to achieve the rank of noble, but without any grant of land. Zybelin was a professor on the medical faculty at the state's Moscow University. Maksimovich-Ambodik held various state positions throughout his career, including a position on the board of the state Medical Collegium and the directorship of the state's midwifery courses. Dr. Khristian Peken's *Domashnii Lechebnik* was commissioned by the Free Economic Society, which, despite its name, was an institution created by the state. Rost writes in his introduction that he had been in government service "to the Russian Empire" since 1745 and had traveled throughout the country as a medic.[70] While some criticism was tolerated under Catherine, it would have been professionally reckless for these medical statesmen to have promoted a vision that either implicitly or explicitly challenged the sociopolitical system—as Novikov learned when he was arrested for publishing works that were not approved by the empress. With the exception of Betskoi, these men were neither wealthy noblemen nor personally connected to the empress. Instead, they depended on their education and status within the civil service for their positions and salaries.

All of the Russian Enlighteners identified their projects with the mercantilist goals of the state. Whether they truly believed in autocracy and the system of serfdom supporting it we cannot know (with the exception of Alexander Radishchev, whose work depicting the cruelty and tyranny of serf owners earned him exile to Siberia, and Novikov, whose critique of autocracy led to prison time).[71] They articulated the state's goals as their own personal and professional goals and benefited from their adoption of Catherine's language of reform. Unlike Rousseau, who adamantly objected to raising children for the good of either society or the French state, these men promoted maternal breast-feeding as a means of achieving a superior Russian society, nation, and state. It is nearly impossible to imagine one of the Russian authors considered here writing as Rousseau did: "Public instruction no longer exists and can no longer exist, because where there is no fatherland, there can no longer be citizens. These two words, *fatherland* and *citizen*, should be effaced from modern languages."[72] Rousseau then dismissed politics altogether as having nothing to do with raising children. For the Russian writers, these categories, fatherland and citizen, had everything to do with raising children. However they imagined the state, society, or the nation, they all imagined these entities—rather than private families or individuals—as the ultimate beneficiaries of their child-rearing reforms. This is the striking contrast with both earlier Russian viewpoints and the beliefs of contemporary French and English maternal breast-feeding proponents. Even Novikov, sometimes posited as a Russian liberal, had much greater ambitions than the liberation of the individual self through a natural upbringing. Like Catherine, he employed the term "citizens" (*grazhdaniny*), indicating the civic content of his prescriptions. While both Catherine and Novikov believed that the ideal upbringing would create virtuous adults who felt responsible to a body politic, Novikov's citizen would be much more self-directed than Catherine's subject-citizen.[73]

The solutions that Maksimovich-Ambodik and Zybelin proposed also depended more on state intervention than did Rousseau's or Cadogan's appeals. Where the latter hoped to influence parents, mostly by petitioning husbands to exercise influence over their wives and convince them to breast-feed, Maksimovich-Ambodik and Zybelin conceived ambitious, far-reaching state reforms. Rousseau suggested that mothers should be given written instructions on how to nurse and raise their infants, but he left the act of converting the women to their husbands. Zybelin proposed a different solution, one that sounds a bit more practical and yet relies upon the intervention of an extra-village authority:

> It would be useful in the countryside to choose one *babka* from among the women of the place, who had given birth herself and was more learned than the others, who would serve as a supervisor for her sex, and especially during the summertime when the mothers are serving in the field, care for the infants.[74]

Zybelin imagined a midwife in each village as an agent of public health who would act as educator and supervisor of other mothers in peasant villages. Catherine's Reform of Local Administration in 1775 provided for hospitals near major towns and for local boards of social welfare.[75] Zybelin's recommendation, published the same year, seems a reasonable extension of these new local institutions.

We might also wonder about the symbolic impact of having a woman and mother on the throne. In Zybelin's text, Catherine is the "mother of the fatherland," from whom "all bliss flows"—like mother's milk. Not only is mother's milk the source of hope for the nation's future according to these medical writers, for Zybelin it even offered an alternative to war. He maintained that improved infant care and the subsequent rise in population would make it unnecessary to expand the empire through force.

> Without conquests I say! For it is known to the whole world that the Russian
> AUTOCRATESS is peace-loving; HER philanthropic soul wishes not for foreign
> acquisitions, but as the benefactress to the human race, the voice of nature, the
> voice of its heart, and the voice of those who come running to her for shelter, she
> ends the strife of others; wishing peace and calm for the whole world.[76]

The political content is evident in this excerpt, in which he preaches population
growth through reforms to infant feeding practices, not war. Thus, the physician, as the agent of change, plays a critical role in the political destiny of the
empire.

It is surely the case that, in Russia, medicine developed as an institution of
the autocracy. Peter established the first medical training schools and also created an institutional structure for entry into the profession. Is it surprising then,
that medical writers adopted a statist analysis in their assessment of infant mortality? Perhaps not. In the impulse to critique and advise mothers, midwives,
and wet nurses, with reference to scientific claims to buttress their advice, these
physicians and the writers who promoted doctors as experts actively worked
to construct their own positions within the Russian state and in society. That
is, as doctors in the Russian context, in which the medical bureaucracy was
first becoming fully established during Catherine's reign, they were seeking to
secure status and privilege. Finally, it seems, on the basis of the anecdotal evidence available, that the prism through which they understood their identities
was informed by Western medicine yet in a distinctly Russian content. These
men wrote from the periphery in Europe, yet understood themselves as both
European and Russian. They referenced a linguistic field created in Europe by
Montesquieu, Diderot, Justi, Linnaeus, and others—but the parameters of that
linguistic field were set by Catherine. As she noted:

> If you go to a village and ask a peasant how many children he has he will say ten,
> twelve, and sometimes even twenty. How many of them are alive? He will say
> one, two, three, rarely four. This mortality should be fought against, one should
> consult able doctors, those of a more philosophical turn of mind than the aver-
> age, and introduce a general rule for the preservation of life among infants which
> is so neglected now; they run about half-naked in the ice and snow; the robust sur-
> vive, but how many of them die! And what a loss for the State![77]

The last sentence underscores Catherine's chief concern: infant and child mortality negatively affects the state's goals.

FOUNDLING HOMES

Catherine's interest in population growth and in raising ideal subject-citizens came together in an institution that facilitated the improvement of midwifery education and also saved abandoned infants. In 1764, Catherine established foundling homes under the name of *Vospitatel'nye Domy* (literally, Houses of Upbringing) in both Saint Petersburg and Moscow. Lying-in hospitals were attached to the homes, where pregnant women could register anonymously two weeks before giving birth, free of charge. Under the directorship of physicians, the hospitals and homes employed a number of women as midwives, nannies, and wet nurses to care for the pregnant women, infants, and children.[78] Women delivered under the hospital's care and surrendered their newborns to the state. Betskoi planned for these infants to be raised at the homes and to become a kind of "third estate" in Russia.[79]

Betskoi articulated Catherine's goals for the institutions of upbringing, including the foundling homes, in 1764's "On the Upbringing of Both Sexes": "in a word, to instill all virtues and qualities that belong to a good upbringing, by which in time they will become upright citizens [*grazhdaniny*]."[80] The moral or spiritual content is foregrounded in the emphasis on raising good "citizens." Betskoi was as preoccupied with inculcating morality as with the wish to "deliver [infants] from untimely death."[81] As this book shows, the moral and physical aspects of child rearing were connected and, in fact, indivisible, in many eighteenth-century minds. Even physicians, with their faith in science and their disdain for the superstitious, viewed the physical world as imbued with moral content. This was never truer or more tragic than at the Moscow House of Upbringing in the early decades of its existence, when it experienced mortality rates of 70 percent and higher due to a shortage of wet nurses.[82]

After a baby's birth or deposit at an eighteenth-century foundling home, no matter the home's location in Europe, finding a suitable means of feeding the infant posed the greatest challenge to the staff. For all foundling home directors at the time, the issue of nourishment proved the toughest obstacle to reducing extremely high mortality rates.[83] Hiring on-site wet nurses proved the most convenient choice and, we now know, the choice most likely to preserve the lives of the infants. But many directors found it difficult to hire enough wet nurses or to keep them on staff.[84] Feeding multiple infants in an orphanage setting was much less desirable employment than feeding one (extra) infant in a noble household or in one's own home. If enough wet nurses could not be employed, a foundling home director had two choices: to feed the babies animal milk or to send them off-site for wet nursing in peasant villages. Either option posed serious problems.[85]

Feeding animal milk to infants, in an era before feeding bottles and rubber nipples, meant using rags soaked in milk or administering milk with spoons or carved wooden instruments or other improvised feeding techniques.[86] This "dry nursing" or "artificial feeding," as it was called then, was recognized as the last resort in a private context or in an orphanage. The other option in face of a wet nurse shortage was to send the infants to be nursed by peasant wet nurses in neighboring villages. This was less convenient than on-site wet nursing and, of course, made supervision of the wet nurses nearly impossible. For Betskoi, sacrificing control over the foundlings' early upbringing was untenable. Sending the infants away defeated his purpose of raising the foundlings according to Enlightenment precepts "for the benefit of the state."[87]

In 1764, the Moscow *Vospitatel'nyi Dom* was opened. In its first year, the home cared for 523 infants. Sadly, only ninety-nine of these infants survived the year, most likely because of a shortage of wet nurses.[88] In the beginning, fourteen wet nurses were hired to nurse the infants. Toward the end of the year, this number was raised to thirty-five. The head supervisor reasoned that each wet nurse could provide sufficient milk for two infants, if she was not also nursing her own infant.[89] However, the number of wet nurses on staff never met the demand. Notes from the home report that "it is difficult to find many good wet nurses."[90] In 1779, Betskoi was again urging the head doctor to hire fifteen to twenty wet nurses to nurse the infants until two months of age; the wet-nursing crisis did not stabilize until the end of the century, for reasons we consider later.[91]

Russia's experience was not unique. In France, at a Parisian foundling home, shortages of wet nurses brought similarly disastrous results for the infants. The French response to the problem, however, was dramatically different and yielded superior results. The Parisian director viewed the problem as a matter of economics and raised the wages for wet nurses until they began to leave private employment for the foundling home. In fact, the private market began to compete with the foundling hospital to attract and retain wet nurses. Wages determined whether nurses changed employers.[92]

At the Moscow House of Upbringing, however, Betskoi focused on the virtue of wet nurses, believing that moral health trumped material concerns when it came to breast milk. He wrote that it was preferable "to give an infant good goat's milk or cow's milk than to give milk from a bad woman."[93] He was continually frustrated at the lack of virtuous wet nurses at the home. Staff complained that the nannies "were of no use at all." Betskoi was loath to entrust *vospitanie* to women he considered unreliable and immoral. He instructed his staff supervisor to keep a close eye on this category of employee, warning "do not rely on the nannies and wet nurses." He seems never to have considered raising the pay for wet nurses in order to attract and keep "good" wet nurses. From 1764 until 1797, the pay for a wet nurse was twelve rubles per year, whereas a municipal midwife earned 150 to 300 rubles annually.[94] To Betskoi, a woman's moral qualities—not the pay—would determine whether she would tenderly care for the infants and show up for work regularly. In 1779, he wrote to the head doctor:

> For the proper care of the children the type of woman is needed who would be a perfect mother for each child; whose heart would be fully committed to the children—and who would not need to complain about the pay. But if such women cannot be found, then everything will be in vain.[95]

Touchingly, but perhaps naively, Betskoi believed it possible to find wet nurses who would serve as substitute mothers for the infants; essentially, he wanted them to nurse the infants out of love, rather than necessity or obligation. He assumed that the success of his entire program rested on finding this ideal type of woman to serve as wet nurse—a virtuous foster mother who would essentially be willing to volunteer her time and give her milk freely. He failed to grasp, however, that wet nursing was a job for women of little or no means, especially women who were unmarried mothers.[96] Wet nurses were able to sell their services precisely because they themselves had given birth recently and, as a result, were lactating. In other words, they were mothers with children of their own to raise.[97] Precisely because Betskoi erroneously believed it better to give infants animal milk than milk "from a bad woman," he pursued means of improving artificial feeding at the Moscow home. He instructed that suitable land near the home be acquired for the construction of a barn so that the home could keep its own cows and goats in better conditions than those found at the municipal stables. Betskoi also directed the staff to keep the feeding apparatus clean: "in relation to cleanliness, see that dishes and rags used for feeding are always clean, for which there should always be a supply of water on hand."[98] Without knowledge of sterilization, lacking modern sanitation and running water, this minimal effort at cleanliness did little to prevent the contamination of the infants' milk and the spread of disease. Of course, before pasteurization and refrigeration, the milk often became spoiled, making the infants sick and prone to dehydration and malnutrition. Betskoi tried to develop creative solutions, including the following suggestion, which he sent to the doctor on staff: "To keep 6 or 8 goats is not difficult—it is possible to tame them, so that they will walk through the children's rooms and give themselves to be milked."[99] Although Betskoi meant well, it is hard to imagine that such a fanciful proposal eased the burdens of the staff and their tiny charges. Despite his efforts, without human milk the infants perished from malnutrition and disease, as they did in foundling homes across Europe in the eighteenth century. In 1772, the Moscow House of Upbringing began to send away as many infants as it could to be wet nursed in peasant villages.[100] Yet Betskoi never completely relinquished his view that the moral aspect of upbringing would be threatened by a coarse village context or by milk from the wrong "type" of wet nurse. Some of Maksimovich-Ambodik's vehement warnings about the dangers of hiring the wrong wet nurses reinforced this view: "Good morals, sobriety, and constancy are the high virtues found in a good wet nurse. Immoral wet nurses not only teach [their bad habits] to the children entrusted to them and make them unhappy for their entire lives, but also cause them to lose their lives; and from drunken wet nurses expect even worse."[101]

The Russian writers and statesmen considered here were indeed a small group, yet the fact that they put pen to paper, imagined great interventions with grand outcomes, and played to an educated Russian audience indicates energy and initiative beyond what was required of them by the state bureaucracy in which they served. Their masculine world of statecraft needed the female task of breast-feeding to conform and to serve their political needs. In the next chapter, we consider how these writers and others interested in *vospitanie* worked to construct a new conception of the child's body, creating at the same time a site for imagining the health and spiritual wellness of the body politic.

4

THE CHILD'S BODY AND
THE BODY POLITIC

The architects of theories of *vospitanie*, as we have seen in the previous two chapters, were keenly interested in saving the lives of infants and children. At the heart of their prescriptions and plans were two rather modern premises. First, these reformers posited infants and children as a special category of the population—a vulnerable group requiring protection. Second, these reformers promoted themselves as the saviors and patrons of this special group. In advocating for reforms in the care and upbringing of young children, these writers and statesmen set out arguments that anticipated the emergence of public health policy. Saving the lives of children and improving their physical well-being became part of the pursuit of a greater good. In this sense, the architects of reform promoted an abstract notion of a public good—and, indeed, a body politic—through the discourse on *vospitanie*. Thus, while constructing a notion of the newborn and immature body as distinct from an adult body and therefore in need of special care, the Russian Enlighteners constructed both a notion of childhood itself as fragile and a conception of the responsibility of state and society to protect children. The indignant and impassioned treatises on child rearing reveal the extent to which these men believed that society, state, country, and even humanity writ large were harmed when infants and children suffered or when their physical infirmities threatened to produce immoral adults.

These Enlighteners did not present a uniform set of prescriptions, but they were united in their tendencies to hold women responsible for the shortcomings in the existing practices of child rearing and to believe that radical interventions in everyday family life were necessary to promote the public good. Most also attributed a supervisory role to men, whether in the home as fathers and husbands or in institutional contexts as medical personnel or directors. These men understood the intellectual aspect of upbringing—the training and education of the mind—as typically reserved for the children of the nobility, and then mostly for boys. However, the reformers explicitly promoted other components of *vospitanie*, identified as physical and moral development, as critical for all children of the empire, regardless of social estate or sex. The Russian Enlighteners perceived the child's body as supple raw material, ready for molding for good or for ill, and gave advice accordingly.

RUSSIAN ENLIGHTENERS AND THE CHILD'S BODY

In the flourishing book market of Catherine's reign, advice manuals were popular. In 1781, Nestor Maksimovich-Ambodik, statesman and author of several medical texts, translated and published Louis Sebastien Sauserotte's work addressing pregnancy, birth, and newborn care.[1] Similarly, a Russian translation of *The Lady's Doctor* addressed health issues specific to women, as the title suggests.[2] In texts like these, authors identified women as both the subjects of and the audience for advice on managing pregnancy, infant care, and all aspects of child rearing. Written in the vernacular and marketed in a context in which physicians were still a rarity, medical and health manuals appealed to the reading public. In 1789, Mark Gorokhovskii, a doctor and member of the Medical Collegium, explained that he translated the medical handbook of the famous Austrian court physician, Anton von Störk, because "in Russia there are few places where medics and doctors are sufficient in number, and in the case of illness, with no one to turn to, it follows that one would make use of printed medical knowledge."[3] Novikov's library contained thirty-six medical titles, which is perhaps an indication of interest among educated readers.[4] Readers of middling means found most medical books fairly affordable at a price of one to three rubles and pamphlets even more so at six to ten kopecks.[5] The first journal to publish exclusively on medical topics, *The Saint Petersburg Medical Register*, also appeared during Catherine's era. In its very first year, the journal devoted considerable space to the issue of *vospitanie* of infants and young children, signaling the importance of this topic to the emerging medical establishment and to the readers of its journal.[6]

While writers focused most on reforming the practices of women who provided direct care for infants and children, they also called upon fathers to assume a supervisory role over upbringing. The famous English physician William Cadogan, whose treatise appeared in Russian during this era, urged men to take an interest in how mothers and nannies raised their children: "I earnestly recommend it to every father to have his child nursed under his own eye, to make use of his own reason and sense in superintending and directing the management of it, nor suffer it to be made one of the mysteries of the *Bona*

Dea, from which the men are to be excluded."[7] Through his association of the feminine world of mothering and child rearing with the all-woman cult of the deity Bona Dea in the Roman state, Cadogan sought to foster a sense of suspicion that would compel fathers to take an active role in the management of child-rearing activities. Cadogan professed the agenda of most, if not all, eighteenth-century physicians who were concerned to reform upbringing: to intervene in the realm of mothering, not by replacing women—an idea that would have been unthinkable—but by instructing and supervising them.

In addition to written texts, physicians imagined this intervention occurring through direct contact with women. As we saw at the end of chapter 3, the physician and professor at Moscow University, Zybelin, imagined a wise woman with a supervisory role in every village, ensuring that women nursed their infants. Maksimovich-Ambodik urged midwives and physicians to begin instructing women on how to care for their children's health before they became mothers:

> In discussions with married women, especially those of weak, tender, and feeble condition, [endeavor to prepare them] for their future duties placed upon them by nature: so that they will have a successful conception, will carry their pregnancy to conclusion, will be prepared for a safe birth and for a well-ordered upbringing of their children from birth, and provide [these women] the necessary and useful means with which they might prevent childhood feebleness, or if it has already occurred, to reverse it successfully.[8]

These reformers sought to create a vehicle for carrying medical knowledge to women, which would travel from European medical faculties to Russian physicians, and then to medics and midwives and finally to future mothers themselves. Through this channeling of scientific information, mediated through men, medically sound and enlightened practices would replace the supposed superstitions of women. In addition to midwives, fathers had a role to play as the deputies of these reforms within the home; they would be the proxies for medical men and reformers of child rearing. The chain of masculine knowledge would thus be secured—if men assumed this important supervisory role over their wives in the raising of children.

In order to convince their readers that the needs of the child's body deserved greater attention and care, these writers had to construct a conception of the young body as different from and more fragile than the adult body. Historians regard the recognition of the unique physiological and cognitive status of

children as one of the hallmarks of a modern notion of childhood.[9] Scholars'
interest in historicizing childhood has led to research that makes visible how
children came to be constructed as beings requiring modified furniture, clothing, nutrition, and even their own branch of medicine, pediatrics.

The development of pediatrics is one of the historically specific ways in which
the human body has been imagined, as historians of the body and historians
of medicine have noted.[10] While is reasonable to assume that bodily sensations
like pain, pleasure, hunger, and fatigue are universals across time and place, those
sensations are interpreted and articulated through culturally specific ways of
conceptualizing the body. In 1998, Barbara Duden underscored the newness of
this line of historical inquiry by noting that "what people in a different age and
culture thought about the inside of the body, about the hidden sphere under the
skin, about stomach, breast, blood, . . . about the 'life inside the body,' is virtu-
ally unknown."[11] An analogy might be made to maps and how they shape perception of the world in historically contingent ways. Dramatic improvements
in cartographic and imaging technologies have given visual maps of the world
a degree of accuracy and detail unimaginable in the eighteenth century, which
in turn has altered humans' mental mapping of the world and, indeed, their
Weltanschauung as well. The Russian Enlighteners considered in this book
offered an increasingly scientific or medicalized conception of the interior of
the infant body as evidence to convince their readers of the necessity of reforming physical *vospitanie*.

The evidence these authors cite rests in large measure on their academic
credentials. The conception of the infant body they created was a medical one
that emphasized the contemporary academic knowledge of anatomy. The life
"under the skin," to speak in Duden's terms, was explained and referenced by
doctors who had observed dissections of corpses in the anatomical theaters of
their medical academies. Whether in Strasbourg, Leiden, or Padua, the anatomical theater became an essential component of an academic medical education
during the early modern period.[12] This type of knowledge of the interior of
the body was, of course, inaccessible to most of the readers of the tracts on
physical care of infants and children. Armed with this privileged knowledge—
available only to men, it should also be noted—the medical writers professed
their authority on the infant body. Readers were, in essence, asked to confirm
that authority by taking on faith the knowledge offered by these new medical
experts.

The physician Zybelin, whose promotion of maternal breast-feeding was discussed in chapter 3, offered a very detailed image of the infant body. Zybelin

created for his reader a mental image of the interior of the newborn body consisting of soft tissues, ducts, and veins. Drawing on the centuries-old theory that the body's well-being depended upon the balance of "humors" (understood then as the four main fluids: black bile, yellow bile, phlegm, and blood), Zybelin's conception also integrated William Harvey's notion of the circulatory system.[13] In order to give a sense of Zybelin's eighteenth-century conception of the interior of the body, it is worth quoting him at length:

> If we look at the composition of the infant body, then we will see that it is nothing so much as it is almost one delicate duct [*kanal*] interwoven with tender, sensitive veins: its instruments are all soft, one finds neither hardness in its limbs, nor strength in its energies: for it is filled only with liquids for comfortable interior circulation, which, when the liquids are thinnest, allows unhindered movement, and nourishment gives growth, health, and life. If however there is a place where a small obstruction is made, it begins to be subject to numerous diseases and ultimately destruction.[14]

Galen's emphasis on balancing humors to achieve optimal health is clearly informing Zybelin's conception, but the circulatory system offers the primary means of conceptualizing the movements of the interior of the body. Zybelin emphasizes the delicate nature of the infant body here, as well, arguing that "given such a build of the infant body, all should easily observe that it is possible to harm it."[15]

The fragility of the infant body is underscored by other writers who addressed early *vospitanie*. These self-appointed child welfare advocates believed it necessary to convince their readers that infants needed more conscientious care than was customary in Russia. The attention given to this issue indicates that these men expected some resistance from their readers. Maksimovich-Ambodik, Peken, and the midwifery instructor Kreizel' all emphasized the helplessness and vulnerability of the infant body in their texts.[16] Kreizel's insistence that a midwife be trained to call a doctor immediately if anything seemed "not right" with a newborn reflects the still very new idea that infant medicine required special training.[17] In emphasizing the vulnerable interior of the infant body, these men claimed a superior ability to see the infant body—to know what is hidden from the lay person—and thus to prescribe the proper *vospitanie* for the youngest children.

As we have seen, the "good mother" was constructed as the natural mother who breast-fed her infant. For Russian Enlighteners, the good mother obeyed natural law and also received instruction in enlightened child-rearing practices from learned men. These instructions were very detailed and addressed every aspect of physical care, from diapering to the proper use of cradles. Three issues in particular engaged deeper political and social questions, along with questions concerning national identity. What should children be fed? How should infants and children be dressed? Is warmth or cold better for infant and child health? These seemingly quotidian issues provoked a questioning of assumptions regarding social estate, obedience, gender, and national identity.

NOURISHMENT AND SOCIAL ESTATE

The issue of what to feed children once they were old enough to be weaned was a central element of physical upbringing. Nourishment, Zybelin insisted, should match the hardness or softness of a child's development, so that the softer, more fluid infant body should be given only liquids until it began to show some firmness. As the child's body developed more "hard" places in its interior, it could accept more substantive food. His reasoning rests on eighteenth-century medical knowledge. He explained to his readers the consequences of feeding the incorrect type of food to small children: "consequently dampness, indigestion, ulcers develop in the interior of all ducts, and their openings become closed, from which the circulation of fluids everywhere finds obstacles; then hard lumps, tightness in the stomach and in other living instruments cause damage and inefficiency."[18] According to Zybelin, managing the interior viscosity of fluids and their circulation was of primary importance.

As food and drink are also very much conditioned by cultural and socioeconomic factors, this aspect of upbringing led to some tensions in dietary prescriptions. Always one to favor the (romanticized) rustic life, Rousseau was unequivocal in promoting a simple, nearly vegetarian diet for children to match the fresh air and exercise that he argued were necessary to develop healthy young bodies. Novikov and Maksimovich-Ambodik encouraged a simple diet closer to that of the peasant family than that of a well-to-do urban one. However, these Russians, along with the famous Russian academician Mikhail Lomonosov, could not adopt an entirely romanticized vision of rural life. The tensions between advocating a peasant or a noble diet were further complicated by the bogey of presumed French influence on certain practices among the nobility.

Maksimovich-Ambodik criticized the nobility for allowing children to drink coffee, tea, and other beverages best reserved for adults, but his warning to stop giving children beer, vodka, and wine was directed to peasants, as well.[19]

Maksimovich-Ambodik, while advocating a Rousseauian upbringing for children in nearly all respects of physical care, could not embrace Rousseau's example entirely. Indeed, he cautioned against applying a peasant upbringing to a child of the nobility, warning that doing so could be dangerous to the child's health.

> The build, nature, and physical strength differ from person to person. . . . And this teaches us that from the very beginning there must be an analysis of children's upbringing [*vospitanie*]; and that not all children should be raised in the same manner everywhere. A well-born, warm, and luxurious life belongs to the nobleman, who raises his small children in a manner contrary to that of the peasant, who is accustomed to ceaseless labor, handiwork, and farming and to the meager nourishment of rural populations. The food and upbringing given to children without analysis would be good for one but harmful and ruinous to another.[20]

Maksimovich-Ambodik begins his passage by appealing to scientific reason, arguing that "build, nature, and physical strength" vary from one child to another. From this, it is logical to conclude, he argues, that not every child should be raised in the same manner. From an argument based on anatomy, however, and one that would be consistent with natural law, he moves to an argument based on differences of social estate. Maksimovich-Ambodik concludes by arguing that noble children in some way would be harmed by a peasant-style upbringing, and vice versa. In this analysis, which contradicts most of his other prescriptions on child care, he makes an argument based solely on the social estate of a child, not on the science he cites to support his arguments elsewhere. Yet Rousseau—and, indeed, most of Maksimovich-Ambodik's prescriptions—supported the opposite notion: what the son of a nobleman needed most of all was to be released from the prison of refinement and luxury.

Novikov similarly criticized noble parents for feeding their children "French confections" as a mark of status and wealth. Indulging children with sweets had become the norm among aristocratic families to such a degree, he argued, that any advice to the contrary was viewed as an "obscenity."[21] He included highly detailed prescriptions for a simple diet consisting primarily of grains and vegetables, devoting twenty-seven paragraphs to educating his readers in what constitutes healthy food for the child's body. Novikov's discourse constructs a new type of parent who is educated and judicious: "This fashion [of feeding children mainly sweets] has become so powerful that only doctors and a few intelligent parents dare to contradict it."[22] In other words, his readers might become the educated parents who choose a simple diet. Novikov, while willing to adopt some aspects of rural child-rearing practices, was explicit in his conception of his readership as elite. He also warned against allowing children to consume vodka, a recommendation that did not originate with Rousseau: "*Vodka* is not given to the children of those estates [*sostoianiia*] for whom we are writing. Only the masses and a few stupid or irresponsible wet nurses give children vodka to drink or to dip bread in so that they will sleep more soundly."[23] Novikov seems to reassure his readers that only the lower orders engaged in such practices, but the implication to keep an eye on one's serf nannies seems evident.

Mikhail Lomonosov likewise did not endorse all aspects of traditional *vospitanie* among the peasantry. A fierce Russian patriot who did not tolerate criticism of Russian culture or history by foreigners, Lomonosov turned a critical, scientific eye toward Orthodox practices that could affect the health and vitality of children.[24] In particular, he condemned the practice of imposing on young children the arduous fasts that were part of Orthodox religious observance, citing the strict and meager diet as an obstacle to population growth. Lomonosov's concern to improve the health of children and thereby increase the peasant population trumped his impulse in other realms to glorify Russian tradition and to preserve Russian culture from change.[25]

SWADDLING, HEAT, AND RUSSIAN TRADITIONS

The Russian medical discourse on the practice of swaddling varied widely, but all Russian Enlighteners engaged with the leading eighteenth-century antagonist of swaddling, Rousseau. In *Emile*, Rousseau devotes several pages to the issue, and his revulsion is both evident and philosophical in nature. Swaddling is a metaphor for the conformity demanded of an individual by society: "At his birth he is sewn in swaddling clothes; at his death he is nailed in a coffin. So long as he keeps his human shape, he is enchained by our institutions. . . . We need to have [our heads] fashioned by midwives on the outside and philosophers on the inside."[26]

Maksimovich-Ambodik opposed the practice of swaddling, arguing that the infant required freedom to move its limbs in order to grow strong and healthy. To make his point, he cited the example of "wild peoples" who "follow nature" and not the "stupid habits of enlightened peoples."[27] "Wild" peoples were superior, according to Maksimovich-Ambodik, because they allowed their children to move freely from birth. Not only did their children learn to walk at an earlier age, they also avoided all sorts of deformity and disease through their "natural" child-rearing practices. Africans and the native inhabitants of North America were his examples. Maksimovich-Ambodik constructed "primitive" as nearly utopian when he claimed that "One doesn't find among them hunchbacked, blind, lame, crippled, or freaks."[28] He attacked midwives, nannies, and mothers for acting against "natural law" and wrapping babies so tightly that they were unable to breathe properly. The only time a baby should be wrapped tightly is in the case of an injury, and then he should be bandaged only by a doctor or surgeon (in other words, a trained male practitioner).[29] Maksimovich-Ambodik's ideas were consistent with Rousseau's. His tendency to look to the natural world for models of maternal care and to make comparisons to other mammals in his analyses seem to suggest that he was also influenced by the French naturalist Buffon, whose thirty-six volume *L'Histoire Naturelle* raised questions regarding the "degeneration" of certain species and the improvement over time of others.[30]

While Maksimovich-Ambodik promoted anti-swaddling practices as a standard for Russia through comparison with "primitive" peoples, Novikov debunked the usual, presumably Russian argument in favor of swaddling—that it was necessary in order to prevent babies from injuring themselves. Novikov trusted natural law: "Nature did not give children so much strength that they could make dangerous movements."[31] Rather than preventing harm, overly tight swaddling could actually injure the child's limbs, he warned.[32] Novikov was concerned not only with the physical harm caused by swaddling but also with the spiritual effects on the infant. He warned that "from the very minute a child is born," care should be taken not to wrap his body too tightly. If the infant's first sensations were "pain and torture," this could have long-term negative effects on the child's spiritual being; in essence, it would corrupt the child's nature. Novikov drew a line from swaddling in infancy directly to compromised virtues in adulthood.[33]

Not all eighteenth-century Russian doctors agreed with Rousseau, however, on the harm of swaddling. Matvei Peken, who revised and expanded his father's health handbook intended for the peasantry, supported swaddling, although in a modified form. Rather than wrapping up the baby immediately after a bath, the mother should allow the baby some time to move his limbs freely, which would serve to "make him stronger." This contradicted the belief among the peasantry that swaddling would make an infant's bones grow straight while protecting him or her from self-injury.[34] Others fully supported traditional swaddling. In the *Saint Petersburg Medical Register*, an anonymous author argued explicitly against Rousseau and in favor of some forms of swaddling—in particular, in order to create a sense of security and obedience in the infant. He cautioned against using wool to swaddle babies, which could cause them to overheat and catch colds, but argued that, in general, swaddling was useful and should not be abandoned. His comment that the objections to swaddling "do more harm than good" suggests an ongoing, passionate debate on the topic in Russia.[35]

Related to swaddling were concerns about how children should be dressed. Proponents of reform in traditional child-rearing practices favored loose, simple clothing over tight garments. The issue of clothing again invokes social and cultural identity: peasant children who from necessity wore loose clothing had healthier bodies and limbs. Girls of the nobility suffered especially from corseting and from wearing shoes that were tight and had high heels. Catherine, Novikov, and critic of serfdom Alexander Radishchev all promoted simple, light clothing for both girls and boys, as did both Locke and Rousseau. Radishchev condemned corseting as an enemy of population growth. Warning that the choice of vanity over health in childhood would have severe consequences, his narrator, in *A Journey from Saint Petersburg to Moscow*, addresses his sister and her husband: "When it comes to childbirth, you will pipe a different tune . . . it is too late. Your distorted joints can't be straightened out now. Weep, my beloved brother-in-law, weep. Our mother, following the lamentable fashion that often leads to death in childbirth, has for many years been preparing sorrow for you, sickness for her daughter and feeble bodies for your children."[36] Novikov, in addressing children's clothing, perhaps rightly judged that some of Locke's suggestions with respect to the outdoors—like bare legs and leaky shoes in all manner of weather—would have been a bit extreme for Russian conditions. However, Novikov sounds positively un-Russian when he recommends sending children outside without hats.[37] The texts, whether written by statesman, doctor, or regime critic, show a willingness to adopt contemporary European practices, but not entirely or to the exclusion of some Russian practices.

The prescription for cold regime, which encouraged moderation in exposure to heat, as the name suggests, proved the most difficult to accept without any exceptions for Russian Enlighteners. European dictates for the physical care of infants and children usually promoted a version of cold regime, which was based on ancient Greek notions of proper hygiene.[38] According to this prescription for good health and longevity, a person must attend to the management of the six "non-naturals": air, diet, sleep, exercise, passions, and evacuations.[39] Overly heated rooms were seen as presenting dangers, as were hot baths, heat-producing beverages, and hot foods. Cold regime attracted followers in Europe in the early eighteenth century and remained the most popular prescription for good health into the nineteenth century.[40] Physicians who recommended cold regime directed mothers to expose their children to cold environments from

Depiction of a Russian merchant mother with a small child. Notice the child's toy.
Jean-Baptiste Le Prince, *Habit of a Merchant's Wife in Russia in 1765. Femme d' un
Marchand Russe.* From *A collection of the dresses of different nations, antient [sic] and
modern.* 1764. Hand-colored engraving.

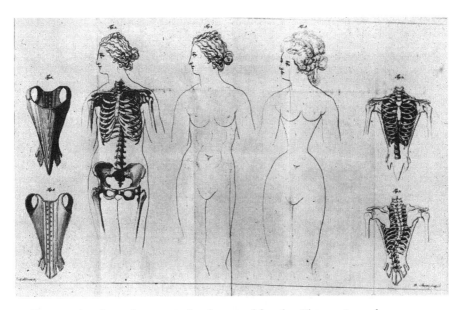

Comparative views of uncorseted and corseted females. Thomas Samuel von Soemmerring, *Über die wirkungen der Schnürbrüste*. Berlin, 1793.
(Courtesy of the History of Medicine Collection, National Library of Medicine, Washington, DC)

infancy, bringing them outdoors in the winter and washing them in cold water. These early modern prescriptions for cold regime differed from their ancient predecessors in their emphasis on scientific explanation; European physicians repackaged the management of "non-naturals" as modern medical science applied to preventing disease and controlling environmental factors.[41]

Russian reformers adopted cold regime unevenly in their prescriptions for child care.[42] In Matvei Peken's chapter on the feeding and care of infants, he wrote that "excessively heated air in rooms and huts, although pleasant if one is accustomed to it from a young age, is however very bad for our health."[43] Similarly, an infant's first bath would be his or her only warm one; Peken believed that cold baths for infants were healthier. He also explained that the practice of covering babies with furs or heavy blankets was dangerous.[44] In a concession to the Russian impulse to keep babies warm, however, Peken did recommend "warm air" for the main room in which they lived.[45] He also made an exception to cold regime for the Russian practice of bringing infants and children into the *banya* or sauna.[46] On this issue, Peken accepted the Russian belief that visits to the *banya* brought long-term health benefits, although the practice ran counter to the supposed wisdom of cold regime: "*Banyas*, if one is accustomed to them from the youngest age, are for the simple folk not only necessary, but also very beneficial." He posited a scientific-sounding reason for endorsing the *banya* for children, explaining that "perspiration consists in freeing the blood from excess moisture and in cleansing it of pungency," which prevents coughs and colds. This advice is absolutely anathema to Locke's belief that exposure to cold prevented illness and to all of Locke's ideas about not heating the head or feet. Peken did caution that one should be careful with newborns in the *banya*, but condoned the practice, nonetheless.[47] Novikov endorsed cold regime only in part. For example, he remarked that fresh air is healthy for infants but that infants should not spend time outdoors during strong winds, severe cold, or humid weather—all of which were fairly frequent weather occurrences in most parts of Russia.[48] Maksimovich-Ambodik, like Peken and Novikov, recommended cold baths and fresh air for infants. He advocated taking infants outside for part of the day, even in the winter.[49] However, on the issue of the *banya*, Maksimovich-Ambodik parted from Peken and criticized peasant women who took infants, especially newborns, to the bathhouse. Even worse, he warned, were negligent women who placed babies on the highest bench in the sauna where the air was hottest and most difficult to breathe. Unforgivable in his mind were those women who, in keeping with Russian bathhouse custom, "beat their [babies'] tender bodies with birch branches."[50] Sensitive to the cruelty of this practice, Maksimovich-Ambodik could not endorse this aspect of Russian peasant tradition.

Thus, Russian Enlighteners adopted cold-regime standards unevenly in their prescriptions for infant care. Peken, who wrote for peasants, was not bothered by seeming contradictions in his blend of Enlightenment recommendations and Russian traditions. Novikov, writing for the elite, was against too much cold, whereas Maksimovich-Ambodik, who wrote for everyone, endorsed the cold regime. On a literal level, these men believed that infancy was the time to intervene in the health of the child—and to begin to condition the child's body toward good moral health. On a metaphorical level, at times more or less explicit, they showed that infancy was also viewed as the time to intervene in the health, and sometimes customs, of the nation as a whole, in terms of both its physical and its moral well-being.

THE PHYSICAL AND THE MORAL

All of the authors examined here shared an assumption that the health of the body was connected to the health of the soul. They believed that physically healthy adults had a greater likelihood of leading contented lives and would be less likely to succumb to temptations of the flesh. Novikov argued that "the care of the body" was the "first important component of upbringing." Preceding the development of reason and intellect, the conditioning of the body laid the foundation for more advanced development.[51] Good health in childhood created the conditions necessary for a peaceful and disciplined adult life. According to Novikov, parents failed in their responsibilities if they did not raise their children to have good health and, thereby, the best chance at happiness. Maksimovich-Ambodik similarly viewed physical health as an essential component of *vospitanie*. He cited Locke's dictum "a sound mind in a healthy body" when stating the goals of upbringing.[52] Andrei Bakherakht, a physician, was convinced that failure to condition the body and its passions in childhood would lead to sinful behavior in adulthood. Then, sin would lead the body further away from good health, thus, infirmity in body and soul would reinforce each other. For instance, Bakherakht believed that a hunched or curved back was a definitive sign of a person's dissolute behavior. He wrote that "it is incontestable that such misfortune occurs from immoderation."[53]

The physical and the moral were most strongly linked in the discourse on venereal disease. Bakherakht warned that syphilis, known as "the French disease" in the politically loaded vocabulary of the time, could be passed from mother to child.[54] He cautioned that children born to "infected people," in this case meaning mothers with syphilis or other venereal diseases, had to literally bear "the sins and weaknesses of their parents."[55] The children produced by such unions were often too sick to be saved. These children, Bakherakht wrote, "are so weak that they can barely be considered alive and the majority will die in childhood or youth."[56] Radishchev sought to make this point forcefully in his writings. His medical training is obvious in his portrayal of the biological inheritance of children born to parents with venereal disease. His narrator encounters a nobleman who has just buried his son and who explains poignantly why he is responsible for his son's death:

> I did not cut short his life with the sword or with poison. No, I did worse than that. I prepared the way for his death before he was born, by giving him a poisoned life. I am a murderer, like many others, but a murderer more savage than any other. I murdered my son before his birth. I, I alone, shortened his days by infusing slow poison into him at his conception. It prevented the development of his bodily powers. During his whole life he enjoyed not a single day of health, and the spread of the wasting poison cut off the flow of his life.[57]

Radishchev's narrator makes clear that the practice of noblemen visiting pros-
titutes caused this tragedy. The narrator himself is guilty, he admits, addressing
his children rhetorically: "I have sinned before you, poisoning your vital
humors *before your birth*. . . . O my beloved ones, how you must hate me!"
Radishchev, alone among these writers, emphasized the damage a father could
do to a child's health and soul even before birth. In this instance, Radishchev
also blamed the Russian government for licensing prostitution, thereby encouraging debauchery and enabling the spread of venereal disease and immorality
in the nation.[58]

The perceived link between the physical and the moral drew physicians'
attention to other prenatal issues. The passions, moods, and sins of the expectant mother were considered a factor in the health of the infant. Maksimovich-
Ambodik, arguing that strong passions could cause the "destruction of the
fetus," advised that pregnant women listen to both "nature" and "reason" and
avoid upsetting situations. A pregnant mother communicated more to her fetus
than simply nourishment: the "purity" of the fetus also depended upon its
mother's health and well-being. Like Bakherakht and Radishchev, Maksimovich-
Ambodik was concerned about the transmission of disease from mother to
newborn, and argued that illness and disease were the biggest killers of children and that these often began at conception, the result of "the improper
life" of their own mothers.[59] Zybelin was one of the few to draw attention to
the role fathers played in producing a healthy infant, but, unlike Radishchev,
he saw the father's contribution to upbringing as ending with conception.[60]

If the correct care was taken, the argument ran, children would grow to be
physically solid, ensuring a healthy society and nation in the future. The proper
physical and moral upbringing included preparation for an adult life of fidelity
and moderation of sexual desires. Bakherakht advocated explicit discussion of
these issues. Children should be taught that masturbation was a "sin which
ruins the mind and the health."[61] He invoked his status as a physician to convince his readers of the need to supervise children in this respect, writing, "I am
certain, and can prove with many examples, as many others practicing medical
science can testify, that this is a frequent occurrence which causes many poor
children to suffer from various illnesses." He warned that this type of behavior
could begin as early as age eight, and thus parents must not delay such discussions.[62] There is a brief window of opportunity in a child's life when *vospitanie*
will be most effective: "If children were taught in their early years, when they
are already displaying some reason and intellect, to understand the different
forms of sin, and if it were made clear to them that every sin leads a person

down the path of destruction . . . then the strong desire toward every kind of sin would be diminished."[63] Although referencing "sin," his warnings focus on earthly consequences. At the end of his book, he offers a frightening list of the effects of promiscuity in order to "put fear before the eyes of young people." He gives them plenty of horrors to ponder: "collapse of the entire body, . . . eclipse of the soul, . . . unnatural imagination, . . . scorn, shame, fear; . . . continuous, tedious, vile and almost intolerable illnesses; . . . Strong convulsions, cramps, seizures, especially in women; . . . Displeasure with oneself and the human race; fear day and night, interminable sadness; . . . Loathing toward life, desire for death; . . . Erratic behavior, rage and even suicide."[64] Bakherakht places the blame for this potential suffering on the parents who fail to provide the proper *vospitanie.*

The perceived connection between physical health and spiritual strength provoked an interesting debate among deputies to the Legislative Commission over medical care, child welfare, and upbringing in peasant villages. The issue of intervention in peasant care for children led to polemics among the Commission's deputies. Many reports from nobility in the provinces lamented the lack of doctors, midwives, and medical personnel available to treat the serfs who worked their land. One deputy, the nobleman Semyon Naryshkin, who also served in the Senate and participated in literary pursuits organized by Novikov, argued passionately for intervening in this sad state of affairs to rescue infants and children especially. Naryshkin underscored the dearth of midwives and the general lack of knowledge about health and hygiene. After describing to the Commission the hardships of peasant life in the village, he went on to lament the profound suffering of infants in particular, whose tender bodies could hardly be expected to bear the hardships created by ignorance and poverty. Continued non-intervention, Naryshkin argued, would only produce more of the same results: "True, even in such careless conditions a few are saved, but they are the minority, and the majority will perish."[65] A Cossack deputy from Orenburg by the name of Samsonov also supported intervention. Like Naryshkin, he too expected no change if the state did not take action: "Although in many cities there are *lekary* [medics or physicians], we have yet to see even one of them going to a suffering peasant and giving him some kind of help."[66]

However, Baron Georg fon Ash, a Russian-born physician representing the state Medical Collegium, argued against any intervention, especially in peasant practices of child rearing.[67] For fon Ash, the issue extended well beyond health care for the youngest children; it invoked profound concerns about how character and masculinity were inculcated in the peasantry. In response to Naryshkin, fon Ash defended the Medical Collegium, insisting that it had already taken great pains to spread information on health, including issues specific to women, by commissioning several books. In 1762, for example, it had published I. F. Erasmus's book *An Instruction on How Every Person in General, and Particularly Women during Pregnancy, Birth, and after Birth, Should Care for Oneself with Respect to Diet*.[68] Fon Ash also reported that the Medical Collegium had already established schools of midwifery in both capitals.[69] It was up to landlords to send peasant women from their villages to be trained. In the words of fon Ash, the Medical Collegium had already accomplished the mission that Naryshkin proposed: "it remains only to wish that the information would always be used correctly."[70]

Beyond defending the reforms of the Medical Collegium, fon Ash also built a case against further state intervention in peasant child rearing. Far from thinking that peasant mothers needed instruction in child care, he held the peasant mother in higher esteem than mothers of the nobility because the peasant mother nursed her own children—and by so doing communicated bravery and strength to her sons.[71] Furthermore, fon Ash argued, because peasant women spent their lives in constant physical movement, working the fields and tending their homes, they were in much better health than noblewomen. Peasant women passed this robust health on to their children, fon Ash explained: "Their children, compared with children of the well-born, are of a much stronger constitution; therefore they rarely need any kind of medicine."[72] The weak and endangered boys were those of the nobility. Whether fon Ash's perspective is romantic or callous is perhaps open to interpretation, but he was certain that the state could not risk softening the physical upbringing of peasant infants and children.

For fon Ash, nothing less was at stake than the security of the Russian state. Peasant boys grew up to become the foot soldiers of the Russian army; thus, the military strength of Russia depended upon their "severe" upbringing, which created strong and brave men. Fon Ash drew a comparison with ancient Rome: "The brave Romans always won while they lived simply, strengthening their bodies through work and toil." Russia's recent military triumphs proved that "the *narod* [the folk]" were healthy and strong, he argued: "Let us turn our gaze to the troops of the entire empire, which are comprised of peasants. What strong health, what steadfastness they have!"[73] To fon Ash, the simple and coarse physical *vospitanie* of the peasantry created the physical and moral strength he saw as characteristic of Russian soldiers—and perhaps missing among their officers.

Thus, a range of opinion existed among Russian Enlighteners concerning the degree and type of intervention necessary in the physical aspects of child-rearing practices. They were in agreement, however, in recognizing the child's body as the site from which the future moral self would begin to grow. Whether too much freedom or too much restriction, too much luxury or too little civilization, the effects of excesses or negligence in the care of children's physical selves would not only determine the health of the individual but would have consequences for the future character of the body politic as a whole. The idea of raising the child to develop a healthy body is echoed in imperial and colonial thinking from this same era. When Catherine sought to "civilize" the "childlike" populations on the periphery of Russia's multi-ethnic empire, she wanted to raise a healthy and strong body politic. As one proponent imagined this process, "the uniformity of State organization wisely helps to bring this along by leading our rude Peoples by giant steps toward the common goal of general enlightenment in Russia, of a wonderful fusion of all into a single body and soul, and of creating, as it were, an unshakeable Giant that will stand for hundreds of centuries."[74] In the next chapter, we consider the vehicles for instilling the Enlightenment and "Russianness" in the children of the empire.

5

MORAL INSTRUCTION FOR
THE EMPIRE'S YOUTH

The architects of the new *vospitanie* recognized the moral component of child rearing as proceeding from the foundation of good physical health established in the earliest years of the child's life. After having been nursed through infancy by mother's milk, the young child's body would be conditioned toward good moral health. At about the age a child learns to read, the reformers argued, moral instruction would be formally introduced to preserve and extend this early training. Consideration of the proper content of the moral aspect of raising a child led these reformers to assess the perceived strengths and weakness of the Russian national character. Novikov predicted that reforming *vospitanie* would transfigure national identity and bring about security and happiness:

> When the rearing of children has reached the acme of perfection, everything else will be made easy. The laws will be universally obeyed; religion, simple in its majesty, will be what it always ought to be, which is to say, the source of every virtue and the mainstay and consolation of the spirit; learning will become an inexhaustible wellspring of genuine benefit to the state; the arts will adorn existence, ennoble emotion, and become a means of encouraging virtue; all citizens will be true to their appointed station in life; and general industry, strengthened by moderation and a good domestic economy, will afford the most populous nation security from want and contentment with its condition.[1]

To reform moral *vospitanie* for juveniles, Enlighteners advocated reinvigorating Russian Orthodoxy along with changing educational sites, methods, and instructors. That is, they sought to establish new schools or to reform existing ones, provide new primers and other didactic texts for teaching children, and change the habit in noble families of hiring foreign tutors to instruct their children. Russian Enlighteners, rather than rejecting or distancing themselves from religion, sought to integrate it within the new teaching methods with the goal of creating and raising subject-citizens with a modern Russian national identity.

The context of the second half of the eighteenth century created the conditions and stimulus for the construction of a revised national identity beginning with Catherine herself. In 1762, Catherine assumed the throne. An impoverished German princess by birth, Catherine learned Russian and converted to the Orthodox faith before her marriage to Peter III. After Peter III was deposed and she was crowned empress, Catherine made a pilgrimage to Rostov to reinforce the public's awareness of her commitment to Russian Orthodoxy. Having no legitimate claim to the throne, Catherine worked hard to create a Russian identity for herself.[2] During her first decade of rule, she solicited proposals in many realms of statecraft, while also encouraging intellectual activity. After the partitioning of Poland in 1772 and the triumph over Turkey in 1774, Russia under Catherine's leadership was firmly established as a fearsome military power.

Catherine and the upper nobility, who traveled in Europe for pleasure and education, had achieved a recognizable cosmopolitan impulse, along with a presence, if not exactly reverence, in the European consciousness. Western European intellectuals viewed Russia with curiosity and caution. European tourists to Russia (a diverse lot that included diplomats, philosophes, and adventurers) perceived Russia as an exotic and wild place not soon subdued.[3] Baroness Elizabeth Dimsdale, whose husband performed variolation against smallpox on Catherine and her heirs, described Russian Orthodox customs as "curious" and "extraordinary," deplored the peasants' "abject state of Slavery," yet found plenty to admire in the generosity of her hosts and Catherine's richly appointed palaces.[4] Montesquieu included Russia among the countries traditionally characterized by "pure despotism."[5] Voltaire tended to flatter Catherine's ambitions, praising her civilizing reforms and prophesying continued conquests over the Turks, and yet he demurred on the issue of visiting and made his pronouncements from afar, as had Montesquieu before him.[6] The admission of Russia into the European "map of civilization" and the simultaneous relegation of the Slavic world to the cultural periphery of Europe pained many intellectuals and the empress herself, who often took up her pen to respond to negative views of Russia in the European press.[7]

Given the historical moment, the drive to reconsider national character and to erect a national identity worthy of respect around the world seemed necessary to representatives of both state and society.[8] Their efforts to forge a new national identity were mostly discursive, to be sure, but the ideas found traction in the support for a reinvigorated Orthodoxy and in a blossoming book market, not only in prescriptive literature for adults but also in primers, grammars, and readers for children. The Enlighteners regarded the new schools for the "folk" (the *narodnye uchilishcha*), residential institutions for raising children like the Houses of Upbringing, and the existing military academies as the perfect sites for framing a new national character through moral *vospitanie*. The perception of a morally diseased Russia that had lost its "true" national identity led the state and public intellectuals alike to pursue means of establishing a reformed and restored Russian national identity through upbringing and education.

Much of the source material in this chapter about the Russian Enlighteners' efforts directed at school-age juveniles includes readers, grammars, and other published literature. Gary Marker notes the problem of inferring social change from publications: the historian cannot know how books were used, why they were purchased beyond assuming general interest, or whether readers learned what the authors intended and put it to use. In the case of primers intended to teach literacy to children, Marker gathered data that show the power of the state to fund incredibly large (for the time) print runs of grammars and primers. Marker concludes that, during Catherine's reign, "millions of printed volumes" intended to teach children the alphabet, grammar, and arithmetic were published and put into circulation.[9] Not only booksellers associated with educational institutions but also private bookshops and book dealers carried these titles, suggesting a demand outside the schools. While it is difficult to know whether children assimilated the moral (and national) lessons embedded in the primers or whether the primers were even effective means of teaching literacy, we can understand from the content of the primers and texts what Catherine and the other writers hoped to instill in pupils. The writers, translators, and publishers believed that primers and lesson books could be vehicles for fostering a national identity. These reformers expected that children, through lessons and reading, at home or at school, would absorb the precepts of "Russianness," as defined by these books.

EDUCATION, ORTHODOXY, AND *Nravouchenie*

Before Catherine's era, education in Russia followed a path of uneven and halting development. The earliest institutions of learning were of Church origin, dating from the 1630s. Two academies, one in Kiev and one in Moscow, flourished or floundered depending upon the gifts or shortcomings of its faculty, but never served more than several hundred pupils each. Recognizing the need for additional institutions that could train and educate his subjects to fulfill his grand ambitions, Peter introduced a range of schools. These included grammar schools that were housed by local churches and served mainly children of the clergy, as well as the so-called cipher schools that emphasized mathematics and were meant to serve the nobility but were beset by disorganization and absenteeism. Peter's crowning glory, the Academy of Sciences, also housed a gymnasium that struggled to attract pupils. Army garrison schools were a source of modest education for a wide swath of impoverished children from families of various ranks. Peter emphasized practical and technical curricula.[10] In 1755, Empress Elizabeth established Moscow University. Its attached gymnasium enrolled twenty or so pupils a year until 1774. The level of instruction report-edly varied, but the gymnasium did educate some of the brightest young minds of this era, including Novikov and Fonvizin. Under Elizabeth, the Academy of Arts was also established. Several schools for noble boys trained and educated the future officer corps. The Noble Army Cadet Corps, founded in 1731, had become by midcentury the premier institution for educating boys of the nobil-ity. At the time of Catherine's ascension in 1762, the Corps of Cadets had six hundred pupils. In addition to the education offered at these state-affiliated institutions, there were other options for educating children privately that were thus open only to the well-to-do. Small private boarding schools run mainly by foreigners could be found in urban areas. Urban and provincial noble families with means often opted to hire tutors to educate their boys (and less often their girls). These tutors tended to be of French extraction, and became the objects of much satire and criticism—the foil against which to measure and negotiate a renovated national identity. Catherine's initial educational projects issued from Ivan Betskoi, whom she appointed to oversee reforms at the Corps of Cadets and the Academy of Arts in Saint Petersburg. In keeping with a growing inter-est in early childhood, a section for younger boys was added to the Corps of Cadets. Catherine also appointed Betskoi to design and implement the Houses of Upbringing for abandoned children (discussed previously) and the Society for the Upbringing of Well-Born Maidens (the subject of chapter 6). The em-press and Betskoi intended for their plan, "On the Upbringing of Both Sexes" (1764), to guide the moral curricula at new and existing institutions.[11]

Later eighteenth-century reformers insisted, first of all, that the Orthodox foundation of Russian national identity must be restored or reinforced through spiritual instruction, with the addition of Enlightenment virtues. The framers of the new upbringing did not perceive a tension in promoting Orthodoxy and Enlightenment, often within the same text. This view of Christianization as Enlightenment helped extend education to the borderlands of the empire.[12] Sec-ond, they perceived a loss of Russian national feeling resulting in large measure from an excess of foreign influence on Russian noble society. Ekaterina Dash-kova, director the Academy of Sciences, worried that an entire generation of children grew up without any connection to Russian history, language, or culture. The critique of French fops and tutors is a well-known part of this period in Russian intellectual history, but the coding of French upbringing as feminine and the need to promote Russian masculinity is less so.[13] The chief problem for those concerned with Russian national character, according to Dashkova and others, resided in the loss of masculinity that such child rearing produced. Many advocated a restoration of patriarchy, but with limits that would inhibit tyranny and arbitrariness (*proizvol'*) within the family. Third, the architects of moral reform were concerned about the harmful effects of sexual license and infidelity on the nation. The immoderation of sexual passions, coded as foreign and dangerous to true Russianness, led not only to physical degeneration but also to spiritual disease. Teaching children virtues and control over their impulses promised to create a morally regenerated Russian society while ensuring the strength of Russian men, the true measure of national character in an era of European Enlightenment.

Protecting children from the infection of moral decay formed one of the conceptual frameworks for reformers of upbringing. The conviction that Russia suffered from spiritual illness was widespread.[14] Evgenii Syreishchikov, a professor at Moscow University and secretary to the Commission on Public Schools, delivered a public speech on the subject of inspiring virtue through *vospitanie* that is representative of this view. Syreishchikov employed the metaphor of disease to convince his audience of the importance of fostering spiritual health in children.[15] While the passage of time would cure or lessen the severity of some childhood diseases that afflict the body, he argued, it would not improve the "illnesses of the soul," which quickly progress to an incurable state. Spiritual sicknesses propagated additional diseases; "one causes another to grow, one makes another stronger and vice versa."[16] Radishchev used the metaphor of contagion, too, to describe the dangers of a tyrannical environment: "The examples of arbitrary power are infectious."[17] A morally diseased environment threatened the spiritual health of children.

The lamentable results of the absence of moral upbringing were already all too evident in the noble classes. The satirical literature of the second half of the eighteenth century created the archetype of the lazy, indifferent, uncouth state servitor of noble rank. The writer Denis Fonvizin addressed the problem of automatic promotion when he asked the empress in a letter published in *Companion for the Lovers of the Russian Word* (1783), "why is it that the chief aim of the majority of the nobility is to make their children, without serving, into guards' officers rather than make them into people?"[18] Catherine answered, "Because one is easier than the other." In her reply, Catherine acknowledged that upbringing, if it existed in noble families, tended toward the path of least resistance, rather than one of moral fortitude. A representative of the local nobility in Smolensk province lamented this reality, yet hoped that the state might provide the remedy so that young men from the provinces would "enter service in a better condition."[19] If parents themselves could not rise above their own upbringing (or lack of it), the state and concerned citizens must seek other solutions.

Vospitanie in the form of moral instruction offered the opportunity to inoculate children against negative influences. Syreishchikov advocated nravouchenie—literally, moral teachings—as part of preparing children "to protect themselves from infection by these [moral] illnesses."[20] Many of Syreishchikov's contemporaries agreed that state or society must address the urgent need for moral education. As is evident from reports from around the empire, provincial noblemen stressed that moral content should take priority over instruction in academic subjects.[21] Novikov argued that nravouchenie ought to be regarded as an important science, necessary especially in childhood but important at every stage of life.[22] He argued that all secular literature ought to both entertain and light a path toward proper behavior and attitudes. Inherent in all of the works directed at improving morals, whether in children or in adults, were assumptions that readers wanted to improve themselves and their children and that reading was an excellent means of achieving this.[23]

With respect to contagion, the chief means for preventing the spread of infection in the eighteenth century was the quarantine of sick persons.[24] The notion of quarantine informed Catherine's projects to establish residential facilities for the raising of orphans and children of the nobility and merchantry. As the general plan from 1764 articulates, by prohibiting holidays at home, allowing only supervised visits with parents, and ensuring the virtuous character of all faculty and staff at the schools, Catherine and Betskoi believed they could establish the ideal virtue incubator for nurturing a novaia poroda—literally, a new breed or race—of Russians.[25] As we saw in previous chapters, Enlighteners had intended that the Houses of Upbringing would function as one such environment, at least in theory. The first state school for girls fell under this plan, as did reforms at the existing state institutions for boys, the Corp of Cadets and the Academy of Arts. Catherine, in turn, adopted Betskoi's new plan for the military academy in 1766, which focused more attention on the moral component of raising the next generation of officers. Betskoi's belief that virtue trumped intelligence is clear in his choice of metaphor: a military without discipline, he insisted, was "like a body without a soul."[26] The making of a good leader depended less on intellectual training than on spiritual and moral preparation. Betskoi created staff positions at the military academy and at the school for noble girls, called "supervisor of morals" at the former and "form mistress" at the latter. The chief responsibility of the employees who held these positions was to inculcate virtue in their charges.[27] Whether one views these goals as naïve or utopian, the commitment to creating a different environment for children and to filling it with positive examples of virtue spoke to the optimistic belief that *vospitanie* could remedy spiritual disease.

Given the attention focused on the spiritual dimension of upbringing, it follows that thinkers expressed anxiety concerning the Church's influence on the Russian population. For both conservative and liberal thinkers, the spiritual decay observable in Russian society indicated that Orthodoxy had lost at least some of its moral authority. A conservative nobleman of ancient lineage, Mikhail Shcherbatov, traced the decline of true Russian identity from the era of Peter the Great, when "the Russians were transformed—from bearded men to clean-shaven men, from long-robed men to short-coated men; they became more sociable, and polite spectacles became known to them." Russians adopted these European customs, but at the expense of their own home-grown virtues. As the religious foundation of Russian culture and society grew weaker, "true attachment to the faith began to disappear." Consequently, the traditional Russian check on immorality—Orthodoxy—no longer served to impede greed, lust, dishonesty, and other vices, Shcherbatov argued.[28]

Some intellectuals expressed concern that the Church was failing in its mission to impart a religious education to Russian children. The publicist and writer Andrei Bolotov despaired in private correspondence that peasants no longer knew basic Christian law, while noble boys grew up indifferent to it. In conversation with peasant men on his estate, Bolotov wrote, he learned that although they attended church regularly and observed Orthodox holidays and rituals, they knew nothing of "the immortality of souls nor about resurrection after death." He lamented that "their understanding of the paramount laws of Christian truth is so insufficient and rather incorrect that I marveled at their ignorance and the great darkness in which they find themselves. . . . 'Oh the shame!' I was forced to exclaim; to hear this from Christians is not right, even more so from Orthodox believers." Bolotov worried that the peasants' illiteracy made them entirely dependent on priests for religious instruction, and the village priests were failing miserably at this duty.[29]

There is more evidence of an uneasiness or disdain for village priests in literature for children. Nikolai Kurganov included in his extremely popular reader for children unflattering, satirical portrayals of ignorant and greedy priests—perhaps further indication of the decline of clergy as moral preceptors.[30] For Bolotov and Kurganov, the antidote to ignorance of and indifference to Orthodox teachings rested partly with members of society. Both men, like other writers of primers and texts for children, believed the renovation of the national spirit would require instruction through *nravouchenie*. Bolotov also wrote with near hysteria about the Francophilia he witnessed among the young men of the nobility, and he associated this with an absence of both national and Orthodox feeling. He complained that the "petits-maîtres" of his era cared only about "romantic adventures" and rather than spending their time usefully in service to the fatherland, "they live in luxury and think only of extravagance, pranks, fashions, ranks, and games." For Bolotov, the ignorance among the peasantry and among the young men of his own social estate posed the main obstacle to true faith and true Russianness. Education and enlightenment were the answer for both groups of ignorant Russians. Through a correct understanding of the Gospels, Bolotov hoped that both peasant and lord would find a renewed Orthodox and thus Russian identity.[31]

Having associated the decline of Orthodoxy's status in Russian culture with the loss of Russian national character, these writers concluded that Orthodoxy must be the foundation of a morally reformed populace. Religious instruction had to be a strong component in the moral *vospitanie* of children. We do not witness an elaborate ideological confrontation between perceived Westernization and Russian Orthodox identity in these texts. Rather, for these writers and for Catherine herself, Orthodoxy could coexist with Enlightenment values that emphasized a positive view of human nature and optimism about the changeability of society. While tensions between these might seem problematic to outsiders' eyes, to the framers of moral instruction for children the contradictions did not pose a philosophical dilemma. Peken reflected a common attitude among these thinkers when he reconciled Enlightenment and Christianity by arguing that God had endowed humanity with reason so that it might improve itself and the world.[32]

The commitment to restoring Orthodoxy to children's upbringing is evident in multiple contexts. The plans for new schools and for reforms at existing schools all posited the teaching of fundamental religious knowledge such as the Ten Commandments as the primary goal of moral upbringing at these state-run institutions. The God of Fonvizin's and Novikov's youth, described by Walter Gleason as the wrathful God of Muscovite Orthodoxy who regarded human nature as inherently sinful, did not disappear from Enlightenment Russia.[33] This God and this view of human nature appear in nearly every primer, grammar, and reader for children published in the eighteenth century.[34] The books that Catherine commissioned—or wrote herself—for use in the *narodnye uchilishcha* and in other state-governed schools included religious instruction without exception. *On the Duties of Man and Citizen*, a commissioned translation for use in schools to be established around the empire, enjoyed six printings during Catherine's reign, reaching a print run of nearly forty-three thousand copies. Professor Evgenii Syreishchikov, who advocated *nravouchenie* as the most important aspect of *vospitanie*, wrote a grammar book for primary-school-age children that enjoyed a total print run of twenty-five thousand.[35]

More significant, the arrangement of these texts for children followed an order that speaks to the imagined national identity that would bridge Russia's past and future. Primers begin with instruction in the Old Church Slavonic alphabet and orthography, with excerpts from scripture providing the material for spelling and grammar lessons. Many also include the Ten Commandments, definitions of sins, and prayers for morning and evening. The moral lessons offered in the religious section of these books are very much rooted in patriarchy, resting on virtues such as unquestioning obedience to male authorities, passivity in the face of punishment, and fear of God's wrath and eternal damnation. On the surface, this content might seem close to a restoration of Muscovite upbringing. However, as Kliuchevskii noted, Muscovite upbringing was essentially an oral experience, without much (or necessarily any) emphasis on written texts.[36] Thus, the emphasis on literacy acquisition in Old Church Slavonic and on learning scripture through reading already signals a new relationship to religious instruction—and perhaps even a new relationship to faith.

After the lessons in religious precepts, primers offered instruction in the civil alphabet, Russian orthography, and lessons in civics, such as the duties of a *grazhdanin*—literally, a "citizen," not a "subject." The message is clear: the Church and faith are primary; civil commitments are secondary but important. The famous eighteenth-century poet and playwright Alexander Sumarokov underscored this in his list of precepts directing children in the proper ordering of one's loyalties: "Love God. Love the Sovereign. Love the fatherland. Love those nearest to you."[37] Worthy of note in this new schema is the space devoted to an emerging notion of the nation: the fatherland is its own entity, separate from the crown, and worthy of loyalty.

Rather than replace the Orthodox view of humans as inherently sinful and fallen, these writers added an Enlightenment notion of human nature as moldable and influenced primarily by environment. Usually placed after sections meant to teach literacy and Orthodox precepts, the primers and readers included moral tales, proverbs and sayings, and health advice translated and excerpted directly from Western European authors. In general, the proverbs and sayings emphasized the values of hard work, honesty, goodwill toward others, and thriftiness and moderation, resembling the common sense advice of Benjamin Franklin's *Poor Richard's Almanack*. For example, *The New Russian ABC with Short Moral Tales and Stories* (1775) emphasized character over status: "A sinful heart often is hidden under jewels and furs, therefore always judge a person by his deeds, not by his attire."[38] The *Primer for the Use of the Youth of the Russian Empire* (1780) taught its young readers "Do not set aside until morning what may be accomplished today," while Barsov's *Church and Civil ABCs* (1768) offered up "Behave toward others as you would like them to behave toward you in the same situation" and "Do not say to yourself: if only I were wealthy and titled, I would be happy."[39] The primer composed by Catherine in the early 1780s included a civics lesson after the standard lessons in the civil and Church alphabets and Orthodox prayers. The primer instructs children on the important function of laws: "without them, society collapses" and explains that "a good citizen is one who fulfills with exactness all of his civil responsibilities."[40] *Russian ABCs for the Instruction of Young Boys* (1795) contains a section entitled "Rules for the Maintenance of Health," which reproduces a lengthy passage from Locke's prescription for good health and hygiene.[41] These primers opened the world of the European Enlightenment to Russian children, teaching them that along with the eternal salvation promised for obeying the Ten Commandments and the credo of the Holy Orthodox Faith, behaving well and hard work would bring the earthly rewards of happiness and contentment. Like Catherine's primers, Barsov's also taught the pupil from a Russocentric perspective. Sprinkled throughout the Enlightenment-inspired moral teachings are geography and history lessons meant to convey Russia's position of prominence among the diplomatic powers of the world. For example, under the heading "European states and territories," the Russian empire leads the list. Similarly, in the section on capital cities, the list begins "Moscow, Saint Petersburg, Vienna, Constantinople or Tsargrad."[42] The world view offered is cosmopolitan yet firmly planted in Russia.

Thus, it might be time to retire the notion of binary oppositions that arises from Kliuchevskii's assessment of *dva vospitanii* (two upbringings), variations of which haunt perceptions of the problem of Russia's borrowing from the West.[43] The notion that a secular, Enlightenment version of childhood was incompatible with Orthodox notions of a child's duty to obey and to learn to avoid sin reinforces an interpretive framework that is based on two oppositional categories. Michelle Marrese challenges historians to consider whether such a framework accurately reflects eighteenth-century noble culture or behavior.[44] Moral lessons in alphabet books were not an invention of the Enlightenment, of course. Prior to the publication of the first secular primers in the early eighteenth century, enabled by Peter's establishment of a civil alphabet, the Holy Synod had a monopoly on publishing primers. Throughout the eighteenth century, the Synod continued to publish primers for the old orthography that taught Christian morals and world view along with the alphabet and grammar.[45] Okenfuss concludes that the Church primers and the new civil alphabet primers offered two incompatible notions of childhood, although he may overstate the extent to which the new primers challenged or dispensed with older notions of the child. Simon Dixon rejects Okenfuss's assessment that the Commission on Public Schools marked Catherine's abandonment of the Enlightenment, as evidenced in particular by *On the Duties of Man and Citizen* (1783) with its emphasis on passive obedience. Dixon argues that, in her choice to import pedagogy and texts from Hapsburg and Hohenzollern educational institutions, "Catherine was not so much rejecting the Enlightenment as adopting its socially and politically conservative German variant, in which raison d'état and reason itself were not only compatible but mutually reinforcing."[46] Jan Kusber, offering another perspective, perceives the chief tension as one between a pedagogy that encouraged individualism and humanitarianism, which he identifies with Catherine's earlier educational projects, and one that privileged order and obedience, which Kusber, like Okenfuss, sees as triumphing over the more "modern" vision of Betskoi. But, long ago, Pavel Miliukov recognized that Russians were not troubled by the same set of issues regarding Christianity and Enlightenment that beset Europeans such as Voltaire and other deists.[47] Franklin Walker observes that educational policy under Alexander I in the early nineteenth century continued and intensified the religious foundations inherited from Catherine's era. Walker argues that both "Enlightened rationalism and Christian-pietism were strong elements in Russian education" from the time of Catherine's earliest projects through the Napoleonic era. Walker and others have recognized that projecting Enlightenment rationalism and Christian-pietism as two oppositional models of education onto the Russian context obscures more than it reveals.[48] In the Russian context, "superstition" was elided not with religion but with ignorance and darkness.[49]

LESSONS AND EMPIRE

Believing Russia to be "the most populous nation" but one lagging in other areas in comparison with other European nations, Novikov imagined that reforms in child rearing would elevate all other aspects of Russia's society, culture, and economy, as this chapter's opening quote illustrates. This conception of a hybrid identity, framed around large-scale goals of national revival and cultivation of population resources, manifested itself in surprisingly detailed advice for children. The lessons for children—*nravouchenie*—often seek to convince children of the pleasures of delayed gratification and of the benefits that they themselves will perceive through their efforts. The secular *nravouchenie* often include illustrations meant to explain why following the rules is really in a child's best interest—and these reasons are communicated on a level likely to be more persuasive to a child than the threat of eternal damnation. For example, obeying instructions related to health means that a child has more time to play and wastes less time indoors, feeling sick. In *The New Russian ABC*, a story is told of a mother visiting the market with her children. The children who beg for a treat are sent home without one, while the well-behaved daughter is rewarded with praise and a pastry. Similarly, a tale of boys who choose to listen to their mother explains the advantages of doing so: such smart boys "do not burn their fingers on candles or get sick from eating too much, so they are not kept from having fun by misfortune that could have been prevented."[50] This is very different from denying the flesh for the good of the eternal soul. The stern, solemn, and even terrifying admonitions of the Orthodox dicta were followed by more personal, nurturing, and secular encouragements toward virtuous behavior.

Nikolai Kurganov's *The Letter Writer* is an excellent example of a reader for children that included a wide range of content, all of it working to promote Russian national pride and worldliness. First published in 1769, the text fulfills all of Novikov's criteria for the ideal useful amusement: it included amusing anecdotes, riddles, and stories—some of them translations from foreign lands— while also offering up lessons in Russian history, Greek mythology, health and hygiene, Russian grammar, and *nravouchenie*. Kurganov gave a sense of the vastness of the Russian land with geography lessons and promoted what might be termed ethnographic information about local peoples around the empire. Folk songs communicated a sense of local culture, while also underscoring that the Russian language, faith, and love of the fatherland united people across a vast territory. Honesty and humility held prominent places in the *nravouchenie*, reinforced by mocking portrayals of corrupt judges and puffed-up foreigners. The book also included a section that introduced the public to Peter the Great's cabinet of curiosities, his *Kunstkamera*, through detailed descriptions of its contents.[51] Originally intended for use in military schools, Kurganov's book quickly became family reading.[52] Because he designed his reader for a child's developing literacy, adults who were not fluent readers also found *The Letter Writer* accessible. Its eighteen printings attest to its popularity; Pushkin referenced it as the book that all noble families possessed in their libraries, no matter how meager the home or how distant from the center.[53] Thus, Kurganov's book allowed many readers, regardless of station or distance from Moscow or Saint Petersburg, to partake in the project of self- and national improvement and to perceive themselves as belonging to a great and vast fatherland.

As if to drive home the importance of reforming juvenile schooling, the powerful empress herself took breaks from partitioning Poland and waging war with the Turks to write texts for children. One of Catherine's publications, *Beginning Notes* (published together with her *Conversations and Tales* in 1782), created and promoted the new hybrid identity of a confident, sophisticated citizen of the Russian empire who is aware of his or her magnificent fatherland.[54] In this engaging and dual-language text for older children, lessons about geography and history are given in Russian, with the opposing page offering a translation in Greek. This text itself is a product of Catherine's imperial ambitions, her so-called Greek Project.[55] Catherine's drive to open the Black Sea to Russian interests fueled war with the Turks in 1768; the defeat of the Ottoman Empire in 1774 led to the annexation of the Crimea. Catherine pursued a colonization effort in Crimea, resettling Germans and Russians there. The gain of Crimea fueled the empress's obsession with conquering and dismantling the Ottoman Empire. After vanquishing the Turks, she planned to restore a Byzantine kingdom under Russian protection, which would include Greece, Bulgaria, and Macedonia. She intended to install her second grandson as ruler. Born in 1779, Catherine had him named Constantine, to presage his destiny. In 1780, she solicited the support of Austria from the recently crowned Joseph II, promising to partition the Ottoman lands between them. At this same meeting, Catherine also took a great interest in Austria's educational system, which she would eventually attempt to import and revise for a Russian context. Her interest appears genuine, but it conveniently may have served a diplomatic purpose as well. The dual-language Greek-Russian text may also have been used to instruct Greek boys who were brought back to Russia at the conclusion of the first Russo-Turkish war in 1774 to study in Saint Petersburg.[56]

Catherine portrayed her interest in establishing schools in the Crimean region (and the dreamed-of revived Russo-Byzantium) as maternal care for her new subjects. Her *Beginning Notes* reflects both her wish to teach children to identify with their status as subjects of the Russian empire and her practicality with respect to regional language differences (something later autocrats would

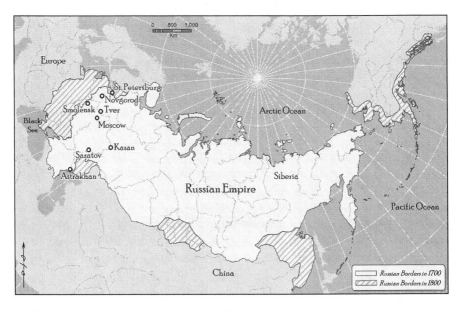

The Russian Empire, showing expansion from 1700 to 1800
(Boundary Cartography)

reject). The lessons in Catherine's Russian-Greek text are not translations from European texts, which is evident from the Russocentric view of the world they offer. The geography lessons all proceed from the vantage point of Moscow, explaining locations of other countries with respect to Russia's boundaries. The text gives directions to major cities in Europe from Moscow, with detours along the way to reinforce the proximity of a greater Slavic world in which the lingua franca includes, rather than excludes, Russian speakers. The lessons depict the peoples and cultures of China, Africa, Persia, Eastern Europe, Central Asia, and the Caucasus. The customs of non-Russian ethnicities within the Russian empire, such as the Kirghiz and the Tatars, receive lengthy, reverent treatment. Children also learn about the spiritual history of ancient Rus'. The linguistic history of the "Slavic language" includes a reference not to the Orthodox church but to the "Greek-Russian Church [*Grekorossiiskaia Tserkov*]."[57] Catherine illuminates every region of the Russian empire with detail and excitement, and one can imagine children longing to see the sites of their fatherland. The message throughout is one of national pride in one's language, history, and culture and in the topography and natural gifts of the Russian land. The message might also be one of imperial pride; throughout the text, Catherine's geography lessons describe the non-Russian borderlands of her empire as "belonging to Russia."[58] In a sense, this text represents Catherine's determination to create her own map of Enlightenment and scale of civilization in which Russia rightfully occupies the top position.

While Enlighteners, including Catherine, embraced some universalism as well as some cultural diversity in the Russian empire, they nonetheless promoted cultural and ethnic particularism in the realms of language and faith. Many shared the belief that native Russians must be the nannies, tutors, and teachers of Russian children. At the Legislative Commission, provincial deputies expressed anxiety over the idea of having non-Russians teach the children of recently converted ethnic minorities. A. Larinov, a deputy from Simbirsk, wanted Orthodox priests, rather than Muslim teachers, to be responsible for educating Chuvash, Mordvinian, and Mari children so that they would "know ecclesiastical law."[59] Betskoi expressed similar concerns about hiring non-Russians at the state orphanages. He wrote, "It is necessary that the *vospitatel'nitsy* be Russian. Would it be possible for children to recognize foreigners as their own parents and to accord them, as duty requires, their love and friendship? If, out of necessity, foreigners will be employed, will they be able to provide an example to the pupils in every respect, to be with them in church and in all places where the rules of faith are enacted?"[60] Thus, it was argued, the national and religious identities of nannies, wet nurses, and teachers would reinforce—or undermine—the national identity of the children they raised.

The same linguistic and religious principles became, for Catherine, a central feature in the design of the national school system and the consolidation of an empire-wide Russian national identity. Within the increasingly multiethnic, multilingual, and multiconfessional character of the Russian empire as it underwent dramatic expansion in this period, the idea of a shared language creating national identity was gaining adherents. Codifying the Russian language through the creation of dictionaries and grammars was part of the process of establishing Russian national identity.[61] The emphasis on having children learn from a native Russian speaker was the moral corollary of arguments in favor of mother's milk.

EDUCATIONAL INSTITUTIONS

Catherine created a commission in 1782 to study the issue of creating a national educational system that would establish new schools and unify all existing schools throughout the empire.[62] Later that year, having decided, on the advice of Joseph II, to adapt the successful Austrian model of school administration, she established the Commission on Public Schools (*narodnye uchilishcha*). She hired

Theodor Iankovich de Mirievo, an Orthodox Serb, because of his experience in implementing a school system within the Hapsburg empire, to work as a consultant to the Commission and to adapt the Austrian model for a Slavic, Orthodox region.[63] Iankovich also spoke Russian, which made him a practical choice. Over the next year, the Commission worked out a plan for an empire-wide school system that would teach children of both sexes from all social estates, including state peasants and serfs with their landlords' permission.

In October of 1782, Catherine approved the Commission's plan and underscored her commitment to promoting a strong Russian national identity through language by insisting that French be removed from the curriculum at all schools. Even at schools for children of the gentry, the empress made clear in an addendum that "French language shall be permitted for home instruction according to personal wishes, but it will not enter the national schools."[64] While the Commission planned that Russian would be the language of instruction in all schools, Catherine wanted second languages added to the peripheral and non-Russian regions of the empire. With her famous attention to detail, she left no room for the Commission to second-guess her meaning: "Greek will be included at least in the Kiev, New Russian, and Azov provinces; Arabic in the schools near Tatar, Persian, and Bukharskii regions; and Chinese in Irkutsk and Kolyvanskii regions."[65] Catherine opted to promote Russian as the unifying language of empire, but her reform did not rise to the level of aggressive Russification of the sort that began after 1825 especially.[66]

The Commission imposed tenets of the new school system on all preexisting schools in the empire—without exception. All schools were expected to adopt new instructional methods based on the Austrian model, which emphasized memorization, group instruction (rather than individual tutorials), and standardized textbooks. To ensure that publications for use in the new public schools had content in keeping with Orthodox perspectives, the Commission appointed the archbishop of Novgorod to review all primers and textbook manuscripts before they were printed. The changes extended to existing schools for the children of the nobility (Smolny and the Corps of Cadets), and privately run boarding schools. The Commission ordered seventeen private schools run by Russians to close immediately, presumably because of the low level of the instruction observed by inspectors. The inspectors allowed other private schools to remain open but placed them under state governance and supervision. Thus, the Commission promoted uniformity and the state's authority over education in theory and in practice.[67]

To staff the soon-to-be-established public schools with domestic Russian teachers, the Commission needed literate, educated Russians. As part of nation-building, Lomonosov had long advocated the development of the next genera-tion of Russian-born academics to replace foreign-born professors at the Academy of Sciences and at Moscow University.[68] Without a well-developed system of primary and secondary schools to feed the universities and graduate programs, the realization of this goal would remain incomplete. The Commission appealed to "local civil and Church authorities" to recruit potential candidates. In 1783, forty-eight candidates arrived from all over the empire to enroll in a new teacher training academy in Saint Petersburg. The bulk of the candidates came from sem-inaries in Tver, Smolensk, Kazan, Novgorod, and Pskov. A few bureaucrats were chosen from Arkhangelsk and Yaroslavl, and even a low-level clerk from Tula was accepted. Somewhat amusingly, the only four university students to appear were judged by the Commission as "absolutely hopeless" and were sent back to Moscow. Once trained as teachers, these recruits would return to their prov-inces to teach in the new public schools.[69] The Commission hoped to realize the goals of spreading the new *vospitanie* to provincial parts of the empire and, with it, a newly fashioned Russian national identity.

The Commission's goals were only partly realized. The distribution of schools across Russia's territory was uneven, and the number of schools opened fell short of the original plans. Compared to Catherine's other projects related to upbringing and the welfare of children, the public school project was always underfunded. While one hundred and fifty thousand rubles per year were ap-portioned for Smolny with additional expenditures for graduations and other ceremonial occasions, Catherine initially set aside only ten thousand rubles per year for the Commission's project; local levies were meant to provide additional revenue.[70] The number of pupils enrolled by 1800 relative to the population of Russia was small: records show that roughly twenty-two thousand pupils were enrolled in the public schools. Of these, 36 percent were peasant children. An even smaller percentage were girls. In a population of 40 million (a number that includes the territories acquired under Catherine), only a small fraction of all school-age children attended school, as Ben Ekloff notes. Yet his assertion that the educational reforms "in practice remained a dead letter," might obscure the longer term significance of the Commission's achievements.[71] Isabel de Madar-iaga and Simon Dixon acknowledge the very real achievement of the schools given the great many obstacles Catherine and the Commission faced, and the drain on state resources caused by wars with Sweden and Turkey.[72]

Whether the Commission's work should be seen as rational, progressive reform or as a turning away from the more liberal aspects of the Enlightenment perhaps cannot be decided.[73] Catherine introduced the aspiration to provide public education throughout the Russian empire and gave legitimacy to the idea that education should be accessible to children of both genders from all echelons in every geographic location. Nonetheless, certain aspects of the reform exercised the autocratic principle by imposing change on existing schools. Finally, Austrian pedagogy emphasized rote memorization, which had more in common with Muscovite culture than with the encouragement of reasoning that Bolotov, Novikov, and Sumarokov hoped to encourage in children. Significantly, the Commission underscored that the pupils at the new people's schools would be provided with an upbringing, with *vospitanie*. In fact, this term was underlined in the plans preserved in the archive of the Ministry of Education. The word choice again signals the emphasis on raising a whole human being, not only instruction; the schools would serve a civilizing mission, not only one of educating the masses.[74]

As part of their civilizing mission, the Commission authorized the publication of a conduct manual for distribution to all matriculating pupils of non-noble status. The small book, entitled *Rules for Pupils of the Public Schools*, went through four printings between 1782 and 1794. Intended for peasant children and children of lower orders, the book explained in simple language the behavioral expectations of the new schools. While the other main publication of the Commission, *On the Duties of Man and Citizen*, has been analyzed by many historians, this companion text has not.[75] The handbook opens with exhortations to the pupil to always remember while at school that "Wisdom begins with the fear of God" and that God approves of learning. The handbook insists that children should know that their internal feelings of love and duty toward the Creator and toward the Savior must be made manifest in external actions and behavior. These rules act as the foundation for learning, the text explains: the fear of God precedes enlightenment. Following this section, the guide focuses on socializing children into their new schoolhouse environment. As the first generation to attend a state school, these pupils needed instructions on every aspect of "going to school." Much of the advice concerns preparing and disciplining one's body appropriately for the school setting: "every pupil must wash his face and hands, comb his hair, and cut, if necessary, his fingernails, every morning before going to school." The body must be prepared for school in every sense; pupils are instructed to take care of their "natural needs" before entering school. The reader will learn that school is a serious place and that he (or she) must learn what behaviors are acceptable. Pupils are instructed to take their books and notebooks to school but to leave behind things that are used for games or amusements. *Rules for Pupils* also instructs children on how to behave outside school, at home, and in public. Instructions on proper table manners at home include remaining standing while one's elders take their seats, eating quietly, and thanking one's parents and kissing their hands at the end of the meal. Children were also advised to avoid unnecessary expenses and to refuse vodka and spirits. In essence, if the *Rules for Pupils* achieved its goals, the product would be not only an obedient and quiet pupil but also a civilized, well-mannered, sober, hard-working member of society.[76] In many respects, the intention to "civilize" the pupils of the public schools mirrored the language and goals of imperialism during this era. The association of enlightenment and civility with cleanliness is evident in both discursive contexts: raising the peasant child in many ways was a project similar to raising and civilizing the nation's multiethnic indigenous peoples.[77]

TEACHING RUSSIAN MASCULINITY

In the overall project to construct an inclusive and unifying national identity through the vehicle of a shared and dominant Russian language, constructions and norms of gender occupied a prominent place. In texts written for a juvenile audience and in practice at boarding schools and residential academies, reformers were concerned in particular with defining and promoting a masculine national identity through moral *vospitanie*. A certain anxiety concerning the boundaries of masculinity and femininity is more than perceptible among the Enlighteners. The identification of French tastes with femininity fueled an assertion of an unequivocally Russian masculinity, which rejected the softness and weakness resulting from an excess of French influence on young noble men. Satire from the period illustrates the concern with the proliferation of vice, especially the negative effects of Francophilia on the moral standards of the Russian nobility. Fonvizin's *The Brigadier* (1769), Elagin's *Jean de Mole, or the Russian Frenchman* (1765), and Kniazhnin's *Misfortune from a Coach* are famous examples. In these works, the loss of national identity is accompanied by a loss of traditional Russian values, such as honor. In *Misfortune from a Coach*, the Frenchified landlord does not want to be called "father" by his serfs, whom he has flogged for addressing him according to Russian custom. Kniazhnin blamed the breakdown of traditional moral relationships, illustrated by this cruel misunderstanding, on the adoption of French manners and tastes.[78]

The French tutor was a ubiquitous stereotype in the satirical literature of the time; he functioned as a symbol of the alienation of the Russian nobility from their national traditions and culture.[79] This was more than a literary trope, however. Many foreign visitors remarked on the prevalence of low-born French expatriates in the employ of Russian noble families.[80] The obsession with French language and fashion had led parents blindly to hire anyone who spoke French, regardless of qualifications. This often meant, according to Dashkova, that the teachers of Russia's next generation were of very low station, having just "staggered off the streets of Paris with barely a thing to eat." According to Dashkova, these people were unfit to teach children anything useful, and, even worse, they in many cases taught young Russians to despise their fatherland.[81]

Love of luxury and idleness were associated with French influence over children. Novikov believed that boys who grew up in households that valued pleasure over work became effeminate, weak, and unambitious:

> Where the morning is spent in sleep or on trifles, and the rest of the day at table and at cards, the children naturally develop a dislike for any serious occupation, come to regard eating, drinking, sleeping, dressing, paying visits, and playing cards as the lot of man, or at least as their own. . . . Thus it happens that the unhappy disposition developed which is most often to be found in young men of good family: a sybaritic softness which weakens a man, makes him incapable of any glorious endeavor [and] a laziness which leads him to regard slumber as the highest good.[82]

Masculinity is clearly at stake in his conception. Peken wrote that having been "raised in luxury and idleness" makes one more susceptible to "hypochondria and hysterical illnesses," especially in persons with "weak constitutions, who are gifted with fine and tender feelings and with ardent, lively imaginations."[83] He also remarked that the only differences in these two diseases are the names. "Although this illness is called hypochondria in men and hysteria or womb disease in women, they are, however, exactly the same disease, arising from the same causes and requiring the same treatment." Other causes of psychological illnesses (nervnye i chuvstvitel'nye bolezni) include lapses in moderation: excess tobacco use, "spiritual passions" like sadness and fear, idleness, and overuse of the mind—all made possible only in an environment of privilege and luxury.[84]

Bakherakht's discourse on this topic also contains a coded reference to homosexual behavior. He warns that boys might develop a "fear of sex with women" from too much masturbation.[85] Boys raised to fulfill, rather than to deny, their sexual urges risk losing their vitality as men: "To verify this, one need only glance at a young man who spent the whole night in loving gaiety, what change shows on his face? Moreover, his limbs are so relaxed he cannot feel them. After such expenditure he can barely walk or even sit."[86] He explained that only a wealthy man could be so indulgent; a working man could not afford to waste his strength. Bakherakht condemned a life of parties, trifles, and debauchery; men who thus indulge themselves eventually are "not competent in any activity" and contribute nothing to society.[87] Bolotov decried the same in his invective against the Russian petit maître who squandered his talents and spent his time in shameless and useless depravity. Peken concurred and warned that excessive sexual pleasure caused by "immoderation of lust" leads to effeminate men subject to other moral weaknesses.[88]

The diminished authority and masculinity of Russian men vexed Fonvizin, as well. His play *The Minor* provides a comedic and dystopic vision of life when a matriarchy replaces Enlightened patriarchy.[89] The title character is a young nobleman who is old enough to enter state service but barely knows the alphabet. His *vospitanie* has been so defective that he is totally unprepared for adult life. Fonvizin names this antihero "Mitrofan," whose name, tellingly, means "like his mother." His mother, Mrs. Prostakova, rules the estate with arbitrary cruelty and ignorance, while his father figures as a nonentity. Fonvizin clearly condemns Mitrofan's mother for his disastrous upbringing. In Russia during this period, noblewomen who owned property and/or ran the estate while their husbands were away in military or civil service did in fact exercise a great deal of power. This reality may have created, in the minds of Fonvizin and other concerned thinkers, the conditions necessary for blaming mothers like Prostakova.[90]

For Dashkova, masculine virtue must be attached to an ethic of service. The noble boy who received the proper upbringing could do "an immeasurable good for society." The ideal upbringing would impart a strong male body with "humanity, fairness, and virtue" to produce a nobleman capable of leadership. He would grow up to be "brave in battle and talented in work and just and fair in his morals."[91] At the Legislative Commission, the report from the Chernigov deputies revealed the same association of proper upbringing for noble boys with an active life in service to society: "Without a good upbringing it is impossible to be a skillful and brave military commander, a wise government servitor, a fair judge, a careful architect, or a useful citizen of society."[92] Thus, a *vospitannyi* or properly raised nobleman was prepared to assume the role of civic leader and moral paragon.

The masculinity of the future officer corps also concerned Betskoi. The aim to establish a boundary between femininity and masculinity is palpable in his efforts to diminish primping and preening in the boys and young men enrolled in Russia's military academies. To this end, he forbade such "overindulgences" as "fancy attire," adornment with "jewels and precious metals," and the immoderate use of "powder and pomade." Large curls and long hair were also forbidden. In place of rampant dandyism and obsessions over coiffure, powder, and costumes, the new masculine upbringing should focus on inculcating "honest virtues" among the future leaders of the state and military.[93]

ENLIGHTENED NOBILITY AND EMPATHY

Reformers further constructed gender and the cultivation of masculinity with respect to considerations of class and estate. Serfdom entered the discourse as a factor in the upbringing of noble children. Many voices—including those of Catherine, Fonvizin, Novikov, and Radishchev—expressed concern about the perpetuation of cruelty from one generation of nobility to the next. Catherine worried about the effect of despotic home environments on children:

> The inclination to tyrannize is cultivated here more than in any other inhabited part of the world; it is inculcated from the tenderest age by the cruelty which children observe in their parents' behavior towards servants for where is the home that has no traps, chains, whips, and other instruments to penalize the smallest mistake on the part of those whom nature has placed in this unfortunate class which cannot break its chains without committing violence?[94]

Some authors created blistering and didactic examples of the emotional or physical cruelty of some noblemen and women toward their social inferiors. Examples include the portrayals by Karamzin in "Poor Liza" and by Radishchev in *A Journey from Saint Petersburg to Moscow*. Others penned moral stories for children meant to teach them empathy for peasants and the poor. *The New Russian Primer with Short Moral Stories and Tales* included the following lesson to encourage empathy: "Do not swear at a poor man . . . he is a human being the same as you, and subsequently no worse than you."[95] In a story in the same primer, a noble girl is insufferably bossy to the house servants, directing them constantly to do things for her. When they rebel and refuse to work, her mother supports them, and the girl is forced to learn to do things for herself. As a consequence, she grows to be a much more pleasant and compassionate lady.[96] Sumarokov encouraged his young readers to be "merciful" and "humanitarian." Barsov's primer reminded children of the Christian duty to help the less fortunate, "to Feed the hungry, give drink to the thirsty, Clothe the naked, go into the homes of the disturbed."[97] Radishchev advocated kindness and friendship in parental attitudes toward their children, reasoning that children would learn to be tyrants themselves only if raised in an atmosphere of violence.[98]

The association of immoral behavior among the nobility with a loss of true Russianness became a theme in prescriptions for improving *vospitanie*. Dashkova invented a history of upbringing in Russia to explain what had been lost over generations of Westernization. In her schema, pre-Petrine upbringing had advantages over contemporary child rearing because of its moral content and national purity:

> Our great-grandfathers called it upbringing when they taught their children their psalters and to count with an abacus, after which they gave their enlightened sons as a reward the Kievan Book of Hours; but they also taught loyalty to the Tsar, obedience to the law, and strict observance of one's word or promises; and as they themselves did not know other regions, they did not allow their children to leave their fatherland, which they valued above other states.[99]

While Dashkova acknowledged the limited intellectual goals of child rearing in the pre-Petrine period, she thought that Muscovite child-rearing practices were superior to eighteenth-century practices because they emphasized moral development: "In this [Muscovite] upbringing, ignorance and not corruption was apparent; that is preferable in my opinion or at least not so disastrous: for ignorance can be corrected more quickly than dissoluteness." Dashkova argued that Peter's reforms, which promoted foreign travel and immoderate appetites for foreign culture, had undercut respect for distinctly Russian values: "Our fathers wanted to raise us in any manner at all, as long as it was not according to Russian customs, and so that through our upbringing we would not become Russians [*Rossiiskie*]." This type of child rearing produced a Russian lacking in the most basic attachments—in Dashkova's words, an "ignoramus" without "love for his fatherland and his parents implanted in his heart." While Dashkova praised the national and spiritual aspects of Muscovite child-rearing practices, she advocated a complete return neither to the old ways of raising children nor to a Muscovite-era patriarchy. While Muscovites received moral instruction, they did not learn "the duty of citizens and natural rights," key lessons of the Enlightenment.[100]

At the Corps of Cadets, Betskoi sought to limit tyranny as well. Betskoi recommended relying on shame rather than physical pain as punishment for major infractions. Minor infractions were not to be punished every few minutes; Betskoi was certain that excessive correction would create an oppressive environment, contrary to the goal of creating an overall pleasant experience in childhood in order to raise happy, virtuous officers. Arbitrariness and physical punishment had no place in raising an Enlightened, rational human being. Betskoi suggested alternative punishments based on creating a sense of shame before one's peers, such as seating the cadet at a separate table during meals or having him kneel on the floor during a lesson.[101]

Russian Enlighteners not only reinvented Russian masculinity and characteristics of the nobility; Bakherakht and other reformers believed that lack of moral *vospitanie* in girls posed a greater societal risk. In one of many examples, Bakherakht reasoned: "Women's build itself is much softer than man's, although this is not because of nature, but from a quiet and idle life and soft *vospitanie* [which is softer and weaker] in homes of luxury; this very softness and idleness hurls them into illness; and especially if a woman, living a quiet and idle life, which arouses in her weak thoughts, sacrifices her marriage with her charms."[102] In other words, her lack of virtue and plenty of idle time predispose this type of woman to use "her charms" to pursue affairs outside of marriage. Dashkova also implied that the upbringing of girls mattered most to the project of renewing Russia's national character. When speaking abstractly about upbringing, Dashkova referenced the grandfathers and fathers of past generations. However, when she turned to practical issues, she illustrated the problem with the story of an imaginary girl living in Catherine's era who had suffered a poor upbringing. The girl's parents had entrusted her upbringing to a French governess and thus ensured their daughter would grow up to sow seeds of anti-Russian feeling, disorder, and immoderation in society:

> This *vospitanie* is not only not useful, it can be called harmful: for it would be better if Taniusha . . . did not have such heinous feelings in her heart and mind which the base and often licentious French wench impresses upon her. She would have been a better wife, mother, and mistress of the household, if, not knowing (poorly) a foreign language, had she learned her native language fluently, and if she had love for her fatherland in place of the scorn that 'Mademoiselle' imparts to children. If Taniusha had learned through example to respect her parents and to love order, modesty, and economy, but not luxury, caprice, and mockery, then it would be possible to conclude that her parents had a proper understanding of the word *vospitanie*.[103]

Thus, Dashkova's construction of the ideal Russian woman reflected the goals of the new Russian national character, imparted through proper child rearing:

a true Russian in speech and patriotic feeling, virtuous in every respect, and yet embodying Enlightenment values like order and industry. For Radishchev, this ideal new Russian woman would also exercise her charms to promote morality in her husband, rather than to corrupt other men: "I know that you lead back to the way of virtue him who has begun to turn aside, and strengthen him who is tending to go astray."[104] Thus, a woman deprived of the correct *vospitanie* threatened to imperil the masculinity of Russian men and order in society, while a properly raised woman ensured an Orthodox yet enlightened patriarchy at home, nurtured patriotic feelings in her offspring, and supported the moral health of society. Indeed, the project of raising a proud, civilized Russian nation rested most of all on her shoulders. In chapter 6, we consider one such site for confronting the issues surrounding the upbringing of Russian girls.

6

THE NEW GIRLHOOD

Many Russian writers and political leaders believed that the long-term success of reforms in upbringing depended upon the creation of a new woman. Accordingly, raising girls became critical to the goals of fostering a new national character and improving the health of the population. Toward these ends, Catherine established one of the jewels of her reign, the Society for the Upbringing of Well-Born Maidens (or Smolny as it came to be known) in 1764. In the charter for the residential school, Catherine and Betskoi professed the aspiration to raise a new kind of *grazhdanka*—literally, a female citizen. They instructed the headmistress to regard the upbringing of the girls with the highest degree of reverence and "as precious to her, to the security of the state, and to the fatherland."[1] The new noble girlhood became one of the most prominent emblems of Catherine's projected image of a new Russia—one that many of her fellow reformers also adopted and promoted. However, the "maidens," who became the first girls in the Russian empire to receive such a comprehensive education, found themselves entirely shielded from the world of adult responsibilities and activities. The specific roles they were being educated to assume remained hazy.

To be sure, educating girls anywhere in the eighteenth century was a tricky business. In even the most enlightened centers of Europe, pedagogues and philosophers argued over how and whether to educate girls at all.[2] A central problem concerned how to prepare girls of the aristocracy and middle classes for adult life while preserving their virtue. (The character of women from the lower echelons of society who worked as midwives and wet nurses vexed reformers, too, as we saw in chapters 2 and 3.) As Nadine Berenguier explains, the authors of advice literature faced "the difficult task of teaching candidates for marriage about the dangers of the world without threatening their modesty or reputation."[3] Mary Wollstonecraft, one of the leading advocates of education for girls, favored some instruction in matters of sexuality as an antidote to immorality. She encouraged parents "to speak to children of the organs of generation as freely as we speak of the other parts of the body." Her detractors were quick to equate education with promiscuity; girls who sought learning, memorably referred to as "botanizing girls" by one critic, risked their modesty and virtue.[4] Catherine rejected Diderot's suggestion that noble girls should study anatomy in preparation for matrimony and maternity. The question of transitioning to the world of adults surfaced only when the first graduation loomed and life beyond the school began to beat a very loud drum. Until then, the Society articulated and constructed—literally and figuratively—the new boundaries of a privileged noble girlhood that explicitly served the goals of the state and the fatherland. This new notion of girlhood became not only a lived experience for an elite few but also a cultural idea with high visibility in Russian culture. This new identity, rooted in a gendered childhood that explicitly articulated meanings for the public and the state, attached to the graduates for their lifetimes. Finally, the new notion of girlhood itself became a feature of Russian culture throughout the remainder of the imperial period, promoting an ideal that had meaning beyond the actual accessibility of such a childhood.

IDEAL GIRLHOOD

Fonvizin provided an early archetype of the "new girl." His character Sophie (from *The Minor*) shared a name with Rousseau's ideal girl, imagined as the perfect helpmeet for Emile, but Fonvizin's Sophie bore closer resemblance to Catherine's ideal noble girl. A calm, reasonable, unaffected girl, Sophie seeks wisdom from her Russian elders and from European philosophers. As an orphan, Sophie (and other girls without mothers) made for the ideal Lockean blank slate. She might be raised free from the contaminating influence of mothers and other female relatives and thus escape both the moral impurity and the ignorance that Russian reformers believed resulted from poor role models. When Fonvizin's elder protagonist, Starodum, meets with Sophie, he finds her reading Fénelon's treatise, rendered by Fonvizin in Russian as *On the Upbringing of Girls*. Fonvizin's Sophie is educated, but not above a level deemed appropriate for her sex, and she reveals her reason by seeking the wise counsel of learned men, like Starodum, whose name and biography references an older Russian morality, of the sort Dashkova had in mind when she invoked with reverence the generation of noblemen who sacrificed in service to Peter the Great and their fatherland. As Fonvizin imagines her, Sophie will not undermine the masculinity of the new Russian nobleman but will support it—and, in so doing, will support an enlightened social order more broadly.[5]

Like Fonvizin, Catherine recognized that orphans would provide the ideal raw material for her project. While her institution did indeed rescue some orphaned noble girls from lives of poverty and tragedy, in fact Catherine's institution transformed all of its pupils into orphans, regardless of their origins, and imposed a narrative of the state's rescue with the goal of improving society. The archive of the Society preserves the sworn affidavits of all the pupils' parents or guardians, who, with a flourish of the quill and the seal of a notary, relinquished all claims to their five-year-old daughters for the remainder of their childhoods. The statements included an explicit promise not to remove their daughters before the end of the twelve-year program for any reason. No girl could matriculate without such a notarized legal document, which made her essentially a ward of the school and, by extension, the state.[6] Indeed, the evidence shows that only in cases of extreme family tragedy did the board release a girl to her home of origin. To preserve the monopoly of the institution's influence, parents and relatives enjoyed only supervised visits with the girls on the campus. For girls whose families lived a great distance from the capital, this meant that they spent very little time with relatives over the course of the year. Thus, the fact of being an orphan did not make a girl a candidate for the Society so much as the Society transformed all the girls into orphans as a precondition to their *vospitanie*.

Within this narrative, teachers and staff raised the girls to regard their upbringing as a special gift and privilege, one that endowed the recipient with a responsibility to serve society and the fatherland. Very wealthy and prominent families placed daughters at Smolny from its earliest years; even Mikhail Shcherbatov, who became Smolny's greatest detractor, sought admission for his daughter. Baron Alexander Ivanovich Cherkassov, the director of the Medical Collegium, enrolled his daughter, as did other prominent families, including the Glinskys, Sheremetevs, and Golitsyns.[7] For the many well-off girls whose parents were living and who paid a hefty tuition bill for this "gift," the figurative orphaning marked the beginning of a new identity as girls. For rich and poor alike, the narrative of a *vospitanie* bestowed for the sake of a greater good became the equalizing message of their girlhood at Smolny. Everyone became an indebted orphan.

EDUCATIONAL SPACE

Catherine and Betskoi, her chief architect of *vospitanie* until 1782, planned an intentional environment for their "orphaned" girls. The designated space for the construction of the Society speaks to the establishment of childhood as important to and highly symbolic of the state's goals. Catherine selected the site of the Smolny monastery, then on the edge of Saint Petersburg, for the year-round raising of girls; hence, the nickname "Smolny" for the school and *"Smolianki"* for the girls who lived there. The emergence of such spaces coincided with the construction of modern childhood, which posited that children needed specific, adult-supervised spaces in the form of orphanages, schools, or playgrounds. In time, the spaces of childhood would become those of institutions—most notably the schoolhouse. In many urban contexts in Europe and America, advocates for children, politicians, and even children themselves competed over the locations and meanings of such spaces. As Marta Gutman and Ning de Coninck-Smith underscore, buildings erected specifically for the raising of children made a grand statement about the importance of children and their welfare and education to the body politic.[8] Thus, the modern state laid a claim to children literally but also symbolically in the dedication of such buildings—the image of which might prove stronger or more enduring than the state's actual reach. As with schools and orphanages in other urban environments, architects and designers freighted Smolny's campus itself with meaning.

First, Catherine might have built her school anywhere in her empire, but she chose the most European of Russian cities, the recently established Saint Petersburg, founded by Peter the Great only sixty years earlier. This choice signals not only the clear connection to westward-looking reforms but also Smolny's importance to the profile of the capital and the state itself. The empress might have chosen Tsarskoe Selo, the site of the royal summer residences, located fifteen miles from the capital itself, had she wanted a completely insulated environment—or if the project of raising girls did not have so much aesthetic appeal to her as a public relations opportunity. The choice of Petersburg proper speaks to the empress's intention to make frequent visits herself, to integrate Smolny into the itineraries of foreign visitors (heads of state, ambassadors, and philosophes), and to host public performances to display the new girls for the elite of Petersburg society. Had Catherine been interested primarily in the product of Smolny (that new *grazhdanka*) but not so interested in the process of upbringing, a sequestered site might have made more sense. The edge of Petersburg proved a perfect compromise: far enough from the center to provide clean air and some insulation from urban influences, yet close enough to court for both supervision and travel to and from by empress and girls alike. Thus, Smolny's location enabled the empress to exhibit her Enlightenment project of raising new girls.

Catherine's choice of an existing convent, with a cathedral as the main feature of the landscape, also speaks to the sort of national identity she and other reformers sought to construct. The building of the cathedral began under Empress Elizabeth, according to the plans of Francesco Bartolomeo Rastrelli, the Italian architect who left his stamp on the Winter Palace, Catherine's summer palace, and other Saint Petersburg landmarks. The baroque and feminine confection featured an azure exterior trimmed in white and gold; while both grand and sumptuous in design, it constitutes a less imposing image than do Rastrelli's other architectural monuments. Catherine came to favor neoclassical architecture and therefore dismissed Rastrelli, yet the Smolny campus retained Rastrelli's cathedral as its baroque central landmark.[9] The residential buildings of the convent, not more than two stories high, were set behind the cathedral and functioned as the first dormitories and classrooms in the early years of the girls' school until the erection of additional wings and buildings. The cathedral itself remained the most prominent architectural feature of the campus for the rest of the eighteenth century (until the construction of Giacamo Quarenghi's neoclassical edifice on the campus in 1806–8), announcing by its presence the primacy of Russian Orthodoxy to the project of raising new noble girls. The schedule governing everyday life at Smolny included morning and evening prayers and church services, underscoring the importance of faith to the overall undertaking.

Smolny Cathedral and Convent. Saint Petersburg, Russia.
(Photo by Tatyana Savvateeva)

As it did in primers and other didactic works for children, Orthodoxy formed the foundation of *vospitanie*, but, as the architecture of Smolny's campus demonstrated, this was an Orthodoxy that departed from earlier versions by allowing some aspects of the Enlightenment to infuse its mission.[10]

The interior spaces of Smolny sought to shape the girls. From the vantage of the history of childhood, an interior space dedicated solely to the overarching goal of nurturing children represents a modern notion. In the case of schools, orphanages, and hospitals with wings for children, this marks the beginning of designing spaces explicitly with children in mind. The creation of child-size tables and chairs and other such innovations in the material world of children considered the physical and emotional comfort of the child.[11] Absent any surviving visual depictions from the eighteenth century, it is possible to infer what was included from the plans, observations of visitors, and items preserved in its archive. Catherine intended a Spartan existence for the girls, yet not one so severe that it created privation. Visitors, such as the British ambassador and the king of Sweden, remarked upon the sense of order, the happiness among the girls, and the attention to detail evident in the surroundings that spoke to the "great care" given to the girls' upbringing within its walls.[12] In addition to dormitory and classroom space, Catherine and the designers planned for public space to accommodate the invited guests—sometimes numbering several hundred—who visited Smolny for dramatic and musical performances, public exams, and celebratory dinners and ceremonies. Classroom walls offered messages in keeping with general Enlightenment precepts for establishing habits of industry and economy. Finally, and sweetly, the girls created handbills and posters to announce upcoming events and gatherings; a few of these survive in the archive. Written in childish script, they speak to an environment in which children participated in constructing their world, and they strike one as a continuing feature of the modern school: children's creations become part of the interior space and décor.[13]

In this world designed explicitly for the raising of girls, Catherine also intended that women would make up the majority of the adults governing the environs and activities within its walls. She and Betskoi subscribed wholeheartedly to the Enlightenment notion that example is the most powerful teacher. Unlike at the flagship convent school for girls in France, Saint-Cyr, Catherine wanted not nuns but virtuous, modest, and refined women of secular society raising the girls. Catherine imagined that the first headmistress to oversee such an upbringing would be a woman who loved to teach, who represented the highest standards in virtuous behavior, and who was "free from other obligations"—

that is, unencumbered by a husband or children.[14] Sophie de Lafond became the first woman to hold this post and by all accounts worked tirelessly, earning the respect of Catherine and even that of her heir, Paul, who in most other matters took joy in opposing his deceased mother's wishes. Her sizable salary of 1,200 rubles per year reflected the importance Catherine placed on her work.[15] Form mistresses acted as nearly constant monitors of the girls' behavior, and, in turn, their own superiors kept an eye on their manners and comportment. Thus, we encounter one of many paradoxes regarding Smolny: it was a pedagogical environment that emphasized teaching through example but there were no wives or mothers for the girls to emulate.

SUPERVISION AND CONTROL

A residential facility offered new liberties and opportunities to girls; at the same time, it created an entirely supervised and controlled environment in which to raise them. The first graduates wrote of their delight in living and learning at Smolny; these girls enjoyed a curriculum and enrichment lessons that exceeded those offered in any other setting available to Russian girls. Within its gates, the careful attention of minders, teachers, and the empress herself kept the girls under continual watch. This type of facility for children was still a novelty in the eighteenth century, as were the Houses of Upbringing and the first hospitals for civilians in Russia. While all of these ostensibly offered their pupils or patients the latest in modern pedagogy or medicine, they also represented the reach of the state and institutionalized medicine into private lives, with, perhaps, a corresponding loss of privacy. Historians of childhood note that adult-free spaces for children came to be seen as problematic and undesirable; the goal of modernizing states and societies was to increasingly manage the activities of children within designated spaces such as playgrounds and schools.[16] In the case of Smolny, as at the Corps of Cadets under Betskoi's authority, one of the key methods of *vospitanie* required nearly totalitarian surveillance by the form mistresses and "observers of morals."[17] Similarly, all of the writers promoting reformed *vospitanie* encouraged parents to provide closer supervision of their children and to be watchful—even suspicious—when their children were in the care of others.[18] This aspiration to constantly watch children and to create environments for doing so that would replace the "free" spaces of childhood represents what has been termed the "panopticon" of modern childhood, in reference to Jeremy Bentham's design for an ideal prison.[19] Bentham's subtitle reveals the myriad applications he imagined for his architectural design: *Containing the Idea of a New Principle of Construction Applicable to Any Sort of Establishment, in*

Which Persons of Any Description are to be Kept under Inspection; and in Particular to Penitentiary-Houses, Prisons, Houses of Industry, . . . Hospitals, Mad-Houses, and Schools. In the chapter devoted to schools, his plan advocates small, individual rooms for children in which they would live, study, and sleep, with a grated door so that they could be under observation at all times.[20] Bentham wrote his treatise describing his design while visiting his brother, Samuel Bentham, who lived in Russia from 1780 until 1791 and served Catherine and her associates in various capacities.[21]

While not confined to individual rooms to live, study, and sleep, *Smolianki* were controlled in other visible ways. Once girls entered Smolny, typically at age five, they adopted a uniform according to age. The dresses were simple by the standards of the court—free from corseting, excessive lace, and crinolines— yet beautiful by any eighteenth-century standard. Each cohort wore dresses of the same color, which marked its social identity within the school. Some girls arrived with trunks full of finery, kid gloves, and linens, but these girls, too, wore the simple uniform of the *Smolianka*. Thus, girls of a certain cohort were nicknamed "the coffee-colored" or the "pale blues," as graduates recalled.[22] The school controlled the appearance of the girls' hair, as well, and departed from the eighteenth-century aristocratic habit of equating elaborate coiffures with status and wealth. The youngest girls wore very short hair, while the older girls could indulge in a little powder and a relatively uncomplicated updo. In one of her satirical pieces, Catherine mocked ladies who spent hours getting dressed and having their hair prepared. Similarly, the empress corrected Friedrich Grimm when he ridiculed her pupils' lack of hair design; she intended this naturalness and wanted nothing to distract from developing their minds and talents.[23] Thus, in appearance, Smolny's pupils surrendered control and any standards imported from home. In this respect, too, Catherine and her faculty deliberately replaced the students' individual identities of origin with a new social identity, thus under- scoring the girls' status as *Smolianki*.

In terms of curriculum, Smolny offered an abbreviated version of the pro- gram at the Corps of Cadets. This included geography, history, catechism, physics, *nravouchenie*, and mathematics, although girls did not learn advanced math. Natural history was added in 1783. Both schools for noble children tended to privilege the study of languages, literature, and drama.[24] As Raeff explains, the relative dearth of scientific and philosophical works in Russian translation made knowledge of other European languages an imperative for the intellec- tual and moral development of eighteenth-century Russians.[25] It is especially important to recognize the emphasis placed on languages, drama, and reading

at state institutions for boys because this contextualizes Smolny's original curriculum, which has been sometimes devalued by suggestions that instruction
was of a "low level" or that the program was exceedingly "light."[26] Boys at the
Corps of Cadets received the following instruction from one of Catherine's
directors: "As soon as you learn to read, you will love reading, and if you read
with curiosity and if you have good and useful books, of course you will teach
yourself how to think, speak, and read well, and finally, how to behave and
act."[27] Smolny's charter states: "above all, [the girls] must be taught Russian
and foreign languages, in order that they will be able to read, write, and speak
them."[28] Proficiency may have been the goal for girls, rather than the pursuit of
scholarly study. Nonetheless, the instruction to teachers to encourage the girls
to develop "an interest in books as personal enjoyment and entertainment"
marks reading as an appropriate pursuit for women.[29] While the contrast might
seem great between encouraging girls to read for amusement and boys to read
in order to develop their minds, it is important to remember that in Europe
during this time debate over "the woman question" invoked questions about
the suitability of fiction, science, and non-religious works as reading material for women.[30] In Russia, Anna Labzina recalled in her memoir that she had
been instructed to avoid reading novels as a girl and young woman.[31] At Saint-
Cyr (Catherine's original inspiration for Smolny), the pupils were actually discouraged from pursuing reading as a pastime, and the lack of a decent library
ensured that girls had access to very few books.[32] In contrast, Catherine and
Betskoi insisted on the necessity of a library at Smolny, stocked with a "reasonable selection of books."[33] Indeed, Smolny departed so significantly in content
and style from the education, everyday life, and image of Saint-Cyr, that the
French school ought not be considered the model for Smolny.[34] Finally, Smolny's
charter instructed the teachers to initiate conversations in foreign languages
with their pupils outside class and to encourage the girls to express their own
opinions by asking them questions.[35] To a certain degree, Catherine viewed reading, thinking, and the development of opinions as appropriate and desirable intellectual activities for women. It seems clear that she desired that the girls at
Smolny have access to the world of Russian and European ideas; perhaps they
would find comfort and inspiration in them, as she had.[36]

THE PUBLIC AND A GIRL'S DUTY

For Catherine and Betskoi, creating an ideal *grazhdanka* figured as a project
worthy of a great degree of cultivation and observation. The narrative constructed about Smolny and at Smolny followed the logic of *vospitanie* in other

contexts: the girls received care (and scrutiny) that would help them become the standard-bearers of a revised Russian national character. The consciousness of the duty to perform this role became part of the Smolny experience and narrative for noble girls from an early age. The school's charter included plans for recognizing and rewarding achievement in *nauka*, broadly understood as learning, knowledge, and sciences at the time. Through public exams—with the empress in attendance, no less—and public award ceremonies to recognize the brightest among them, the girls learned that they had to demonstrate their abilities and talents before an audience of high-status adults.[37] Self-confidence was an imperative. The board spent a great deal of time preparing for such events, posting notices in newspapers and issuing invitations to special guests. Betskoi also instructed teachers to encourage a healthy competition among the girls to stimulate their ambition and work ethic.[38] Girls who did not perform could expect to be sent home—and they routinely were, with comments as spare and direct as "untalented" and "not competent in sciences."[39]

The girls also performed plays and operas through Smolny's theater program. Dramatic arts constituted a significant part of the curriculum at Smolny, as at Catherine's other schools; many eighteenth-century pedagogues regarded theater as a progressive means of instilling virtue and even national character. Diderot and Voltaire flattered Catherine by praising her girls as gifted dramatists. Girls also began appearing in Saint Petersburg society from the age of fifteen, attending balls and accompanying Catherine at her request in other settings.[40] After some of the older Smolny girls joined the empress on a promenade (*gulian'e*) in the Summer Gardens on May 2, 1770, Betskoi wrote to them as a group. His letter underscores the high expectations placed on the girls' public behavior and performances:

You would not know, nor could you imagine, Ladies, in what satisfaction I found myself yesterday, learning from the Lips of your Gracious Sovereign in the presence of all the court, the praises full of goodness that she spoke to me of her contentment with your class. Judge, Ladies, the infinite pleasure that it caused me; I believe to give much to you also in repeating it to you today. All of you flattered Her Imperial Majesty; your candor, your modesty, your carriage, your expressions, nothing escaped her observation until the least of your actions found its place in her good heart.

The letter reveals the stakes: the girls should earn the praise of the empress and Betskoi to remain in their good graces. One does not like to imagine the type of letter he would have written if the empress had been displeased. The letter continues, making very clear the narrative of indebtedness:

> Ladies, such is the privilege of virtue, such is the fruit of the good Education that Madame de Lafond inspires you to and for which you are all indebted. I repeat that it is good to hear the praises escape the lips of one of the premier sovereigns of the world, and that it is sweet to merit the praises and to attract new favor [from her].[41]

Later that month, he wrote another gushing note to the girls, reporting the empress's further positive impressions and those of the audience around her—clearly, the other constituency that the girls needed to impress. Betskoi reported Catherine's praise: "'Explain, Mr. Betskoi, to these likeable, very lively children how I was struck by their zeal and their intelligence, how I feel joy at such a charming assembly, who on this occasion entered into my view and seconded my intentions with as much dignity as they did.'"[42] Thus, the girls learned of their very public role as pet projects of the empress, expected to be intelligent, lively, and charming in the presence of many important people. Betskoi ended with a postscript to underscore the point: "The happiness and satisfaction of the public is inexpressible."[43]

The "public" in question could represent thousands of Catherine's guests. In this same year, 1770, the empress wrote to Voltaire to boast of the success her girls displayed on stage. Girls ages eight, nine, and ten performed as part of the program for an opulent ball she hosted, with 3,600 guests in attendance.[44] Thus, the upbringing at Smolny offered these girls new experiences and opportunities to study theater, music, and the arts, but it demanded no small payment in return. Beginning with the abandonment of their families and their origins, the payback quickly progressed to high-stakes performances before the empress, thousands of her guests, and reminders of the girls' eternal indebtedness.

Letters from the first *Smolianki* to Betskoi, de Lafond, and Catherine reveal that this narrative became a hallmark of their *vospitanie* and their identities. If judged by the graduates' words, Catherine succeeded in her goal of creating *vospitannye* women at Smolny. The letters convey a profound learned gratitude. The similarity of sentiment in these letters is remarkable; all of the letters express, in flowery eighteenth-century Russian (not French!), the heartfelt appreciation of the writer for having been honored with an upbringing at Smolny. The following excerpt from Elisaveta Shcherbatova is typical: "Your efforts to instill in me the laws of honor and gratitude motivate me now to fulfill my first duty, which is to express to you, as far as is possible, my gratitude."[45] Writing the letter itself figured as evidence of proper upbringing and of the manners and morals taught at Smolny. Another example comes from Elisaveta Simonova: "Exercising the fruits of your philanthropy, my first duty is to express to you my sincere gratitude."[46] Using almost the same phrasing, Serafima Zvereva explains to the staff at Smolny that, in the act of expressing thanks, she was illustrating for her teachers "the fruits of your labor."[47]

These letters also conveyed the notion that proper morals were the guide to correct behavior, another lesson Catherine and Betskoi hoped to instill. Many girls wrote that their Smolny upbringing would guide them throughout life, as Anis'ia Svistunova noted in this letter: "You guided my limited efforts on the path toward enlightenment. . . . Your tireless effort gave me the means to a peaceful and fortunate life."[48] A sense of duty to exercise one's morals, to put virtue into action, is also evident in a letter by Natal'ia Borshcheva: "Thanks to you, these gifts to me are, and will be, motivation throughout my whole life to glorify your great blessings and to guide all of my actions."[49] This equation of one's education and upbringing with a "gift" that requires gratitude and re-payment throughout one's life also reveals how the Smolianki understood their importance to the state. They would repay their debt not only through loyalty to the crown and the fatherland but also through good actions, as Borshcheva's letter indicates. Similarly, Afim'ia Dunina expressed a sense of responsibility and a consciousness of being a role model: "the realization in action of these virtu-ous rules, instilled in me from my early years, will be one of my greatest achieve-ments. . . . I will be an example to my peers."[50] These girls clearly thought of themselves as invested with a duty—imposed by the highest secular authori-ties—to lead through virtuous example and service.

In the 1770s, Catherine commissioned portraits of some of her favorite Smo-lianki from D. G. Levitskii, who also created the famous depiction of Cather-ine as a Solon-style "lawgiver." Portraiture, along with ceremonies and parades, functioned in the early modern era as a powerful means of communicating messages visually and provides visual evidence of Catherine's enlightenment ideals.[51] Levitskii's contemporaries and later critics recognized him for the warmth and humanity he captured in his subjects; he depicted them as human beings outside their social estate. His series of Smolianki portraits evidence Catherine's intention to promote these girls as emblems of the Enlightenment in Russia and of noble girlhood itself. While some scholars have interpreted Levitskii's portraits as depictions of the muses, the portraits of the girls are strikingly natural departures from some of his more formal head-and-shoulders portraiture.[52] Rather than depicting allegory or myth, Levitskii rendered the personalities and joyfulness of the girls in a very lifelike manner, which no doubt accounts for the pictures' enduring popularity in Russian culture. The girls shine with a kind of self-confidence and lack of self-consciousness at the same time. The fact that no adults appear in the series, while two of the paintings depict more than one girl, underscores the community of girls at Smolny. All of the girls are smiling—which is unusual in an era that favored a more somber countenance in most portraits—and, whether the smiles were at Catherine's behest or because of the temperament of the girls themselves, the subjects' sunny demeanors serve to promote an idea of girlhood as animated, natural, active, and exuberant. The refinement and luxury of noble life are apparent in the settings, yet Levitskii conveys a new image of noble girlhood (or, indeed, of any girlhood). The girls are not passive objects or ornaments but fully possess their own subjectivity: these are girls with passions, whether for music, drama, friendship, or even science and reading. Finally, we can read the portraits themselves as the first effort in Russia to aestheticize girlhood—to celebrate it and render it as beautiful because it is girlish.[53] Levitskii's portraits also represent a secular celebration of feminine purity and innocence. Following the Enlightenment precepts of character building, Levitskii shows that, in the absence of vice, virtue and talent may flourish. Thus, his portraits capture Catherine's goal of constructing a hybrid Russian national identity; the portraits project the new Russian girls as the ideal Enlightenment-era beings, free from any artifice or vice that might mar their civilizing potential.

Novikov believed that the Smolny girls would not only be models but would actively improve society. In 1773, in his journal *Zhivopisets* (*The Painter*), he wrote of the *Smolianki*, before any had graduated: "they are an example to us of all the virtues; they correct the ruined hearts and morals of all wicked people."[54] But how exactly would the girls correct "ruined hearts"? The actual content and meaning of such feminine virtues and in what contexts they might be exercised beyond girlhood is vague and takes us back to the issue of how to raise girls while protecting their modesty. This issue attaches to girlhood in many historical contexts. As Sally Mitchell underscores, culturally the adolescent girl occupies a "provisional free space"; her upbringing might lead her toward a chaste womanhood, or she might still develop the destructive attributes of vice and sexual promiscuity. For the moment, she is no longer a child, but she is not yet a woman.[55] Berenguier captures the conundrum thus: "Caught between childhood (connected with animality) and womanhood (tainted with relations with a man), the female adolescent also stands on the threshold between the space of education (home or convent) and the space of the world (salon, theater, ball) from which she will access married life."[56] Thus, the boundaries of girlhood become a very charged issue. In the context of Smolny, two boundaries defined girlhood: *soslovie* (social estate) and graduation. The name itself, Society for the Upbringing of Well-Born Maidens, indicates an institution for well-born "girls" and interests us because it uses the term *devitsy*, a now-obsolete term that translates as "maidens" or "girls." Catherine later decided to add another section to the Society, which eventually became its own separate division for daughters of soldiers, urban commoners, and other lower orders. Unlike the "Society," this facility was called simply an *uchilishche* (school), intended not for *devitsy* (maidens) but for *devushki* (girls). The distinctions between the two schools, both located on the same campus, reveal a great deal about the boundaries of the "girlhood" that was meant to represent an Enlightened Russia.

The section designated for non-nobles had its own set of rules of conduct and its own curriculum, and these were explicit in preparing girls for their future roles as wives, mothers, and keepers of a domestic economy. The pupils of this section were often referred to as the *meshchane*, a term that indicated the low-born status of those whose parents worked in trades, crafts, or service of some kind, and paid taxes. These girls did not enjoy the personal attention of Catherine and of course they received no invitations to court. While they received awards for needlepoint and other handiwork, their intellects were neither examined nor celebrated publicly, nor were their awards preserved as important artifacts in the archive, as they were for noble girls. The *meshchane* girls were expected to display "honest behavior," rather than refinement. Instead of performing plays, they learned bookkeeping, home management, and how to produce lace and other handmade items to sell for a little profit. Certificates of completion awarded to *meshchane* girls praised their diligence in "handiwork and home economy."[57] The *meshchane* section of Smolny also demanded the building of separate quarters to keep the non-nobles from disturbing or corrupting the noble girls. Alexandra Levshina, one of Catherine's favorite girls, with whom the empress corresponded, complained to her of "the loudness and impropriety" of the *meshchane* girls, writing that she would be glad when construction of a separate building for this section of the school would be complete.[58] Most tellingly, however, the school's charter revealed that childhood ended for these girls at age twelve, when they would begin to study or practice "every feminine handiwork and labor, that is: to sew, to weave, to knit, to cook, to wash, to clean, and to perform all services related to domestic economy." From age fifteen to eighteen, these girls were to perfect their abilities and knowledge in "all aspects of physical *vospitanie*" and to acquire "cleanliness, order, good manners, and appropriate behavior."[59] From the very beginning, the original charter of the *uchilishche* also anticipated the day that the girls would leave the school. For each girl admitted, the school placed fifty rubles in a bank account, which would accrue interest until the girl received the payment. In order to qualify for this small dowry, the girls had to either present a marriage certificate or reach the age of twenty-one.[60] If a girl finished her years at the school and did not yet have a marriage proposal or an invitation for employment, she would be allowed to stay on at the school with a room, candles, and firewood provided free of charge. She would be expected to earn her own funds to pay for food and clothing by selling her handiwork—or by working in the school for noble girls.[61] The fact that the charter considers, in very practical terms, the future for these girls speaks to the necessity of such considerations for girls without means, but it also indicates that the privilege of a girlhood free of worry about the future belonged to girls of nobility and wealth.

The board at Smolny also strictly observed the boundaries between nobility and other ranks. Sentries posted at the gates received specific instructions about whom to admit for "public" events; the board instructed them that "during public gatherings persons of lower officer rank or those without any title at all were not to be admitted."[62] The archive shows that the board spent a great deal of time considering petitions from families of questionable noble provenance. In fact, non-Russians found it easier to gain admittance to Smolny than did Russians of uncertain lineage. Families submitted lengthy and complicated genealogies in usually futile attempts to prove their nobility and thus have their daughters considered for admission.[63] However, in some years girls of non-Russian ethnicity enjoyed a sort of "affirmative action" through Catherine's decrees to reserve a certain number of spaces for them.[64] Wealthy patrons who hoped to curry favor with Catherine donated large sums to support pupils without means. Girls whose board was paid from these funds wore sashes that indicated by color their benefactor or benefactress. Ekaterina Shtakelberg established a scholarship explicitly for the purpose of supporting twenty girls of Livonian origin.[65] Lutheran girls from the Baltic provinces received permission to continue to practice their own faith and were exempt from attending Orthodox services.[66] While Protestant girls appear to have been under no pressure to become Orthodox believers, Muslim girls presented the empress with an opportunity to enact and display the narrative of "civilizing" the near East that was at the heart of Catherine's Greek project. The board celebrated the conversion and baptism of Muslim girls with ceremonies and gifts from the empress. For example, in 1771, Catherine gave three thousand rubles for one such event honoring "three Turkish girls" who were christened.[67] The conversion of Muslim girls to Orthodoxy enacted Catherine's celebration of the civilizing potential of Russian culture and faith; it also served a public relations purpose.[68] By the acculturation of non-Russian girls at Smolny, even though their numbers were small, the empress furthered her imperial goals in a practical sense by raising them to be *rossiiskie* elites.[69] The "civilization" of these non-Russian girls into Russian-speaking, Orthodox, and well-mannered maidens illustrated the power of Catherine's institutions of upbringing.

In contrast to the planning for the girls of the *meshchane* section to enter the world of adults, the charter for noble girls gave very little attention to life after Smolny, when the students would cross the boundary from girlhood to adulthood. "Shielding us from worldly sorrows and providing us with innocent joy," Glafira Alymova wrote, "they taught us to be content with the present and not to think about the future."[70] The future may have been abstract because Russian society did not yet have many preexisting social spaces for the type of woman being raised at Smolny; perhaps it remained vague in an effort to prolong girlhood. In practice, however, Smolny provided its graduates with options that most other young Russian women of any social estate did not have.

In 1775, the board of directors started preparing for the first graduation of noble girls. Along with planning the ceremony, the board confronted the issue of the graduates' welfare. Notices were sent to parents and guardians, informing them of when they were expected to resume responsibility for their daughters.[71] Discussions also considered the problem of parents of little means. Catherine authorized the disbursement of life-long annual pensions "according to merit and need."[72] From the first graduating class of fifty-one girls, thirty-seven received stipends, ranging from 100 to 250 rubles per year.[73] While not a large sum of money, these pensions certainly had practical value to those without means. By way of comparison, it should be noted that teachers at Smolny earned an annual salary of two hundred rubles per year at this time.

We can guess that these pensions were not designed to enable these young noble women to live independently. However, given that women controlled their own property in Russia, even after marriage, these stipends had the effect of giving their recipients a degree of limited autonomy in their marriages or in whatever position they found themselves after leaving Smolny. For a young woman without a family inheritance or with very little property, a pension could mean avoiding total dependence on the men in her family or postponing marriage for a while. In this way, graduating from Smolny provided a little insurance against the vagaries of a system that allowed women few means of earning their own living. For a lucky few, graduating from Smolny meant ascending into the highest echelon of society by becoming maids of honor in Catherine's court. The top five students from Smolny's first graduating class (Catherine's well-known favorites: Alymova, Molchanova, Levshina, Borshcheva, and Nelidova) all received gold medals, the highest pensions, and positions as maids of honor at Catherine's court.[74] Not only did this afford access to the most desirable bachelors; it also meant, upon marriage, receipt of an immense dowry. By the end of Catherine's reign, these dowries were twelve thousand rubles each.[75]

In addition to protecting girlhood, the board of directors at Smolny took action in several instances to protect the property of its girls. By advocating on behalf of students, the directors sought to ensure that *Smolianki* were not taken advantage of by male relatives in inheritance disputes. There were at least four such incidences affecting girls from Smolny's first two classes involving Glafira Alymova, Natal'ia Zherebtsova, Serafima Zvereva, and Nadezhda L'vova.[76] These cases usually involved brothers and/or uncles who were attempting to divide an inheritance in a manner that would have been unfavorable to the girl who had rights to a portion of it. In two cases, brothers tried to designate small, unsalable strips of land in different villages as their sisters' inheritance. In each case, Smolny's board got involved, calling on the Votchina Chancellery (the administrative unit that adjudicated in cases involving ancestral lands) for assistance and going so far as to have the Bank of the Nobility freeze the assets of Serafima Zvereva's uncle.[77] Having advocates in high places meant that these girls received an equitable inheritance and protection from arbitrary male power.

Smolny also provided shelter from patriarchy in a literal sense. Graduates might be allowed to stay at Smolny for up to three years.[78] In seeking funds to make this option available to most members of a graduating class, Betskoi explained the reasoning for keeping the young women at Smolny. He worried that, at age seventeen or eighteen, "a person could still be torn from the proper path." A few extra years would ease the girls into adult life by allowing them to "become used to living on their own and guiding their own behavior" while still under some supervision.[79] He also proposed that, if the board of directors approved of a prospective bridegroom, a young woman be allowed to leave.[80] Clearly, he wanted to protect these young women from harmful situations, even after they were no longer students, and to give them a safe place to live when they had no other options.

Friendship was yet another protection. Growing up at Smolny meant giving up one's own family for an adoptive family of sorts. The staff at Smolny encouraged friendship as an expression of appropriate virtues: charity, kindness, and service. In character evaluations, teachers praised girls who attracted many friends and those who expressed loyalty to their friends.[81] Glafira Alymova remembered Smolny and her cohort fondly: "It was a community of sisters, all subject to the same rules."[82] The shared identity and experience led to life-long friendships between *Smolianki*, which provided them with emotional and financial support networks after they graduated. Maria Golitsyna, after hearing of her Smolny friend's financial troubles, wrote to Smolny's board of directors to ask that half of her own yearly pension be diverted to her friend, Anis'ia Svistunova. Her letter speaks of the passionate and committed nature of their friendship: "I am obliged to Anis'ia Matveevna Svistunova, who was raised with me, and my duty to her demands zeal, and as I know of her lack of means, I give Madam Svistunova half of my pension as a sign of my love for her, until I die."[83] Betskoi granted her request but concealed Svistunova's financial troubles. Protecting her pride and privacy, he edited the letter and cited friendship, rather than need, as the reason for the gift.[84] An ardent friendship between Elisaveta Rubanovskaia and Glafira Alymova lasted throughout their lives, as well. When Rubanovskaia, who was Radishchev's second wife, died during her return from her husband's exile, her Smolny friend took on the responsibility of raising her three children. Alymova described this as a duty she gladly fulfilled as a way of repaying Rubanovskaia for her friendship.[85]

Finally, in some cases, Smolny provided jobs. Anna Ushakova and Nadezhda L'vova became teachers, for instance, and at least one woman went on to have a "career" at Smolny.[86] Baroness Elisaveta Aleksandrovna Cherkassova, a graduate from the class of 1779, taught at the school and later became headmistress during the early nineteenth century.[87] Smolny could be a place to go in one's old age, as well. Ekaterina Nelidova, one of the first graduates and the famous favorite of Emperor Paul I, retired to Smolny.[88] By providing stipends, a place to stay, and even sometimes a means of earning a living, Smolny helped usher these women through the transition from schoolgirl to adult and gave them a few options not available to most young women in the Russian empire. Thus, in addition to friendship networks, the Smolny experience offered for some women what we might call a respite from patriarchy: an in-between space that provided twelve to fifteen or more years of being neither daughters in their fathers' households nor wives or subordinates in the home of another man.[89] For some this likely also meant postponing motherhood. Arranged marriage in the teen years was common for noble girls, as memoirs attest. Already middle-aged, Andrei Bolotov chose a reluctant twelve-year-old girl as a bride. She married him at age thirteen and at fourteen endured a pregnancy, traumatic labor, and the death of her first child. Catherine and Dashkova were also given in marriage at similarly tender ages, as was Anna Labzina, who experienced the loss of her family and friends as grievously painful and unjust. While the *Smolianki* performed in plays, studied history, attended balls, and practiced piano or the harp, Bolotov's wife Aleksandra spent her teen years continuously pregnant.[90]

REFORMS

In April 1783, the head of the Commission on Public Schools, Peter Zavadovskii, sent a letter to Betskoi informing him of the decision to reform Smolny's curriculum and teaching methods to bring it into compliance with the new plans for people's schools.[91] Accompanying the letter was an extensive new plan for Smolny, preserved in its archive, which set out the details of the changes.[92] The letter presented the reform to Betskoi as a fait accompli. From Betskoi's marginal notes on the reform document, it is clear that he had not been included in Catherine's new plan; he was outraged.

According to Zavadovskii, the new plan replaced Smolny's existing charter, thus altering both the main objectives and the day-to-day management of the school. The new plan called for fewer total hours of instruction, the implementation of a new pedagogical style based on the memorization of tables (the Felbiger method), and the replacement of French with Russian as the language of instruction, an edict that was at odds with the lack of Russian-speaking instructors. Music instruction would take place not one-on-one but in groups (an idea that Betskoi found preposterous). The new plan also granted the Commission on Public Schools control over the hiring and firing of teachers at Smolny, stripping the board of most of its powers. Members of the Commission on Public Schools would also supervise classes to ensure compliance with the new methods.[93] Betskoi quickly penned a response to the empress, impressing upon her the need to reconsider some aspects of the reform, in particular the plan to have the Commission handle the staffing and to place an observer in the classrooms. He reminded Catherine that the Smolny board had responsibility "for everything that concerns upbringing and instruction." In the face of criticism regarding the language of instruction, Betskoi wrote that he always intended to hire Russian teachers—as soon as Russia produced some.[94] Betskoi's defense was not an exaggeration; as we know from chapter 5, the Commission had created a teacher-training academy to respond to the dearth of Russian-born instructors. Zavadovskii's critique of Smolny on these grounds was either ignorant of actual teacher availability or deliberately malicious. In either case, while it may sound like the death of Catherine's ideal, as it certainly did to Betskoi, the Commission's reforms were unevenly implemented. Although little actually changed, the new reforms were important for their attempt to solve the problem of preparing noble girls for their future as wives and mothers.

In defining the revised goals of *vospitanie* for girls in the Russian empire, the Commission on Public Schools left no room for guesswork. Its new plan was penned by Theodor Iankovich, the author of the general plan for a system of public schools. Sanctioned by Catherine and the Commission's members, the plan stated that the overarching purpose of the entire program at Smolny should be "to make [the girls] into good mistresses of the house [*khoziaki*], faithful spouses, and trustworthy mothers."[95] Rather than raising girls who would become "*grazhdanki* [citizens]" and "useful members of society," in Betskoi's words from twenty years earlier, Smolny's faculty must focus on raising girls for specific—and domestically defined—roles.[96] The new plan also discouraged independent intellectual activity, stipulating that free time "should be spent on the study of handiwork and aspects of homemaking specific to the female sex."[97] Betskoi objected to the reforms in general, especially the switch to all-Russian instruction, which would require replacing most of the predominantly European teaching faculty. He doubted that replacements with similar credentials could be found. Furthermore, the problem of transition time, or the lack of it, troubled him. He noted that the new handbooks for the teachers were in Russian, which the French teachers would not be able to read. "This is impossible!" he scribbled in the margins on his copy of the reform plan.[98]

More worrisome still, from Betskoi's perspective, was the introduction of instruction in "immodest subjects." The original charter for Smolny never mentioned the relationship between husband and wife. In contrast, the Commission's new plan promised a handbook that would instruct girls "in the rules of marital relations [and] how to behave toward their husbands."[99] The girls would study this handbook "under the supervision of their teachers" and would have it in their possession for future reference.[100] The girls would also study the new textbook, *On the Duties of Man and Citizen* (1783), translated from the German original and chosen by Iankovich as the foundational text for all existing and future elementary schools as part of the project to create schools for the folk.[101] This textbook gives explicit instructions on power relations in the home: "Everyone in the household, that is, the lady of the house, the children, and the servants must love the head of household or master as a benefactor and guardian. They should honor him as their superior and obey him in everything, unless his orders are in conflict with the Holy Commandments or regulations of the government."[102] The introduction of this book into the Smolny curriculum marks the first explicit effort to address marriage and future familial relations. The Commission on Public Schools approved this text as mandatory reading for every child attending school in the Russian empire. Smolny and other elite schools, including privately run schools, were not granted an exception, reflecting the Commission's principle of promoting certain kinds of uniformity in education, especially concerning the "civic" instruction represented by this manual.[103] In this principle, the imperial and administrative goals of the educational reforms are clear, as is the awareness that pupils will constitute the future body politic. It is worth noting that the Commission's members were concerned with instruction for noble boys at the Corps of Cadets, but they spent much more time and energy on their review of instruction for girls at Smolny and their plans for reform.[104]

The understanding of what it meant to raise good mothers also underwent a transformation. According to Smolny's original charter, preparation for becoming a mother meant learning to be a teacher. Under the new plan, the biological dimension of motherhood would be taught. The new plan stipulated that the girls would learn "how to act as mothers in relationship to their children: 1) during pregnancy, 2) during breast-feeding, 3) during their [children's] infancy and adolescence."[105] These first two points struck Betskoi as particularly offensive. He was livid at the suggestion that noble girls would be taught about such provocative things as marital relations, pregnancy, and breast-feeding at Smolny, as his marginal comments reveal. He was concerned about preserving the modesty of his pupils; teaching them about sex and pregnancy would, he believed, harm their innocence. In drafting a letter of protest to the empress, he complained: "It is written that the girls should, under the guidance of supervisors read a book on how to behave in marriage, how to keep oneself during pregnancy and so forth—they do not need to know any of this!"[106]

Betskoi may have expected Catherine to agree, since she too had once been concerned about the girls' adolescence and innocence. In 1772, Catherine wrote to Voltaire asking for recommendations for plays that would not focus on love; she did not want "passions" aroused too early. Voltaire wrote back: "It is true that all our plays are concerned with love; it is a passion for which I have the deepest respect, but I agree with your Majesty that it should not be developed too soon. One could, I think, take several selected comedies, and cut out the parts most dangerous to young minds, while retaining the interest of the play." Voltaire offered to order tragedies and comedies from Paris with additional blank pages sewn in so that he could "dictate the changes necessary to preserve the virtue of your fair young ladies."[107] In 1781, a few years before the reforms, Betskoi wrote that the primary goal of upbringing at Smolny was to raise women who would "occupy a place in society as useful citizens [*zanimat' v obshchestve mesta poleznykh grazhdanok*]."[108] In fact, he was the one to remind the board of directors that the girls would also have private lives and might need help finding "suitable husbands."[109] Nonetheless, Betskoi never imagined that this would involve any discussion of "immodest subjects." Before a certain age, he worried, such instruction might create a curiosity that could "turn the useful into something harmful."[110] His remarks show how much he differed on this issue from Russian physicians who advocated that noblewomen become more aware of the importance of upbringing, including the idea that it "starts with conception," and the importance of breast-feeding their children.[111] Recall the accoucheur Kreizel' from chapter 2, who argued that the *vospitanie* of girls in Russia needed to be altered to make them less modest and to condition them to accept examinations by male physicians. In this matter, the medical men and Betskoi had competing notions about whether more or less modesty was necessary in women. Zavadovskii and Iankovich sided with the doctors, isolating Betskoi.

The imposition of reforms at Smolny marked the beginning of Betskoi's retirement; he became ever more disillusioned and eventually withdrew from life at Smolny. As it turns out, the prospect of long-term, profound changes at Smolny ought not to have worried him so much. The Commission seemed concerned primarily that the girls demonstrate fluency in Russian. In March 1783, representatives of the Commission attended the public exams and reported that the girls performed well—and in Russian.[112] Catherine was satisfied and issued monetary rewards to all of the teachers. One wonders how such a feat was possible in only a year's time; one explanation is that the pupils' Russian language abilities were never as poor as the Commission had charged. Noble schools seemed, in the end, to have been granted exemptions from the ban on French. Years after the reforms, the Smolny teachers and form mistresses were still conducting portions of instruction and evaluations in French.[113]

In 1784, a year after the reforms, Novikov published a new text for Russian noble girls, the *Pocket or Memory Book for Young Girls*, possibly compiled by Anton Barsov.[114] Ostensibly for use at Smolny, this conduct manual followed the general outline of Barsov's and Novikov's other publications for children and advice manuals. A professor at Moscow University and an academic at the Academy of Sciences, Barsov was an active contributor to the Russian Enlightenment. Trained as a linguist, he authored numerous primers and alphabet books. The

Pocket or Memory Book is another illustration of the syncretic nature of the Russian Enlightenment and of how little the reforms changed the instruction at Smolny. The fifty-five-page text begins with religious instruction, includes a very lengthy section on health habits and cold regime (with the suggestion to consult and respect doctors!), and concludes with a section of *nravouchenie*. Despite Iankovich's instructions, the *Pocket or Memory Book* did not include any material on pregnancy or infant care. The section on moral instruction includes a Russian translation of a famous French advice manual for girls, written by the *salonnière* Madame de Lambert. The following excerpt from the *Pocket or Memory Book* was taken from Lambert's *Avis d'une mère à sa fille*. Here the importance of an enlightened, yet modest, education for girls is underscored:

> The use, which you will receive from your knowledge, will be such that you will not be constrained, for the avoidance of boredom and for the repulsion of inactive life, to occupy idle hours with games, sights, useless visiting, and empty conversation, and that you will find yourself in a condition, having satisfied the proper decorum of your title, to preserve for yourself precious minutes, in which, being free and solitary, you may exercise yourself in reading, conveniently nourish your intellect with pleasantness, and fill your heart with firm and steadfast joy, showing it only the good, the better to make it happy.[115]

In this advice, embedded within a renewed Russian Orthodoxy, we can perceive an enlightened version of patriarchal domesticity. The daughter, educated and governed by reason, chooses wisely to stay home and read, rather than seek situations in society that might lead to compromises in virtue and fidelity. Her choice not only serves to develop her own intellect in her moments of solitude but also to support her husband's status as an enlightened, benevolent patriarch. With a quiet and virtuous wife at home, keeping an orderly house, patriarchy and reason govern. It was a slight refocusing of the girls' education to include their expected future roles as wives and mothers, but hardly the wholesale transformation of instruction at Smolny that Zavadovskii and Iankovich had proposed.

LASTING EFFECTS

The impact of Smolny and the general interest in girls' upbringing in Catherine's era had a lasting effect on the lives of women and on Russian culture. By the end of the eighteenth century, the notion that girls should receive an upbringing that required hired tutors or a school setting was becoming a norm for noble families. Bolotov lamented that he could neither afford to send his daughters to an institute nor hire language tutors, which indicates that these options represented an established standard in his mind.[116] Memoirs indicate that, by the early nineteenth century, noble families of some means that did not provide a "correct" (*pravil'noe*) upbringing for their daughters risked criticism by their peers. Labzina wrote that a family considering an early marriage for a daughter drew the comment that "it would be a sin" to remove the girl from school before she had completed her education. She remarked, "she is still a child," a conclusion not drawn by adults when Labzina herself had been the same age.[117] Given that marriage in the early teen years was not uncommon, Smolny and the other schools for girls that were established in its image in Moscow and other urban areas of the empire provided an extended girlhood in a literal sense. In the span of fifty years, the notion that girls should have a girlhood, with some instruction from non-family members at home or from teachers at school, became a new ideal for noble girls.[118] Although the Holy Synod considered the minimum age for marriage for a girl to be twelve, judging by memoir and diary evidence, this age appears to have crept upward.[119] Thus, it seems likely that the new upbringing for girls established girlhood as a recognizable stage of life, one that made it worthwhile to postpone marriage. Given the many pregnancies that child brides were subject to (as in the case of Bolotov's wife), extending the age of marriage meant postponing pregnancy, thus limiting a woman's "fertile years" and the potential number of pregnancies over her lifetime. Future research may reveal whether this change improved mortality rates for educated women. One might also reasonably imagine that the "valorization of the maternal" and the warmer familial relations that came to characterize the noble domestic ideal were facilitated by a healthy mother with fewer children.[120]

By the mid-nineteenth century, boarding schools for girls had proliferated in urban areas around the empire, attesting to the now culturally entrenched notion that daughters of noble families of all strata and geographic location and girls born to ambitious families in middling ranks should be sent away to an urban girls' school for their education. One memoirist recalled that the institute she attended in Moscow was populated mainly by noble girls of modest means, girls whose fathers were teachers, professors, and "provincial or state functionaries with bent backs," who were known to take "bribes in order to support their families and save every hard-earned kopeck."[121] Girls came from all over: from the provincial regions of central Russia, from Moscow suburbs, and from the periphery of the empire—Ukraine, Siberia, Georgia.[122] Impoverished noble families were known to scrimp, save, and beg the help of potential patrons in order to send their girls to boarding school. For gentry families without means, securing entry to such a school became an obsession focused on survival: "The daughter must get an education. An education will let her earn her crust of bread."[123]

The literary archetype of the school girl, the *institutka*, had also become a standard character in Russian literature by midcentury. While naïveté usually made up a significant aspect of this literary personality, the *institutka*'s innocence regarding the flirtatious locution and innuendo common to mixed-sex social gatherings could be read as a positive attribute. The stifling atmosphere of a sealed boarding school protected the girls from the adult world and preserved their girlishness until graduation.[124] Indeed, the fact that women began to write autobiographies during the nineteenth century also suggests that girlhood, education, and subjectivity are correlated. Anna Labzina's memoir stands out for its exceptionality in the eighteenth century; a hundred years later, many more women thought of their lives as worthy of contemplation, had the literacy and skill to produce a memoir, and had the "private" psychological or mental space necessary to develop the desire to write and to value writing as an activity worthy of their time. After all, writing one's autobiography (or even writing at all) might be seen as selfish for a woman and at odds with the feminine ideal of self-sacrifice and service to others. This private, individual act was for many writers the source of their female subjectivity and gendered consciousness.[125]

Fonvizin's Sophie received advice on creating matrimonial happiness from her wise and dear uncle. Starodum explains to her the unhappiness of a home in which the spouses have strayed from reason and virtue: "Let's take as an example an unhappy home, of which there are many, where the wife has no heartfelt friendship for her husband, nor he any trust in his wife; where both have strayed from the path of virtue. Instead of a sincere and forbearing friend, the wife sees in her husband a coarse and corrupted tyrant. On the other hand, instead of gentleness and openheartedness, the attributes of a virtuous wife, the husband sees in his wife's heart only willful arrogance."[126] Starodum does not advocate a return to patriarchy without restraint, a Muscovite tyranny. Having witnessed the kind of Hobbesian state of nature—and the chaos of matriarchy—in the home ruled by Prostakova, Sophie is ready to accept his advice. His counsel on matrimony illuminates not only Fonvizin's imaginary ideal but also Catherine's. Like Sophie, the girls at Smolny were being raised, all those involved hoped, to respect reason over passions. Catherine corrected Voltaire when he referred, in typical banter with the empress, to the girls at

Smolny as "a battalion of Amazons."[127] Catherine dismissed his reference to female warriors; her girls would be wives and mothers governed by reason.[128] Sophie's uncle advises her on the ideal relationship in marriage: "The husband—prudent! The wife—virtuous! What can be more respectable! It is necessary, my friend, for your husband to obey reason and for you to obey your husband, then you will both be perfectly happy."[129] Raising virtuous girls would lead them to grow into women who were governed by reason and thus able to recognize a reasonable man—and submit to him. In this respect, the "new girls" might light the path toward a more civilized Russia, without any compromise to masculinity and order.

CONCLUSION

Reform-minded Russians began to construct ideas of infants and children as precious resources for the state beginning in the mid-eighteenth century. Their ambitions to rescue babies and to raise them into new Russians—whether strong peasant soldiers or Enlightened noble women—created an opportunity to conjure the ideal body politic. These new Russians would embody both the best of European civilization and a revised and renewed attachment to faith and fatherland. This book has demonstrated how these crusading impulses led to a wealth of schemes and publications aimed at intervening in every aspect of a child's life, from the womb to the brink of adulthood. The visionaries of the new *vospitanie* needed an army of supporters willing to make changes in the everyday lives of infants and children; thus, they had to seek the complicity of women as agents of change in a range of contexts. Their optimistic propositions included licensing and educating midwives (and taxing parents to pay for it), convincing mothers to nurse their own infants, finding virtuous wet nurses willing to work for very little pay, educating peasant and noble mothers alike on the proper cultivation of the child's body, and creating new spaces for children in the form of schools and residential institutions in cities and towns. The state demonstrated its symbolic commitment to the *vospitanie* of the empire's children by these actions, while also working to establish the literal boundaries of childhood, shaped by social estate, gender, and conceptions of national identity.

Taken together, my analyses of these projects to reform upbringing make three primary incursions into our perception of eighteenth-century Russia. First, I have drawn attention to how gendered categories shaped the discourse of and programs for reforms in child rearing. Gendered hierarchies of knowledge, critiques and redefinitions of femininity and masculinity, and anxieties about the relationship between unchecked patriarchy and Russian national identity influenced how Russian Enlighteners proposed to reform *vospitanie*. Second, I have cast light on the widespread appeal of the uniquely Russian notion of *vospitanie*. The voices presented in this book demonstrate the rhetorical power of this concept, which promised nearly limitless potential for renewing and strengthening the Russian population. The Russian notion of an Enlightened upbringing became more than an importation of Locke's guide for raising citizens or Rousseau's for raising a natural man. The embrace of children as an untapped political and national resource produced especially ambitious projects and fueled dreams of rapid and profound progress toward robust health, civilized behavior, and moral renewal on the individual, societal, national, and imperial levels. Third, I have positioned physicians and medical men in the wider cultural and social milieu of Enlightenment Russia in which they themselves sought authority. Like eighteenth-century physicians in other parts of Europe, these men applied themselves to more than treating the sick; they hoped to influence and shape society, as evidenced by their publications and civic activities. By writing in Russian rather than Latin, by working for the Legislative Commission, and through their participation in the Free Economic Society, they explicitly pursued cultural and political sway beyond the boundaries of academic or state medicine.

By identifying pregnancy, birth, and infancy as vital to the overall health of Russia's population of children, reformers brought these issues into public discourse. Chapters 2 and 3 showed the range of contexts in which physicians, statesmen, and the empress discussed these topics. While some elder statesmen like Betskoi found such topics indelicate, plenty of others explicitly—and even passionately—called attention to pregnancy, birth, and breast-feeding. The public discourse on these matters, evidenced by the market for home health manuals, might have contributed to the use of reproductive metaphors in other contexts.[1] The metaphor of birthing a nation, of bringing a new Russia to life, appears in a number of contexts. For a country as old and as autocratic as Russia, even considering the upheaval initiated by Peter the Great, the appeal of this type of rhetoric seems worthy of greater consideration. Catherine described one of her primers as the "midwife" that would help to birth a new type of Russian. One might wonder who or what represented the laboring mother in Catherine's metaphor.

The masculine attributes of Catherine's carefully constructed image—from her legendary work ethic to her political agility—have perhaps obscured from our view the invocation of maternity as a component of her identity as ruler. Catherine's contemporaries and subjects frequently addressed her as the mother of the Russian empire and the mother of enlightenment in Russia. Although Catherine officially declined the title "Mother of the Fatherland" when it was offered to her at the beginning of her reign, the frequency with which she was addressed this way in official correspondence and promulgations suggests that the usage of the title pleased her.[2] Catherine's female anatomy appears explicitly and implicitly in some allusions and depictions. Even the discreet Betskoi refers to her "maternal blessed womb," which gave birth to all of her projects for the upbringing of children.[3] Catherine's maternal symbology was quite distinct from the royal maternity of nineteenth-century empresses of Russia, whose images as mothers were thoroughly contained within a tableau of domesticity and marital fidelity.[4] Having replaced her deposed husband on the throne, Catherine's royal maternal image had to draw from abstractions. Her relationship with her heir was notoriously strained, and after she assumed her role as autocrat, official portraiture featured her independent of her son Paul.[5] As the beneficiary of a coup d'état, she was not eager to remind her subjects of an alternative autocrat waiting to take her place. The writers who lauded her in their prefaces, as the literary form dictated in an autocratic context, frequently referred to her maternal love, maternal protection, and maternal care, which "flowed" from her to her subjects, like a mother's milk.[6] These dedications to the empress required the approval of the royal censor; clearly, Catherine approved of this imagery. Catherine placed herself in a maternal tableau for the benefit of Diderot, who wrote of his impressions of the empress with her Smolny favorites: "[she has founded] a magnificent establishment for girls . . . these children who are no higher than cabbages . . . gather around her, embrace her, put their arms around her neck and head . . . The sovereign of a huge empire? That was not considered either by her or by them."[7] This image of little girls around her neck evokes a mother who gives physical comfort and care to the children nestled in her bosom. The maternal images of the empress are ripe with sensuality; the empress's womb is the source of her enlightenment—not only her mind or her will—while her maternal body nurtures her figurative children. Catherine controlled her image carefully, as we know. Thus, Catherine's panoply of ruler imagery must be expanded to include feminine tropes of motherhood more often reserved for fully "domesticated" empresses like Maria Fedorovna or the Muscovite tsaritsas.[8]

Catherine did not raise her own offspring because of Empress Elizabeth's wishes and royal traditions. This may have contributed to the emphasis on other aspects of Catherine's personality as ruler. Yet, even in the midst of pursuing aggressive expansion of the empire's borders, battling the Ottomans and Swedes, and struggling to snuff out a persistent Cossack and peasant rebellion in the provinces, Catherine wrote tales for children, created pedagogical texts, and published advice on child rearing. Her enduring interest and faith in *vospitanie*, evidenced by her projects and publications, along with her manipulation of maternal imagery within political rhetoric, suggest the need for a more complex consideration of Catherine's own maternal impulses.

In another play on maternal imagery, Catherine adopted the literary persona of a grandmother in her journal, *Vsiakaia Vsiachina (All Sorts)*. Modeling her writing on the English *Spectator*, the empress intended to both entertain and instruct her readers through the voice of the imaginary editor, a wise babushka who counseled young and old alike that character would always trump wealth and rank.[9] Why a grandmotherly figure—rather than simply maternal? Within this conceit, Catherine is freed from the maternal body and its imperative to provide comfort, yet she is still entitled as grandmother to scold her grandchildren. Thus, the figure of the babushka instructs her most problematic descendants, many of whom are the same antiheroes identified in the discourse on *vospitanie*—superstitious women, adulterous wives, vapid young women, and lustful young men. *All Sorts* might represent a kind of upbringing, or instruction in *vospitanie*, delivered directly to its readers. In Catherine's version, the solutions issue from a wise matriarch—not from any would-be patriarchs, and certainly not from the "children" themselves.

For the writers who addressed upbringing, however, solutions did issue from sources other than the crown and the state, especially (but not exclusively) the medical men who deployed their own potentially subversive strategies for communicating their messages. This might explain why their publications contain a whiff of flattery directed not only at the empress but at the "public," as well. Bakherakht sought the approval of the public explicitly, giving this abstraction the power to judge the worth of his book. "If the public [*publika*] recognizes my work as useful," he wrote, "I will be honored."[10] Kreizel' gave his readers the same respect and authority, writing, "It is left to knowledgeable people to judge whether this small book may be put to good use."[11] In some ways, this was a bold and clever move. In an autocratic context, the approval of the monarch determined which books lived or died (and which authors would suffer in exile for their words), yet these men constructed a judging, discerning, educated public with the power to evaluate their advice. Whether such a public existed or whether members of society thought of themselves as constituting a "public" is less the point than what this rhetorical device signals about the shifting cultural landscape in Russia. These writers curried favor—and legitimacy—outside the traditional channels of influence. If readers confirmed the worth of the new experts by buying and circulating their works, then the readers also confirmed the legitimacy of the new science of maternity and child rearing. Matvei Peken expressed exactly this when he claimed that the market success of his father's original *Home Healer*, which went through multiple printings over thirty years, "was honest and faithful proof of its worth."[12] In other eighteenth-century contexts, the discursive construction of a public anticipated and encouraged the emergence of a public sphere. While the notion of a "public" became highly charged in the revolutionary politics of eighteenth-century France, in Russia it worked to confirm new sources of authority in society.[13] In some cases, these experts did use their authority to make political commentary; Zybelin, for example, called for alternatives to violent conquest and expansionism for increasing the size of the empire's population.

By construing their readers as fit to judge the merit of the book before them, these authors also invited readers to perceive themselves as peers and to identify with the author and his goals. No doubt then, treatises on the reform of upbringing functioned as vehicles for the self-promotion of authors. They also helped these writers to present themselves as learned experts in matters previously managed almost exclusively by women. In most cases lacking in actual experience of monitoring pregnancy, delivering babies, and managing breast-feeding, these physicians and medical writers cited their degrees and medical titles as confirmation of their superior knowledge. As we have seen, legitimizing their scientific perspective sometimes meant denigrating women as their would-be competitors in the world of advice on child rearing. Women's ways of knowing and making decisions, whether rooted in peasant tradition (and therefore coded as superstitious and ignorant when this served writers' claims) or in the norms of high society (and therefore coded as shallow and selfish), could occupy only the lowest rungs on the hierarchy of Enlightenment heuristics.[14] Thus, all women needed instruction from men on pregnancy, birth, infant care, and child rearing—whether the peasant woman who should be taught by a local priest, physician, or licensed midwife, or the noblewoman who should be instructed by learned works, physicians, or her husband.

The outcome of reforms in child rearing would be not only improved rates of infant mortality and healthier children, according to the explicit claims of the new experts, but also greater status for male expertise on such matters. The faith or belief among the public in the efficacy of medicine practiced by these eighteenth-century physicians and the advice they offered on pregnancy, birth, public health, and a host of other issues depended less on their ability to prove their claims than on their ability to convince the public to take their advice on faith. The French anthropologist Bruno Latour's theory of the "Janus-face" of scientific endeavor posits an ambiguity or conundrum at the heart of the production of knowledge within most fields of science (or natural philosophy in the eighteenth century). While new "knowledge" is always provisional, scientists must nonetheless advance their findings or theories as incontrovertible truth.[15] In the Russian context, persuading the public of their claims was paramount to establishing the legitimacy of the emerging medical profession and to the continued availability of resources for the pursuit of new "truths." Appeals by men of science directly to the public for ratification of their knowledge is evidence of their ambitions to unseat "feminine" knowledge on such matters and of the gathering steam of the professionalization of medicine. To address the shortage of doctors in the provinces, enlightened types like Naryshkin, Novikov, and Bolotov had advocated training village priests to treat the sick. Physicians protested the idea. Bakherakht wrote in the *Saint Petersburg Messenger* that "there is nothing more humorous and stupid" than the idea of a layperson practicing medicine.[16] The efforts by medical men to claim authority over midwifery and pediatrics and to buttress the boundaries of medicine as a profession support the earlier periodization of J. T. Alexander and Andreas Renner for the professionalizing activities of physicians.[17]

In seeking influence beyond the realm of academic medicine, these Russian physicians were acting very much like Europeans. Having studied abroad, Russian doctors returned with an outlook that seems very similar to that of other eighteenth-century physicians who also trained at Leiden, Strasbourg, and Padua. To take one example, a study of seven physicians in Geneva from this same era found that the men who had studied in Edinburgh and Leiden approached their careers "not simply [as] practitioners but medical researchers, intellectuals, and promoters of collective professional goals."[18] Given the peripatetic nature of the careers of many physicians in the eighteenth century, the transnational networks of Russian physicians seem like another rich avenue for more research. As Renner underscores, the Russian context presented a different set of challenges, with its still underdeveloped tradition of academic medicine.[19] The Russian physicians and medical men in general faced the need to establish status; they were not an elite seeking to maintain status. Thus, like the German bureaucrats of Andre Wakefield's *The Disordered Police State*, these physicians had practical reasons to promote medical knowledge—not only altruistic reasons or a sense of duty to the state, but also a desire to secure for themselves a livelihood and a social identity.[20] In the case of the physicians and accoucheurs who populate this study, that action also rested upon establishing a gendered hierarchy of knowledge.

With the exception of those in the highest posts, Catherine did not appoint these men to their positions. Instead, the ambitious among them had their titles confirmed by a committee of physicians, who would become their professional peers. Thus, they advocated for, participated in, and enjoyed the benefits of a nascent meritocracy. The concept (and enactment) of a meritocracy, enforced by a discerning public, implicitly usurped other authorities on the basis of status and tradition. A hundred years earlier, in Muscovite Russia, it was not unusual for bureaucrats to fear taking any action without direct orders from the tsar. For example, a seventeenth-century provincial governor wrote to the tsar: "We have no ink, no candles, no paper, and my last literate scribe has been conscripted to chase bandits, but without your decree, Sovereign, I dare do nothing."[21] While the eighteenth-century medical men were not governors, they were working as state servitors and lacked noble status; nonetheless, they took independent initiative and presented social criticism in their treatises on health and child rearing. Rather than orienting the content of their works and projects exclusively toward the crown for approval, the medical writers sought to appeal to multiple constituencies and acted like the moral citizens they and other reformers of *vospitanie* hoped to raise.

The Russian Enlighteners embodied in other ways the national character they imagined themselves to be instilling in children through changes in patterns of upbringing. Those who had obtained medical degrees abroad had first studied in seminary academies, which were the only institutions of higher learning in Russia before Moscow University, founded in 1755, became fully established. Like the hybrid Orthodox yet Enlightened identity that reformers constructed in various contexts, these men shared in common a spiritual education to which they added the education and training they received in European academies. They also became the sort of self-made men, like Fonvizin's Pravdin, who owed their success to their education and their honorable traits, rather than to their lineage, and who would lead the country toward moral renewal. This new masculine identity informed the reforms at the Corps of Cadets, for example, and the content of *vospitanie* for boys.

The person of Maksimovich-Ambodik is particularly emblematic of the new masculine identity. His Orthodox faith informed his self-conscious expression of his identity, which was based on his medical training. In the preface to his midwifery textbook series, he articulated his spiritual reasons for choosing a life of science. After finishing his studies at the Kiev academy (a seminary), he was called by God to study medicine, he explained: "And thus Providence, who tirelessly guards the good of every creation, . . . expecting the best for me and for the general good, selected me for a different worldly title."[22] Maksimovich-Ambodik became a doctor, rather than a priest. He found biblical justification in God's dictum "go forth and multiply" for choosing obstetrics as his specialization. An excerpt from his soliloquy gives a sense of his defense: "What could be more noble and more important, more necessary and useful to human society? . . . There is hardly another science that possesses a subject so important, necessary, and beneficial to the human race as midwifery. . . . How noble is the science of midwifery; how necessary is its knowledge to everyone."[23] It is interesting to note that Maksimovich-Ambodik may have been perfectly positioned, with his background, to move into the intimate realm of reproductive health. Angus MacLaren argues that, in early nineteenth-century France, the doctor began to replace the priest in some intimate matters by intruding "on that terrain previously dominated by the dictates of religion—the area of sex and the family."[24] More research might reveal whether physicians like Maksimovich-Ambodik replaced priests and midwives in the Russian context and what this might have meant for women.

Finally, Maksimovich-Ambodik represents the new masculine identity shaped by physicians in Russia by a gesture of self-fashioning borrowed from the likes of Voltaire: he gave himself a nom de plume. Born in Ukraine as the son of an Orthodox priest, Maksimovich-Ambodik's birth name reflected both his Polish-Ukrainian roots and the Russian linguistic tradition of adopting patronymics as middle names. With a father named Maksim Maksimovich, the son became Nestor Maksimovich Maksimovich. As a young physician he began to add the made-up surname "Ambodik" (from a riff on the Latin for "twice written"). He used this name not just as a witticism but adopted it as his professional name. His dissertation thesis, defended at the University of Strasbourg, bears this name, as do his many publications and his professional correspondence, all signed "Professor Ambodik" or "Doctor Maksimovich Ambodik."[25] In pursuing a medical education abroad (funded by a wealthy Russian noblewoman) and in choosing a new surname from Latin, Maksimovich-Ambodik made himself one of the archetypal new men in Enlightenment Russia. His humble origins, European education, Russian national pride, and self-conscious act of naming himself all bear the traces of the Russian Enlightenment.

In stepping outside the social identities to which they were born, these writers adopted and indeed created a new identity that negotiated the relationship between state and society. Mary-Louise Pratt coins the term "seeing-man" to capture the imperial gaze of Englishmen in the colonial "contact zone."[26] In the colonial context, these men possessed what they saw, or imagined that they possessed it, with the authority of the British Empire legitimizing their vision. I suggest a similar usage to describe how these reformers of child rearing viewed themselves: they could "see" what their peers could not, and they ascribed to themselves the power not only to diagnose social (and even political) problems but also to prescribe solutions. In his journal, *Truten*, Novikov adopted the persona of a doctor diagnosing moral illnesses, for which he then offered prescriptions for "cures."[27] The term "seeing-men" works here also to suggest the way in which the population of children became, through this discourse, something that belonged not only to parents but also to society and to the state; as children gained visibility, they became the objects of the reformers' plans. As in a colonial context, "seeing" can imply possession or, at least, proprietary entitlement and the subsequent right to intervene.

The new noblewoman of the sort Smolny hoped to create might have functioned as a cultural counterpart to the seeing man. In the first play to be staged in Russia that featured a *Smolianka*, A. D. Kopiev's *The Converted Misanthrope*, the main character is able to "see" high society through the lens of the Enlightenment.[28] Because of her upbringing at Smolny, Liubov (literally, "Love") does not know the social rules, but this is shown to be her greatest virtue. She is able to observe—and judge—the nonsense and frivolity of those around her and thus is the ideal woman to lead the male misanthrope toward a new life. Like other emerging literary types at the end of the eighteenth century, Liubov exerts a civilizing force on men. Like the new masculine experts, she sees moral shortcomings, diagnoses them, and cures them. In 1841, in the first short story featuring Smolny girls to be written by a woman, the girls are shown to retain their powers of observation once they leave school. While socializing for the first time beyond Smolny, they are mocked and teased for their inability to flirt and play games. Like Liubov, however, these *Smolianki* are not insulted but recognize the intellectual and moral inferiority of such noblemen and women; they are armed with an ability to step outside their own social estate and "see" what is true.[29] Indeed, some of the new men chose Smolny brides; Radishchev, for one, found a companion willing to follow him into exile.

Finally, a redefinition of beauty away from artifice and toward "natural" beauty marked both the new femininity and the new masculinity. One of the "letters" to *All Sorts* mocks the upbringing of an imaginary girl of fifteen, who writes to the editor seeking help in finding a mate. Her main charms include obsessions with high heels and high coiffure; she mumbles in French and hides her face behind powder and rouge. To this fictitious antiheroine we should compare Catherine's praise for Alexandra Levshina, one of her favorite *Smolianki*;

her comments capture the redefinition of feminine beauty that emerged as consensus in the discourse on upbringing: "I love that [her] beautiful nature has followed its own course, without affectation or refinement, and I find the dark-skinned Levushka [her nickname] with her playfulness and antics exactly to my liking."[30] Levshina's beauty resided in her unspoiled quality; she is dark skinned because she does not wear powder. She is beautiful because her own inclinations have not been destroyed through an improper upbringing focused on external appearances. Radishchev promoted a new version of feminine beauty in print, too: "Natural charm, although roughened by heat and cold, is delightful without any false front of sophistication."[31] In terms of the new masculinity, the reformers condemned artifice, as well. The reforms at the Corps of Cadets sought to make the lads into something more closely resembling Rousseau's natural man—or fon Ash's Romans—than French dandies. Although Rousseau's liberalism might have caused a flap at the academy, were it outright discussed or taught, his rejection of wigs and artifice did not pose any overt political obstacle for Betskoi and Catherine. Betskoi's attempt to limit the amount of time spent primping, the use of pomade on hair and wigs, and the use of powder on faces speaks to the fashioning (or un-fashioning) that some proponents of a new masculine identity hoped to strengthen. Thus, the new ideals for masculinity and femininity promoted less artifice, natural looks, a simple style (for the age), and the restraint and fidelity imparted by a good upbringing. The fact that these were also the markers of a new "respectability" among the middle classes in other parts of Europe and often reflected a conscious rejection of aristocratic style (as in the case of men's wigs and cosmetics, especially) might be a connection worth exploring further.

As we saw in several chapters and in Maksimovich-Ambodik's autobiographical notes, for the reformers and architects of *vospitanie*, joining faith and reason posed no philosophical problems. Marcus Levitt writes of an "Enlightened Orthodoxy," referencing the Enlightened clerics whose educational background was similar to that of many of the luminaries of the secular world of eighteenth-century Russia, such as Lomonosov. Before Moscow University began granting degrees, the only available institutions of higher learning in Russia were seminaries.[32] Drawing on Viktor Zhivov, Levitt underscores that religious and secular culture were no longer in contest under Catherine, an idea that has some resonance in Elise Wirtschafter's research on Father Platon.[33] Within this cultural milieu, might we speak of an Orthodox Enlightenment as well? The version of a new Russian identity that we find in Kurganov's *Pismovnik*, in the Catherinian primers, and embedded in the curriculum at all of the later eighteenth-century schools suggests that we might. As reformers constructed it, *vospitanie* would be the vehicle by which to unite the Enlightenment and Orthodox Christianity in the Russian national character.

Many of the reformers of *vospitanie*, male and female, exhibited a crusading zeal and commitment beyond the requirements of their positions. In this sense, these reformers enacted the sort of active citizenship that they hoped reforms in *vospitanie* would bring into being. Bolotov observed that children in his environs were poorly informed—and he began a salon for children, organized a children's theater, and wrote a book for children. Among his many activities on behalf of improving child rearing, Novikov produced a beloved book for children and families, *Children's Readings*. Kondoidi and other physicians in the employ of the state suffered constant shortages of revenue, yet continued to pursue their programs. As we saw, the earliest efforts to license midwives suffered for lack of funding to support the licensing programs, while later midwifery training programs continually lacked necessary pedagogical and technical supplies. Maksimovich-Ambodik regularly sent letters requesting more funding and better textbooks, instruments, and chemical preparations to teach his students. In the provinces, occupants of the recently established posts for physicians in every guberniya sent reports to the central medical authority that reveal continual concern over very tight budgets and shortages of essential items like surgical spirit.[34] When physicians or pharmacists could not obtain this preparation of alcohol, they made do with twice-distilled wine. At the lowest level, we might think of the wet nurses who did their best to nurse five and six babies at once, while begging their superiors to hire more women. The accoucheur Georgii Gamen, hired to deliver babies at the Saint Petersburg lying-in hospital attached to the House of Upbringing, implored the Medical Collegium to reassign him to another post after only a few months, claiming exhaustion from attending births "around the clock." Meanwhile, the midwife on staff managed to fulfill her duties for much less remuneration for fifteen years, finally retiring when the infirmities of old age made it impossible for her to stay on. Maksimovich-Ambodik never did earn as much as his foreign-born predecessor, despite his significant contributions to Russian medicine and to midwifery, including the first dictionary of Russian medical terms.[35] Madame de Lafond comes to mind, as well; she committed herself entirely to the institution she was hired to direct, with no separation between her professional and personal life. Each one gave personally and modeled the new active citizen-subject.

The eighteenth-century discourse of *vospitanie* provided reformers a means and a language for promoting themselves as experts and professionals worthy of respect and status in society. The attention to all aspects of upbringing generated reforms that led to salaried occupations for some women, who found work as municipal midwives, teachers, and staff at Smolny and the Houses of Upbringing. As we know from first-person accounts, the notion of moral citizenship consciously infused the actions of many of the reformers and their front-line agents. They held in common the optimistic belief that their service to society and the fatherland on behalf of infants and children would create an enlightened, robust, morally upright Russia—a nation prepared to lead the way among its European peers. What happens in the nineteenth century to this optimism and these dreams of a healthy Russia is a story for another time.

Notes

INTRODUCTION

1. Ekaterina Dashkova, "O smysle slova vospitanie," *Sobesednik liubitelei rossiiskogo slova* 2 (1783): 21.

2. David L. Ransel, *Mothers of Misery: Child Abandonment in Russia* (Princeton, NJ: Princeton University Press, 1988); N. A. Lavrovskii, *O pedagogicheskom znachenii sochinenii Ekateriny Velikoi* (Kharkov, 1856); E. Likhacheva, *Materialy dlia istorii zhenskogo obrazovanii v Rossii (1086–1796)* (St. Petersburg, 1890); N. P. Cherepnin, *Imperatorskoe vospitatel'noe obshchestvo blagorodnykh devits: Istoricheskii ocherk, 1764–1914* (St. Petersburg, 1914); J. L. Black, *Citizens for the Fatherland: Education, Educators, and Pedagogical Ideals in Eighteenth-Century Russia* (Boulder, CO: East European Quarterly, 1979); Max Okenfuss, *The Discovery of Childhood in Russia: The Evidence of the Slavic Primer* (Newtonville, MA: Oriental Research Partners, 1980); George K. Epp, *The Educational Policies of Catherine II: The Era of Enlightenment in Russia* (New York: Peter Lang, 1984); I. P. Maklakova, "Reformy obrazovaniia vtoroi poloviny XVIII veka," in *Otechestvennaia istoriia: Liudi, sobytiia, mysl'*, ed. A. A. Sevast'ianova (Riazan', 1998), 95–106.

3. David L. Ransel, ed., *The Family in Imperial Russia: New Lines of Historical Research* (Urbana: University of Illinois Press, 1978); Jessica Tovrov, *The Russian Noble Family: Structure and Change* (New York: Garland, 1987); Robin Bisha, "The Promise of Patriarchy: Marriage in Eighteenth-Century Russia" (PhD diss., Indiana University, 1994); Natal'ia Pushkareva, *Chastnaia zhizn' russkoi zhenshchiny: Nevesta, zhena, liubovnitsa* (Moscow, 1997); Olga E. Glagoleva, *Dream and Reality of Russian Provincial Young Ladies, 1700–1850* (Pittsburgh, PA: Center for Russian and Eastern European Studies, University of Pittsburgh, 2000).

4. On the later nineteenth century, see Samuel C. Ramer, "Childbirth and Culture: Midwifery in the Nineteenth-Century Russian Countryside," in Ransel, *Family in Imperial Russia*, 218–35. For the twentieth century, see Nancy M. Frieden, "Childcare: Medical Reform in a Traditionalist Culture," in Ransel, *Family in Imperial Russia*, 236–59, and also Natalia Chernyaeva, "Childcare Manuals and Construction of Motherhood in Russia, 1890–1990" (PhD diss., University of Iowa, 2009). With respect to the eighteenth century, I have in mind the following excellent general works on women's

history and collections of essays and primary sources related to women's history: Natal'ia Pushkareva, *Women in Russian History: From the Tenth to the Twentieth Century*, trans. and ed. Eve Levin (Armonk, NY: M. E. Sharpe, 1997); Barbara Alpern Engel, *Women in Russia, 1700–2000* (New York: Cambridge University Press, 2004); Robin Bisha et al., eds., *Russian Women, 1698–1917: Experience and Expression; An Anthology of Sources* (Bloomington: Indiana University Press, 2002); Wendy Rosslyn, ed., *Women and Gender in Eighteenth-Century Russia* (Burlington, VT: Ashgate, 2003); Wendy Rosslyn and Alessandra Tosi, *Women in Russian Culture and Society, 1700–1825* (Basingstoke, UK, 2007).

5. Marta Gutman and Ning de Coninck-Smith, eds., *Designing Modern Childhoods: History, Space, and the Material Culture of Children* (New Brunswick, NJ: Rutgers University Press, 2008). On eighteenth-century European experiments in child rearing, see Julia V. Douthwaite, *The Wild Girl, Natural Man, and the Monster: Dangerous Experiments in the Age of Enlightenment* (Chicago: University of Chicago Press, 2002); Jennifer Popiel, "'Education Is but Habit': Childhood, Individuality, and Self-Control in France, 1762–1833" (PhD diss., University of Pennsylvania, 2000). For nineteenth- and twentieth-century Russian and Soviet childhood studies, see Lisa A. Kirschenbaum, *Small Comrades: Revolutionizing Childhood in Soviet Russia, 1917–1932* (New York: RoutledgeFalmer, 2001); Boris Gorshkov, *Russia's Factory Children: State, Society, and Law, 1800–1917* (Pittsburgh, PA: University of Pittsburgh Press, 2009); Catriona Kelly, *Children's World: Growing Up in Russia, 1890–1991* (New Haven, CT: Yale University Press, 2007).

6. See note 2. Also, Jan Kusber, "Individual, Subject, and Empire: Toward a Discourse on Upbringing, Education, and Schooling in the Time of Catherine II," *Ab Imperio*, no. 2 (2008): 125–56.

7. Philippe Ariès, *Centuries of Childhood: A Social History of Family Life* (New York: Alfred A. Knopf, 1962), 33–49. For a summary of earlier responses to Ariès, see Richard Alan Meckel, "Childhood and the Historians: A Review Essay," *Journal of Family History* 9 (Winter 1984): 415–24, and for a quick but useful account of some of the subsequent historiographical debates, see Rudolf Dekker, *Childhood, Memory, and Autobiography in Holland* (London, 2000), 3–4.

8. The most recent review of Ariès's influence is offered by Colin Heywood, "*Centuries of Childhood*: An Anniversary—and an Epitaph?," *Journal of the History of Childhood and Youth* 3, no. 3 (2010): 343–65.

9. Ibid.

10. Gutman and Coninck-Smith, *Designing Modern Childhoods*; Allyson M. Poska, "Babies on Board: Women, Children, and Imperial Policy in the Spanish Empire," *Gender and History* 22, no. 2 (August 2010): 269–83; Lisa Forman Cody, *Birthing the Nation: Sex, Science, and the Conception of Eighteenth-Century Britons* (New York: Oxford University Press, 2005); Liane McTavish, *Childbirth and the Display of Authority in Early Modern France* (Burlington, VT: Ashgate, 2005); Eve Keller, *Generating Bodies and Gendered Selves: The Rhetoric of Reproduction in Early Modern England* (Seattle: University of Washington Press, 2006).

11. Margaret L. King, "Concepts of Childhood: What We Know and Where We Might Go," *Renaissance Quarterly* 60, no. 2 (Summer 2007): 371–407.

12. Okenfuss, *Discovery of Childhood*.

13. Ransel, *Mothers of Misery*, 8–61.

14. Glagoleva, *Dream and Reality*, 1–73; Natal'ia Pushkareva, "Materinstvo i materinskoe vospitanie v rossiiskikh sem'iakh XVIII–nachala XIX v.," *Rasy i narody* 25 (1998): 104–24. Using memoirs, Pushkareva investigates the feelings women had about motherhood and different styles of mothering as expressed in affectionate or distant relationships between mothers and children. Feelings about pregnancy, miscarriage, and the physical aspects and challenges of maternity are not addressed, either by design or because memoirists did not include observations on these issues.

15. Lynn Hunt, *The Family Romance of the French Revolution* (Berkeley: University of California Press, 1992). Private life, public virtue, and political culture are also central analytical categories explored through an array of advice literature, satirical prints, and contemporary fiction in *Eroticism and the Body Politic*, ed. Lynn Hunt (Baltimore: Johns Hopkins University Press, 1991). More recent inspiration for employing understudied or non-traditional sources can be found in Cindy McCleary, *The Satirical Gaze: Prints of Women in Late Eighteenth-Century England* (New York: Oxford University Press, 2004); and Cody, *Birthing the Nation*.

16. Hans Rogger, *National Consciousness in Eighteenth-Century Russia* (Cambridge, MA: Harvard University Press, 1960); Richard Wortman, *Scenarios of Power: Myth and Ceremony in Russian Monarchy* (Princeton, NJ: Princeton University Press, 1995); Iurii Lotman, *Besedy o russkoi ku'lture: Byt' i traditsii russkogo dvorianstva (XVIII–nachalo XIX veka)* (St. Petersburg, 1994).

17. Cynthia Hyla Whittaker, "The Idea of Autocracy among Eighteenth-Century Historians," *Russian Review* 55 (April 1996): 149–71; Elise Kimerling Wirtschafter, "Thoughts on the Enlightenment and Enlightenment in Russia," *Journal of Modern Russian History and Historiography* 2, no. 2 (January 2009): 1–26; Thomas Newlin, *The Voice in the Garden: Andrei Bolotov and the Anxieties of Russian Pastoral, 1738–1833* (Evanston, IL: Northwestern University Press, 2001); Andreas Schönle, "The Scare of the Self: Sentimentalism, Privacy, and Private Life in Russian Culture, 1780–1820," *Slavic Review* 57, no. 4 (Winter 1998): 723–46; Michelle Lamarche Marrese, "'The Poetics of Everyday Behavior' Revisited: Lotman, Gender, and the Evolution of Russian Noble Identity," *Kritika: Explorations in Russian and Eurasian History* 11, no. 4 (Fall 2010): 701–39.

18. Helen King, *Midwifery, Obstetrics and the Rise of Gynaecology: The Uses of a Sixteenth-Century Compendium* (Aldershot, UK, 2007), 189–94; Peter Wagner, "The Discourse on Sex—or Sex as Discourse: Eighteenth-Century Medical and Paramedical Erotica," in *Sexual Underworlds of the Enlightenment*, ed. G. S. Rousseau and Roy Porter (Chapel Hill: University of North Carolina Press, 1988), 46–68.

19. While Catherine ordered all copies of Radishchev's *Journey* destroyed, Gary Marker's work has shown that recalling banned titles from bookshops around the empire in this era was a haphazard endeavor at best. Gary Marker, *Publishing, Printing,*

and the Origins of Intellectual Life in Russia, 1700–1800 (Princeton, NJ: Princeton University Press, 1985), 226–32.

20. Lotman, *Besedy o russkoi kul'ture*; Wortman, *Scenarios of Power*; and Richard Wortman, "The Russian Empress as Mother," in Ransel, *Family in Imperial Russia*, 60–74.

21. Andre Wakefield, *The Disordered Police State: German Cameralism as Science and Practice* (Chicago: University of Chicago Press, 2009). Wakefield's work addresses Marc Raeff's "Well-Ordered Police State" and other historical scholarship that adopts this interpretive framework: Marc Raeff, "The Well-Ordered Police State and the Development of Modernity in Seventeenth- and Eighteenth-Century Europe: An Attempt at a Comparative Approach," *American Historical Review* 80 (December 1975): 1221–43.

22. Kusber, "Individual, Subject, and Empire"; Whittaker, "Idea of Autocracy."

23. Colum Leckey, *Patrons of the Enlightenment: The Free Economic Society in Eighteenth-Century Russia* (Newark, DE: University of Delaware Press, 2011); Newlin, *Voice in the Garden*, 85–87.

24. John T. Alexander, *Bubonic Plague in Early Modern Russia: Public Health and Urban Disaster* (Baltimore: Johns Hopkins University Press, 1980).

25. Rebecca Friedman, *Masculinity, Autocracy, and the Russian University, 1804–1863* (New York: Palgrave Macmillan, 2005). Another example of a study that considers the interplay between masculinity and femininity is Abby M. Schrader, "Unruly Felons and Civilizing Wives: Cultivating Marriage in the Siberian Exile System, 1822–1860," *Slavic Review* 66, no. 2 (Summer 2007): 230–56. See also Laura Engelstein, *The Keys to Happiness: Sex and the Search for Modernity in Fin-de-Siècle Russia* (Ithaca, NY: Cornell University Press, 1992); Barbara Evans Clements, et al., eds., *Russian Masculinities in History and Culture* (New York: Palgrave, 2002).

26. See Joan Wallach Scott, *Gender and the Politics of History* (New York: Columbia University Press, 1988); Ludmilla Jordanova, *Nature Displayed: Gender, Science, and Medicine, 1760–1820* (London, 1999); Hunt, *Family Romance*; Hunt, *Eroticism and the Body Politic*; Regina Schulte, ed., *The Body of the Queen: Gender and Rule in the Courtly World, 1500–2000* (New York: Berghahn Books, 2006).

27. Marker, *Origins of Intellectual Life*, 17–31.

28. Alexander Vucinich, *Science in Russian Culture: A History to 1860* (Stanford, CA: Stanford University Press, 1963); Ludmilla Schulze, "The Russification of the St. Petersburg Academy of Sciences and Arts in the Eighteenth Century," *British Journal for the History of Science* 18, no. 60 (November 1985): 305–35.

29. Alexander, *Bubonic Plague*, 38–39.

30. Marker refers to Peter's influence as constituting a "Petrine revolution" in the history of printing in Russia. Marker, *Origins of Intellectual Life*, 17.

31. On censorship, see Marker, *Origins of Intellectual Life*, 212–32. For the vagaries and uneven application of autocratic support for the academy, see Schulze, "Russification" and Vucinich, *Science in Russian Culture*.

32. On these terms, see Yuri Slezkine, "Naturalists versus Nations: Eighteenth-Century Russian Scholars Confront Ethnic Diversity," in *Russia's Orient: Imperial*

Borderlands and Peoples, 1700–1917, ed. Daniel R. Brower and Edward J. Lazzerini (Bloomington: Indiana University Press, 1997), 31–32. Slezkine's work on the eighteenth century illuminates the problematic relationship between nation and empire and the slipperiness of these categories in the Russian context. For the nineteenth and twentieth centuries, and for more on these categories as historians have employed them, see Alexei Miller, *The Romanov Empire and Nationalism: Essays in the Methodology of Historical Research*, trans. Serguei Dobrynin (Budapest, 2008), as well as Ilya Gerasimov, et al., "New Imperial History and the Challenges of Empire," in *Empire Speaks Out: Languages of Rationalization and Self-Description in the Russian Empire*, ed. Ilya Gerasimov, Jan Kusber, and Alexander Semyonov (Leiden, 2009), 3–32.

33. Vucinich, *Science in Russian Culture*, 34.

34. Elise Kimerling Wirtschafter, *The Play of Ideas in Russian Enlightenment Theater* (DeKalb: Northern Illinois University Press, 2003), 83; Douglas Smith, "Freemasonry and the Public in Eighteenth-Century Russia," in *Imperial Russia: New Histories for the Empire*, ed. Jane Burbank and David L. Ransel (Bloomington: Indiana University Press, 1998), 281–304; Leckey, *Patrons of the Enlightenment*, 180–81.

CHAPTER I. THE MEANINGS OF VOSPITANIE

1. N. I. Novikov, "O vospitanii i nastavlenii detei," in *Izbrannye sochineniia*, ed. G. P. Makogonenko (Moscow, 1951), 417–506. An excerpt is published in translation in Marc Raeff, ed. and trans., *Russian Intellectual History: An Anthology* (New York: Harcourt, Brace, and World, 1966), 68–86. All translated quotations are my own except when noted. This excerpt is from Raeff's translation, 79. For more on Novikov, see G. P. Makogonenko, *Nikolai Novikov i russkoe prosveshchenie XVIII veka* (Moscow, 1951). On Novikov's Masonic activities, see Douglas Smith, *Working the Rough Stone: Freemasonry and Society in Eighteenth-Century Russia* (DeKalb: Northern Illinois University Press, 1999).

2. Many scholars of early modern Europe have written on the gendering of natural science. I found the following very useful: Carolyn Merchant, *The Death of Nature: Women, Ecology, and the Scientific Revolution* (San Francisco: Harper & Row, 1980); Londa Schiebinger, *Nature's Body: Gender in the Making of Modern Science* (Boston: Beacon Press, 1993); Jordanova, *Nature Displayed*; Mary Terrall, "Metaphysics, Mathematics, and the Gendering of Science in Eighteenth-Century France," in *The Enlightenment*, eds. Dena Goodman and Kathleen Wellman (Boston: Houghton Mifflin, 2004).

3. *Polnoe sobranie zakonov Rossiiskoi Imperii, poveleniem Gosudaria Imperatora Nikolaia Pavlovicha sostavlennoe, sobranie pervoe s 1649 po 12 Dekabria 1925 goda, 1-aia seriia* (St. Petersburg, 1830) (hereafter cited as *PSZ*), I, vol. 16, no. 12103 (1764).

4. Novikov, "O vospitanii i nastavlenii," Raeff's translation, 75.

5. Douthwaite, *Wild Girl, Natural Man*; Anja Müller, *Fashioning Childhood in the Eighteenth Century: Age and Identity* (Burlington, VT: Ashgate, 2006); Karin Lee Fishbeck Calvert, *Children in the House: The Material Culture of Early Childhood, 1600–1900* (Boston: Northeastern University Press, 1992); David Hamlin, "The Structures of Toy Consumption: Bourgeois Domesticity and Demand for Toys in Nineteenth-Century

Germany," *Journal of Social History* 36, no. 4 (2003): 857–69. See also the essays addressing the eighteenth and nineteenth centuries in Mary Jo Maynes et al., eds., *Secret Gardens, Satanic Mills: Placing Girls in European History, 1750–1960* (Bloomington: Indiana University Press, 2004) and in Gutman and Coninck-Smith, *Designing Modern Childhoods.*

6. V. V. Kolesov and V. V. Rozhdestvenskaia, eds. *Domostroi* (St. Petersburg, 1994). See Carolyn Pouncy's introduction to her translation of *The Domostroi: Rules for Russian Households in the Time of Ivan the Terrible* (Ithaca, NY: Cornell University Press, 1994), 1–54, and remarks in Gary Marker, "God of Our Mothers: Reflections on Lay Female Spirituality in Late Eighteenth- and Early Nineteenth-Century Russia," in *Orthodox Russia: Belief and Practice under the Tsars*, ed. Valerie Kivelson and Robert H. Greene (University Park: Pennsylvania State University Press, 2003), 194, note 5.

7. *Iunosti chestnoe zertsalo ili pokazanie k zhiteiskomu obkhozhdeniiu. Sobrannoe ot raznykh avtorov* (St. Petersburg, 1717).

8. Catriona Kelly, *Refining Russia: Advice Literature, Polite Culture, and Gender from Catherine to Yeltsin* (Oxford, 2001), xxiv.

9. Kelly, *Refining Russia*, 16; Lindsey Hughes, *Russia in the Age of Peter the Great* (New Haven, CT: Yale University Press, 1998), 288–90.

10. Hughes, *Russia*, 289; Marker, *Origins of Intellectual Life*, 37.

11. Zh. B. Bel'gar'd [Jean-Baptiste Morvan, l'abbé de Bellegarde], *Sovershennoe vospitanie detei* (St. Petersburg, 1747).

12. N. A. Kopanev, "Rasprostranenie frantsuzskoi knigi v Moskve v seredine XVIII veka," in *Frantsuzskaia kniga v Rossii XVIII veka: Ocherki istorii*, ed. S. P. Luppov (Leningrad, 1986), 81–83. On the importation of French and German books into Russia for retail sale, see Marker, *Origins of Intellectual Life*, 172–77.

13. V. G. Berezina and A. V. Zapadov, *Istoriia russkoi zhurnalistiki XVIII–XIX vekov* (Moscow, 1973), 25; "Ezhemesiachnie sochineniia," in *Sbornik materialov k izuchenii istorii russkoi zhurnalistiki*, ed. E. P. Koz'min and V. D. Koz'mina (Moscow, 1952), 46.

14. Dzh. Lokk [John Locke], *O vospitanii detei* (Moscow, 1759). On the uneven and sometimes idiosyncratic importation of foreign works, see Thomas Barran, *Russia Reads Rousseau, 1762–1825* (Evanston, IL: Northwestern University Press, 2002).

15. Publication data gathered from *Svodnyi katalog russkoi knigi grazhdanskoi pechati XVIII veka, 1725–1800* (Moscow, 1962–67); A. K. Pokrovskaia and N. V. Chekhov, eds., *Materialy po istorii russkoi detskoi literatury, 1750–1855* (Moscow, 1927); and from the catalog *Russkaia kniga grazhdanskoi pechati XVIII v., 1708–1800 v fondakh bibliotekakh RF* at the Russian National Library, St. Petersburg, Russia.

16. Marker, *Origins of Intellectual Life*, 55.

17. *PSZ*, 1, vol. 16, no. 12103 (1764).

18. Catherine II, *Nakaz Eia Imperatorskago Velichestva Ekateriny Vtoryia Samoderzhitsy Vserossiiskiia dannyi Komissii o Sochinenii Proekta Novago Ulozheniia* (1797; repr., St. Petersburg, 1893), chapter 14.

19. On the Free Economic Society, see Leckey, *Patrons of the Enlightenment.*

20. N. G. Kurganov, *Pismovnik* [sic] *soderzhashchii v sebe nauku rossiiskago iazyka so mnogim prisovokupleniem raznogo uchebnago i poleznago veshchesloviia* (St. Petersburg,

1769). *Pismovnik* was reprinted in 1777, 1788, 1790, 1793, and 1796; A. A. Barsov, *Azbuka tserkovnaia i grazhdanskaia s kratkami primechaniiami o pravopisanii* (Moscow, 1768).

21. A. P. Sumarokov, *Nastavlenie mladentsam: Moral', istoriia i geografiia* (St. Petersburg, 1774).

22. N. I. Novikov, *Detskoe chtenie dlia serdtsa i razuma* (Moscow, 1785–89); A. P. Babushkina, *Istoriia russkoi detskoi literatury* (Moscow, 1948); R. V. Dlugach, "Deti i knigi, 1770–1860," in *Materialy po istorii russkoi detskoi literatury, 1750–1855* (Moscow, 1927), 1:265–301.

23. P. A. Plavil'shchikov, "Teatr," *Zritel': Ezhemesiachnoe izdanie* 2 (June 1792): 128–29.

24. A. P. Berdyshev, *Andrei Timofeevich Bolotov: Vydaiushchiisia deiatel' nauki i kul'tury, 1738–1833* (Moscow, 1988), 278–80.

25. A. T. Bolotov, *Detskaia filosofiia, ili nravouchitel'nye razgovory mezhdu odnoiu gospozheiu i eia det'mi sochinennye dlia pospeshestvovaniia istinnoi pol'ze molodykh liudei* (Moscow, 1776).

26. Catherine's works in their Russian titles, with publication dates: *Skazka o Tsarevich Khlore* (1781), *Rossiiskaia azbuka* (1781), *Razgovor i rasskazy* (1782), *Zapiski pervoe chasti* (1782), *Skazka o Tsarevich Fevee* (1782), *Vybornyia Rossiiskie poslovitsy* (1783), *Grazhdanskoe nachal'noe uchenie* (1783), and *Prodolzhenie nachal'noe uchenie* (1783). For more on these works see Lavrovskii, *O pedagogicheskom znachenii*, and Babushkina, *Istoriia russkoi detskoi literatury*, 72–127. On other children's books from this era, see Dlugach, "Deti i knigi," 265–301. On primers, see also Gary Marker, "Faith and Secularity in Eighteenth-Century Russian Literacy, 1700–1775," in *Christianity and the Eastern Slavs*, vol. 2 of *Russian Culture in Modern Times*, ed. Robert P. Hughes and Irina Paperno (Berkeley: University of California Press, 1994), 3–24.

27. N. M. Maksimovich-Ambodik, *Iskusstvo povivaniia ili nauka o babich'em dele: Na piat' chastei razdelennaia i mnogimi risunkami snabdennaia* (St. Petersburg, 1784–86).

28. Kh. Peken, *Domashnii lechebnik* (Moscow, 1765); M. Kh. Peken, *Novyi domashnii lechebnik* (Moscow, 1796). I use the Russianized versions of German names as they appeared in the original Russian publications.

29. A. G. Bakherakht, *O neumerennosti v liubostrastii oboikh polov*, published with his *Sobranie raznykh poleznykh lekarstv* (St. Petersburg, 1779).

30. S. G. Zybelin, *Slovo o pravil'nom vospitanii s mladenchestva* (Moscow, 1775); S. G. Zybelin, *Slovo o sposobe, kak predupredit' mozhno ne malovazhnuiu mezhdu prochimi medlennago umnozheniia naroda* (Moscow, 1780).

31. Kh. Rost, *Derevenskoi vrachebnik, ili legkoi sposob pol'zovat'sia nedostatochnym liudiam ot vsiakikh boleznei prostymi ili domashnimi veshchami, ne imeia nadobnosti v lekarstvakh aptekarskikh* (Moscow, 1793).

32. Rikhter, *Istoriia meditsiny v Rossii*, 3:336.

33. I. Kreizel', *Nastavlenie nachinaiushchim uprazhniat'sia v povival'nom iskusstve, sostiashchee v dvukh chastiakh* (Moscow, 1792).

34. For example, V. M. Rikhter also began in seminary.

35. Rikhter, *Istoriia meditsiny v Rossii*, 3:467.

36. Ia. Chistovich, *Ocherki iz istorii russkikh meditsinskikh uchrezhdenii XVIII stoletiia* (St. Petersburg, 1870), 199–201. An excellent and succinct summary of the development of the medical bureaucracy during the eighteenth century can be found in Alexander, *Bubonic Plague*, 36–45, although I have a different reading of Catherine's refusal to intervene in the matter of credentialing physicians. On the nineteenth-century profession of medicine in Russia, see Nancy Mandelker Frieden, *Russian Physicians in an Era of Reform and Revolution, 1856–1905* (Princeton, NJ: Princeton University Press, 1981).

37. Leckey, *Patrons of the Enlightenment*, 3–4, 20–27, 141–42; Paul Dukes, *Catherine the Great and the Russian Nobility: A Study Based on the Materials of the Legislative Commission of 1767* (Cambridge, MA: Harvard University Press, 1967); V. N. Bochkarev, "Vrachebnoe delo i narodnoe prizrenie v Rossii XVIII veka: Po materialam Zakonodatel'noi Komissii 1767 goda," in *Sbornik statei v chest' Matveia Kuz'micha Liubavskago* (Petrograd, 1917), 468–72; B. D. Petrov, *Ocherki istorii otechestvennoi meditsiny* (Moscow, 1962), 247.

38. Maksimovich-Ambodik, *Iskusstvo povivaniia*, 1:xviii.

39. For example, George K. Epp translates *o vospitanii iunoshestva* as "on the education of youth." Epp, *Educational Policies of Catherine II*, 193. Seeking an idiomatic rendering, perhaps, Max Okenfuss opts to translate *dva vospitanii* as "two childhoods." See his translation of V. O. Kliuchevskii, "Two Childhoods," *History of Education Quarterly* 17 (Winter 1977): 417–47. For the original Russian text, see V. O. Kliuchevskii, "Dva vospitanii," *Russkaia Mysl'* 14, no. 3 (1893): 79–99.

40. Iu. S. Sorokin, ed., *Slovar' Russkogo iazyka XVIII veka* (Leningrad, 1988), 4:84.

41. Dashkova, "O smysle slova vospitanie," 23.

42. Novikov, "O vospitanii i nastavlenii," Raeff's translation, 72.

43. Catherine II, *Instruktsiia Kniaziu Nikolaiu Ivanovichu Saltykovu pri naznachenii ego k vospitaniiu Velikikh Kniazei* (1784), reprinted as *O vospitanii i obrazovanii vnukov* (St. Petersburg, 1994).

44. Novikov, "O vospitanii i nastavlenii," Raeff's translation, 73.

45. See chapter 3.

46. Novikov, "O vospitanii i nastavlenii," Raeff's translation, 72.

47. Dashkova, "O smysle slova vospitanie," 21.

48. Wortman, *Scenarios of Power*, 128–31.

49. Dashkova, "O smysle slova vospitanie," 23.

50. Novikov, "O vospitanii i nastavlenii," 448.

51. These are discussed in chapters 5 and 6 of this book.

52. M. D. Kurmacheva, "Problemy obrazovaniia v ulozhennoi komissii 1767 g.," in *Dvorianstvo i krepostnoi stroi Rossii XVI–XVIII vv: Sbornik statei, posviashchennyi pamiati Alekseia Andreevicha Novosel'skogo*, ed. N. I. Pavlenko (Moscow, 1975), 240–64.

53. An extensive literature exists on this topic. For some of the most recent research on noble attitudes toward their serfs, see Leckey, *Patrons of the Enlightenment*, 61–100.

54. Ransel, *Mothers of Misery*, 58.

55. Historians who study women, children, peasants, and/or lower classes in the early modern period or earlier are well aware of the irregularity of sources. For discussion, see King, "Concepts of Childhood"; Adrian Wilson, "Participant or Patient? Seventeenth-Century Childbirth from the Mother's Point of View," in *Patients and Practitioners: Lay Perceptions of Medicine in Pre-Industrial Society*, ed. Roy Porter (New York: Cambridge University Press, 1985), 136; and Hilary Marland, Introduction to *The Art of Midwifery: Early Modern Midwives in Europe* (New York: Routledge, 1993), 1–8.

56. Two works that provide compelling discussion on this issue are Schiebinger, *Nature's Body*, and Keller, *Generating Bodies*.

57. Adrian Wilson, "William Hunter and the Varieties of Man-Midwifery," in *William Hunter and the Eighteenth-Century Medical World*, ed. W. F. Bynum and Roy Porter (New York: Cambridge University Press, 1985), 343–70; Edward Shorter, "The Management of Normal Deliveries and the Generation of William Hunter," in Bynum and Porter, *William Hunter*, 371–84.

58. See chapters 3 and 4.

59. Denis Fonvizin to I. I. Bulgakov, 1778, quoted in Walter Gleason, *Moral Idealists, Bureaucracy, and Catherine the Great* (New Brunswick, NJ: Rutgers University Press, 1981), 185.

60. Wortman, *Scenarios of Power*. I borrow from Wortman this useful phrase for referencing a semiotic approach to her reign. On nineteenth-century Russian empresses, see also Wortman, "The Russian Empress as Mother," in Ransel, *Family in Imperial Russia*, 61–74.

61. Catherine II to Friedrich M. Grimm, 1781, quoted in I. P. Kornilov, Introduction to *Sbornik materialov dlia istorii prosveshcheniia v Rossii: Izvlechennykh iz Arkhiva Ministerstva narodnago prosveshcheniia* (St. Petersburg, 1893), 1:xxxv.

62. Barbara Duden, *The Woman beneath the Skin: A Doctor's Patients in Eighteenth-Century Germany* (Cambridge, MA: Harvard University Press, 1998), 159; Maksimovich-Ambodik, *Iskusstvo povivaniia*, 1: preface.

CHAPTER 2. THE STATE AND MIDWIFERY

1. Green belongs to a generation of historians who are revising the narrative of the history of midwifery that had been constructed by historians in the 1970s and '80s as a response to (and critique of) the history of obstetrics and gynecology. Monica H. Green, "Gendering the History of Women's Healthcare," *Gender and History* 20, no. 3 (November 2008): 487–518. For a consideration of some of the assumptions of historians who claim impartiality, see Isobel Grundy, "Sarah Stone: Enlightenment Midwife," in *Medicine in the Enlightenment*, ed. Roy Porter (Amsterdam, 1995), 128–44.

2. Ia. Chistovich, *Ocherki iz istorii russkikh meditsinskikh uchrezhdenii XVIII stoletiia* (St. Petersburg, 1870). His chapter 4 addresses the first schools of midwifery in Russia. In the tradition of nineteenth-century Russian historians, Chistovich includes the text of many primary sources, upon which I rely. Another short narrative of the history of medicine in Russia is B. N. Palkin, *K istorii russkoi meditsiny XVIII veka*

(Alma-Ata, 1953). V. A. Kovrigina, E. K. Sysoeva, and D. N. Shanskii, "Meditsina i zdravookhranenie," in *Ocherki russkoi kultury XVIII veka*, ed. B. A. Rybakov (Moscow, 1988), 3:50–84, offers a consideration of public health measures. Medieval childbirth is treated by Eve Levin, "Childbirth in Pre-Petrine Russia: Canon Law and Popular Traditions," in *Russia's Women: Accommodation, Resistance, Transformation*, ed. Barbara Evans Clements, Barbara Alpern Engel, and Christine D. Worobec (Berkeley: University of California Press, 1991), 44–59. Nineteenth-century midwifery is the subject of Ramer, "Childbirth and Culture." See also Samuel Ramer, "Who Was the Russian Feldsher?" *Bulletin of the History of Medicine* 50, no. 2 (1976): 213–25.

3. Mary Lindemann, "Professionals? Sisters? Rivals? Midwives in Braunschweig, 1750–1800," in *The Art of Midwifery: Early Modern Midwives in Europe*, ed. Hilary Marland (New York: Routledge, 1993), 176–91.

4. Levin, "Childbirth in Pre-Petrine Russia," 45–51; Ramer, "Childbirth and Culture," 219.

5. By citing an example here, I do not mean to criticize the author, who cannot cite work that has not yet been done; rather, I reference this explicitly in order to demonstrate that Green's theory holds water in the Russian case. See Elizabeth Waters, "The Modernization of Russian Motherhood, 1917–1937," *Soviet Studies* 44, no. 1 (1992): 123–35. See 132, note 51.

6. A brief overview of eighteenth-century medicine can be found in Aleksandr Nikitin, *Kratkii obzor sostoianiia meditsiny v Rossii v tsarstvovanie Imperatritsy Ekateriny II* (St. Petersburg, 1855). Alexander, *Bubonic Plague*, 36–60.

7. Alexander, *Bubonic Plague*, 36–38.

8. Andrew Curran, "The Faces of Eighteenth-Century Monstrosity," *Eighteenth-Century Life* 21 (May 1997): 1–3; Paul-Gabriel Boucé, "Imagination, Pregnant Women, and Monsters in Eighteenth-Century England and France," in *Sexual Underworlds of the Enlightenment*, ed. G. R. Rousseau and Roy Porter (Chapel Hill: University of North Carolina Press, 1988), 86–100.

9. Curran, "Faces of Eighteenth-Century Monstrosity," 12.

10. T. V. Staniukovich, *Kunstkamera Peterburgskoi Akademii Nauk* (St. Petersburg, 1953), 21.

11. Ibid., 21.

12. See chapter 6 in L. J. Blyakher, *History of Embryology in Russia from the Middle of the Eighteenth Century to the Middle of the Nineteenth Century* (Washington, DC: Smithsonian Institution, 1982).

13. Ransel, *Mothers of Misery*, 27–28.

14. Letter from Empress Anna and reply from Lavrentii Blumentrost, 1740, in Rikhter, *Istoriia meditsiny v Rossii*, 3:93–96, italics in original. Rikhter's work is useful, but it should be noted that it is incomplete. Rikhter, who practiced midwifery in the late eighteenth century, omitted from his book one of the key reformers, his apparent rival Nestor Maksimovich-Ambodik.

15. Nadia Filippini, "The Church, the State, and Childbirth: The Midwife in Italy during the Eighteenth Century," in Marland, *The Art of Midwifery*, 163.

16. Roy Porter, *The Greatest Benefit to Mankind: A Medical History of Humanity* (New York: W. W. Norton, 1997), 245–303. Barbara Duden also underscores the fact that medical policy began to focus on women as reproducers of the "body politic." Duden, *Woman beneath the Skin*, 17.

17. In the case of Mary Wollstonecraft's death, the use of forceps may have hastened the fatal infection. Vivien Jones, "The Death of Mary Wollstonecraft," *Journal for Eighteenth-Century Studies* 20, no. 2 (September 1997): 187–205. Jane B. Donegan, *Women and Men Midwives: Medicine, Morality, and Misogyny in Early America* (Westport, CT: Greenwood Press, 1978), 164–65.

18. David Harley, "Provincial Midwives in England: Lancashire and Cheshire, 1660–1760," in Marland, *The Art of Midwifery*, 27–48.

19. Ibid., 43.

20. Porter, *The Greatest Benefit*, 273–74; Wilson, "William Hunter," 343–70; Shorter, "Management of Normal Deliveries," 371–84; Harley, "Provincial Midwives in England," 27–48.

21. Jones, "Death of Mary Wollstonecraft."

22. Lindemann, "Professionals? Sisters? Rivals?," 176–91.

23. Hilary Marland, "The '*Burgurlijke*' Midwife: The *Stadsvroedvrouw* of Eighteenth-Century Holland," in Marland, *The Art of Midwifery*, 204.

24. Nina Rattner Gelbart, *The King's Midwife: A History and Mystery of Madame du Coudray* (Berkeley: University of California Press, 1998). See 60–63 on du Coudray's model, including a photograph of one preserved in a museum.

25. Rossiiskii gosudarstvennyi istoricheskii arkhiv (hereafter cited as RGIA), f. 758, op. 17, d. 4, l. 2.

26. Gelbart, *The King's Midwife*, 60.

27. Merry E. Wiesner, "The Midwives of South Germany and the Public/Private Dichotomy," in Marland, *The Art of Midwifery*, 77–78; Johanna Geyer-Kordesch, "German Medical Education in the Eighteenth Century: Prussian Context and Its Influence," in Bynum and Porter, *William Hunter*, 203.

28. See the essays cited earlier in Marland, *The Art of Midwifery*.

29. Chistovich, *Ocherki iz istorii*, 130.

30. Alexander, *Bubonic Plague*, 37–41.

31. Kovrigina et al., "Meditsina i zdravookhranenie," 50–52; Nikitin, *Kratkii obzor*, 4.

32. Kovrigina et al., "Meditsina i zdravookhranenie," 58.

33. Alexander, *Bubonic Plague*, 52–53.

34. RGIA, f. 730, op. 2, d. 1, ll. 15–17 ob.

35. Schulze, "Russification of the St. Petersburg Academy"; Vucinich, *Science in Russian Culture*, 104–47.

36. Rikhter, *Istoriia meditsiny v Rossii*, 3:495–96.

37. Kovrigina et al., "Meditsina i zdravookhranenie," 56.

38. P. Z. Kondoidi, "Uchrezhdenie babich'iago dela" (1754), reprinted in Chistovich, *Ocherki iz istorii*, 137–46.

39. Ibid., 137.

40. George D. Sussman, *Selling Mothers' Milk: The Wet-Nursing Business in France, 1715–1914* (Urbana: University of Illinois Press, 1982), 28–29.

41. This is developed further in chapter 3.

42. Kondoidi, "Uchrezhdenie babich'iago dela," 145.

43. Ibid., 142.

44. The engagement with Western ideas and the concern for Russia's position in the world are generally acknowledged by historians as characteristic of this era for members of the urban nobility and educated elites. Interpretative differences continue among historians over how educated Russians responded and what meaning they attached to European standards. See, for example, Rogger, *National Consciousness*, 253–81; Vucinich, *Science in Russian Culture*, 110–16; Iurii Lotman, "The Poetics of Everyday Behavior in Russian Eighteenth-Century Culture," in *The Semiotics of Russian Culture*, ed. Iurii Lotman and B. A. Uspenskii (Ann Arbor: Department of Slavic Languages and Literatures, University of Michigan, 1984), 239–56; Marc Raeff, *Origins of the Russian Intelligentsia: The Eighteenth-Century Nobility* (New York: Harcourt, Brace, and World, 1966), 148–71; David M. Griffiths, "Eighteenth-Century Perceptions of Backwardness: Projects for the Creation of a Third Estate in Catherinian Russia," *Canadian-American Slavic Studies* 13, no. 4 (Winter 1979), 452–72; Marrese, "'The Poetics of Everyday Behavior,'" 701–39.

45. Kondoidi, "Uchrezhdenie babich'iago dela," 142.

46. Wiesner, "Midwives of South Germany," 176–91.

47. Kondoidi, "Uchrezhdenie babich'iago dela," 137.

48. Rikhter, *Istoriia meditsiny v Rossii*, 3:525.

49. Kreizel', *Nastavlenie nachinaiushchim*, x.

50. Kondoidi, "Uchrezhdenie babich'iago dela," 137.

51. Ibid., 138.

52. Ibid.

53. Ibid.

54. Marland, "The '*Burgurlijke*' Midwife," 192–213.

55. Wiesner, "Midwives of South Germany," 79.

56. Kondoidi, "Uchrezhdenie babich'iago dela," 138.

57. Marland, "The '*Burgurlijke*' Midwife," 192–213.

58. P. Z. Kondoidi, "Prisiaga povival'nykh babok po dolzhnosti zvaniia ikh" (1754), reprinted in Chistovich, *Ocherki iz istorii*, 148.

59. P. Z. Kondoidi, "Iz Meditsinskoi Kantseliarii opredelennym prisiazhnym povival'nym babkam Instruktsiia" (1754), reprinted in Chistovich, *Ocherki iz istorii*, 150.

60. Ibid.

61. Chistovich, *Ocherki iz istorii*, 128–36; Alexander, *Bubonic Plague*, 36–50.

62. Wiesner, "Midwives of South Germany," 83.

63. Catherine II, *The Memoirs of Catherine the Great*, ed. Dominique Maroger, trans. Moura Budberg (New York: Macmillan, 1961), 223–24.

64. Porter, *The Greatest Benefit*, 245–303.

65. Kondoidi, "Uchrezhdenie babich'iago dela," sections 18–19, 23.

66. Marland, Introduction to *The Art of Midwifery*, 1–8.

67. Andrei Bakherakht, "Nechto o iskusnykh i nesmyslennykh vrachakh," *Sankt-Peterburgskii vestnik* (December 1779): 425–26.

68. Kondoidi, "Uchrezhdenie babich'iago dela," 141.

69. Ibid.

70. Ibid.

71. Mark Jackson, "Developing Medical Expertise: Medical Practitioners and the Suspected Murders of New-Born Children," in *Medicine in the Enlightenment*, ed. Roy Porter (Amsterdam, 1995), 145–65; Bochkarev, "Vrachebnoe delo," 442–89.

72. Chistovich, *Ocherki iz istorii*, 155.

73. Ibid., 155–56.

74. Lindemann, "Professionals? Sisters? Rivals?," 179.

75. Daniel H. Kaiser, "The Poor and Disabled in Early Eighteenth-Century Russian Towns," *Journal of Social History* 32, no. 1 (Autumn 1998): 137–38.

76. In Spain and Italy in particular, issues of confession intersected with the midwifery business. See the essays by Teresa Ortiz and Nadia Maria Filippini in Marland, *The Art of Midwifery*; Wiesner, "Midwives of South Germany," 85.

77. P. Z. Kondoidi, "Rospisanie po rangam, skol'ko ot rozhanits imat' v kaznu dlia soderzhaniia babich'iago dela i proizvozhdeniia uchenykh iskusnykh babok," reprinted in Chistovich, *Ocherki iz istorii*, 147.

78. P. Z. Kondoidi to the Senate, January 15, 1757, reprinted in Chistovich, *Ocherki iz istorii*, 157.

79. Rikhter, *Istoriia meditsiny v Rossii*, 3:329.

80. Chistovich, *Ocherki iz istorii*, 174.

81. Ibid., 164, 176–77.

82. Wiesner, "Midwives of South Germany," 78.

83. Lindemann, "Professionals? Sisters? Rivals?," 176–77.

84. Rikhter, *Istoriia meditsiny v Rossii*, 3:525–26.

85. Wiesner, "Midwives of South Germany," 80.

86. Ibid., 80–81.

87. Isolde Thŷret, "'Blessed Is the Tsaritsa's Womb': The Myth of Miraculous Birth and Royal Motherhood in Muscovite Russia," *Russian Review* 53, no. 4 (1994): 479–96; Isolde Thŷret, *Between God and Tsar: Religious Symbolism and the Royal Women of Muscovite Russia* (DeKalb: Northern Illinois University Press, 2001); Adele Lindenmeyr, "Public Life, Private Virtues: Women in Russian Charity, 1762–1914," *Signs: Journal of Women in Culture and Society* 18, no. 3 (1993): 562–91; Anna Labzina, *Days of a Russian Noblewoman: The Memories of Anna Labzina, 1758–1821*, ed. and trans. Gary Marker and Rachel May (DeKalb: Northern Illinois University Press, 2001), 8.

88. Lindemann, "Professionals? Sisters? Rivals?," 184.

89. Raeff, "Well-Ordered Police State," 1221–43.

90. Alexander, *Bubonic Plague*, 42.

91. RGIA, f. 1294, op. 1, vn. op. 18, d. 12; f. 1294, op. 1, vn. op. 24, dd. 726–28; f. 1294, op. 1, vn. op. 28, d. 785.

92. Medical Chancellery Ukaz, May 1, 1757, reprinted in Chistovich, *Ocherki iz istorii*, 162–63.

93. Chistovich, *Ocherki iz istorii*, 160–62, 186.

94. Nikitin, *Kratkii obzor*, 52–53; Chistovich, *Ocherki iz istorii*, 164–65.

95. Chistovich, *Ocherki iz istorii*, 160.

96. Ibid., 170. See also Nikitin's biographical entries for Erasmus, Lindeman, Fonmellen, and Pagenkampf. Nikitin, *Kratkii obzor*.

97. Chistovich, *Ocherki iz istorii*, 191–92.

98. Nikitin, *Kratkii obzor*, 46.

99. Chistovich, *Ocherki iz istorii*, 193.

100. Correspondence between Erasmus and the Medical Collegium is reprinted in Chistovich, *Ocherki iz istorii*, 177–84.

101. Ibid., 164.

102. Ibid., 176–77.

103. I. F. Erasmus, *Nastavlenie kak kazhdomu cheloveku voobshche v razsuzhdenie diety, a osoblivo zhenshchinam v beremennosti, v rodakh i posle rodov sebia soderzhat' nadlezhit* (Moscow, 1762).

104. Rikhter, *Istoriia meditsiny v Rossii*, 3:348; Jane Eliot Sewell, *Cesarean Section: A Brief History* (Washington, DC: The American College of Obstetricians and Gynecologists, 1993), 2–8; John Harley Young, *Cæsarean Section: The History and Development of the Operation from Earliest Times* (London, 1944).

105. Chistovich, *Ocherki iz istorii*, 176.

106. *Materialy dlia istorii Imperatorskogo Moskovskogo vospitatel'nogo doma* (hereafter cited as *MIIMVD*), ed. V. Drashuvov (Moscow, 1863–68), 2:2.

107. Iogan van der Gorn [Johan von Hoorn], *Povival'naia babka ili Dostovernoe nastavlenie chrez voprosy i otvety*, trans. I. Pagenkampf (Moscow,1764).

108. Alexander, *Bubonic Plague*, 38; Isabel de Madariaga, *Russia in the Age of Catherine the Great* (New Haven, CT: Yale University Press, 1981), 488–501.

109. Rikhter, *Istoriia meditsiny v Rossii*, 3:337. In 1792, Catherine granted the Medical Faculty the right to bestow the title and license of medical doctor upon its graduates. As mentioned, until that date, only the Medical Collegium had the authority to license physicians.

110. Chistovich, *Ocherki iz istorii*, 187.

111. Catherine II, *Memoirs*, 224–25.

112. RGIA, f. 1294, op. 1, vn. op. 18, d. 12.

113. Maksimovich-Ambodik, *Iskusstvo povivaniia*, 1:xxviii.

114. Ibid., 1:xxix–xxx.

115. Documents from the Legislative Commission in *Sbornik Imperatorskogo Russkogo istoricheskogo obshchestva* (hereafter *SIRIO*), 8:303. For a very good, brief description of the various activities and participants that constituted the Legislative Commission, see John T. Alexander, *Catherine the Great: Life and Legend* (New York: Oxford University Press, 1989), 113–19.

116. Quoted in Alexander, *Bubonic Plague*, 53.

117. Maksimovich-Ambodik, *Iskusstvo povivaniia*, 1:xxxiii.

118. *MIIMVD*, 2:3. Letter to the St. Petersburg *Opekunskii sovet* is reprinted in Chistovich, *Ocherki iz istorii*, 214–15.

119. Amanda Carson Banks, *Birth Chairs, Midwives, and Medicine* (Jackson: University Press of Mississippi, 1999), 33–74.

120. In the eighteenth century, the binding of a particular title could vary greatly, even within the same printing. If a patron wished, some leaves might be arranged in a particular order, for example, or omitted altogether. It is not unusual to find variations from one eighteenth-century copy of a work to another. For Maksimovich-Ambodik's work, some bindings included a sixth volume and others did not. Sometimes the sixth volume included herbal remedies and recipes for medicines; in others it included Maksimovich-Ambodik's translation of Sauserotte's work. In the original copies preserved at the Russian National Library, the sixth volume contains engravings and the title page discussed above.

121. Some of the engravings from Maksimovich-Ambodik's volume are reproduced as illustrations in this book. The famous English physician William Smellie produced a similar work, but the somewhat fanciful or horrifying aspects of Maksimovich-Ambodik's illustrations appear to be of his own creation. See William Smellie, *A Set of Anatomical Tables with Explanations, and an Abridgement of the Practice of Midwifery; With a View to Illustrate a Treatise on that Subject, and a Collection of Cases* (Edinburgh, 1780).

122. This copy is now held by the National Library of Medicine on the campus of the National Institutes of Health, Washington, DC.

123. Kreizel', *Nastavlenie nachinaiushchim*, x–xi. Relatedly, the perceived potential for sexual impropriety is addressed in Roy Porter, "A Touch of Danger: The Man-Midwife as Sexual Predator," in *Sexual Underworlds of the Enlightenment*, ed. G. R. Rousseau and Roy Porter, 206–24.

124. Kovrigina et al., "Meditsina i zdravookhranenie," 55.

CHAPTER 3. MOTHER'S MILK

1. Valerie Fildes, *Wet Nursing: A History from Antiquity to the Present* (London, 1988), 43–100, 111–26; Sussman, *Selling Mothers' Milk*, 1–35.

2. Pushkareva, "Materinstvo," 104–24; Joanna Hubbs, *Mother Russia: The Feminine Myth in Russian Culture* (Bloomington: Indiana University Press, 1988); Eve Levin, *Sex and Society in the World of the Orthodox Slavs, 900–1700* (Ithaca, NY: Cornell University Press, 1989).

3. Levin, "Childbirth in Pre-Petrine Russia," 49–50.

4. Pushkareva, "Materinstvo," 104–24.

5. Pouncy, *Domostroi*.

6. Levin, "Childbirth in Pre-Petrine Russia," 50. Levin's research also shows that during this era the term *baba* could indicate a midwife, a wet nurse, or an old woman rumored to practice witchcraft.

7. Dmitrii, "Mudrye sovety roditel'iam" and "O dolge materei," in *Russkaia pedagogika v glavneishikh eia predstaviteliakh*, ed. M. I. Demkov (Moscow, 1898), 12:45–47.

8. Dmitrii, "O dolge materei," 47.

9. Ibid., 48.

10. Ibid., 47–48.

11. Evgenii Anisimov, "Petr I: Rozhdenie imperii," *Voprosy istorii*, no. 7 (1989): 3–20; Marc Raeff, "Imperial Policies of Catherine II," in *Major Problems in the History of Imperial Russia*, ed. James Cracraft (Lexington, MA: D. C. Heath, 1993), 234–43.

12. Maksimovich-Ambodik, *Iskusstvo povivaniia*, 1:xiv.

13. Ibid. For a brief summary of the Legislative Commission's composition and activities, see John T. Alexander, *Catherine the Great: Life and Legend* (New York: Oxford University Press), 113–19. The Legislative Commission involved the work of 564 deputies from around the Russian empire. Of these, thirty-eight represented government offices; 162 were drawn from assemblies of nobles; 206 came from assemblies of townspeople; fifty-eight were state peasants; fifty-six were categorized as non-Christian peoples; and fifty-four represented Cossack communities.

14. Maksimovich-Ambodik, *Iskusstvo povivaniia*, 1:xiv.

15. Ibid., 1:xv.

16. Ibid., 1:165.

17. Ibid.

18. Ibid., 5:26. Italics added.

19. S. G. Zybelin, *Slovo o sposobe, kak predupredit' mozhno ne malovazhnuiu mezhdu prochimi medlennago umnozheniia naroda* (Moscow, 1780).

20. Ibid., 5.

21. Ibid., 13.

22. Ibid.

23. Ibid., 15.

24. Novikov, "O vospitanii i nastavlenii," 444.

25. Ibid., 417.

26. Ibid., 440.

27. I. Betskoi, *Kratkoe nastavlenie, vybrannoe iz luchshikh Avtorov s nekotorymi fizicheskimi primechaniami o vospitanii detei ot rozhdeniia ikh do iunoshestva* (1766), reprinted in Demkov, *Russkaia pedagogika*, 12:56–76.

28. Ibid., 56.

29. Quoted in Fildes, *Wet Nursing*, 112–13.

30. Sussman, *Selling Mothers' Milk*, 85–86.

31. Christine Theré, "Women and Birth Control in Eighteenth-Century France," *Eighteenth-Century Studies* 32, no. 4 (1999): 559–60.

32. Kondoidi, "Uchrezhdenie babich'iago dela," 140. See also chapter 2.

33. Ibid., 141.

34. Zybelin, *Slovo o pravil'nom vospitanii*, 22; Novikov, "O vospitanii i nastavlenii," 441.

35. Carol Blum, *Strength in Numbers: Population, Reproduction, and Power in Eighteenth-Century France* (Baltimore: Johns Hopkins University Press, 2002), 11–12.

36. Jacqueline Hecht, "From 'Be Fruitful and Multiply' to Family Planning: The Enlightenment Transition," *Eighteenth-Century Studies* 32, no. 4 (1999): 536–51; Michel

Foucault, "Governmentality," in *The Foucault Effect: Studies in Governmentality*, ed. Graham Burchell, Colin Gordon, and Peter Miller (Chicago: University of Chicago Press, 1991), 87–104.

37. Walter Gleason, *Moral Idealists, Bureaucracy, and Catherine the Great* (New Brunswick, NJ: Rutgers University Press, 1981), 53–85, 159–96.

38. Eric Voegelin, *From Enlightenment to Revolution* (Durham, NC: Duke University Press, 1975), 110–35.

39. Zybelin, *Slovo o sposobe*, 4–5.

40. Ibid., 4.

41. Ibid., 11.

42. Ibid., 13.

43. Sussman, *Selling Mothers' Milk*, 12–13.

44. Theré, "Women and Birth Control," 559.

45. Sussman, *Selling Mothers' Milk*, 27–28.

46. Theré, "Women and Birth Control," 552.

47. Quoted in ibid., 559.

48. William Cadogan, *An Essay upon Nursing, and the Management of Children from Their Birth to Three Years of Age. By a Physician in a Letter to One of the Governors of the Foundling Hospital. Published by Order of the General Committee* (London, 1773), 9. Published in Russian as Vil'gel'm Kadogan, *Sredstvo kakim obrazom bez povrezhdeniia zdorov'ia detei vospityvat' s nachala ikh rozhdeniia do okonchaniia tret'iago goda ikh vozrasta* (Moscow, 1789).

49. Antoine-Léonard Thomas, "Essay on the Character, Morals, and Mind of Women across the Centuries (1772)," in Goodman and Wellman, *The Enlightenment*, 163.

50. Jennifer Popiel, "Making Mothers: The Advice Genre and the Domestic Ideal, 1760–1830," *Journal of Family History* 29, no. 4 (October 2004): 339–50; Jeremy Jennings, "The Debate about Luxury in Eighteenth- and Nineteenth-Century French Political Thought," *Journal of the History of Ideas* 68, no. 1 (January 2007): 79–105.

51. Leiselotte Steinbrügge, "The Moral Sex," in Goodman and Wellman, *The Enlightenment*, 181.

52. Ibid., 181–82.

53. Linda Kerber, *Women of the Republic: Intellect and Ideology in Revolutionary America* (Chapel Hill: University of North Carolina Press, 1980); Ruth Bloch, "American Feminine Ideals in Transition: The Rise of Moral Motherhood, 1785–1815," *Feminist Studies* 4, no. 2 (June 1978): 100–26; Jacqueline S. Reinier, "Rearing the Republican Child: Attitudes and Practices in Post-Revolutionary Philadelphia," *William and Mary Quarterly* 39 (January 1982): 150–63.

54. William Coxe, *Travels into Poland, Russia, Sweden, and Denmark: Interspersed with Historical Relations and Political Inquiries* (London, 1785; repr., New York: Arno Press, 1971); Larry Wolff, *Inventing Eastern Europe: The Map of Civilization on the Mind of the Enlightenment* (Stanford, CA: Stanford University Press, 1994), 79–81.

55. Quoted in Wolff, *Inventing Eastern Europe*, 190.

56. Mary Wollstonecraft, "A Vindication of the Rights of Woman," in Goodman and Wellman, *The Enlightenment*, 178.

57. Rost, *Derevenskoi vrachebnik*, xi; Peken, *Novyi domashnii lechebnik*, 157–61.

58. Peken, *Novyi domashnii lechebnik*, 157–62; Rost, *Derevenskoi vrachebnik*, xi; Zybelin, *Slovo o pravil'nom vospitanii*, 17; Maksimovich-Ambodik, *Iskusstvo povivaniia*, 5:26; Marylynn Salmon, "The Cultural Significance of Breastfeeding and Infant Care in Early Modern England and America," *Journal of Social History* 28 (Winter 1994): 247–60.

59. Maksimovich-Ambodik, *Iskusstvo povivaniia*, 5:39; Novikov, "O vospitanii i nastavlenii," 441–43.

60. Maksimovich-Ambodik, *Iskusstvo povivaniia*, 1:168.

61. Novikov, "O vospitanii i nastavlenii," 443.

62. Maksimovich-Ambodik, *Iskusstvo povivaniia*, 5:3–4.

63. Rost, *Derevenskoi vrachebnik*, xi–xii.

64. Ibid., 49.

65. Zybelin, *Slovo o sposobe*, 9, 14–15.

66. Maksimovich-Ambodik, *Iskusstvo povivaniia*, 5:3–4.

67. Ibid., 1:165.

68. Ibid.

69. Jean-Jacques Rousseau, *Emile; or, On Education*, trans. Allan Bloom (New York: Basic Books, 1979), 362, 45.

70. Rost, *Derevenskoi vrachebnik*, v–vi.

71. Nearly any work on the Russian Enlightenment will include a discussion of both Radishchev and Novikov. See Avrahm Yarmolinsky, *Road to Revolution: A Century of Russian Radicalism* (Princeton, NJ: Princeton University Press, 1986); Andrzej Walicki, *A History of Russian Thought from the Enlightenment to Marxism*, trans. Hilda Andrews-Rusiecka (Stanford, CA: Stanford University Press, 1979).

72. Rousseau, *Emile*, 40.

73. Novikov, "O vospitanii i nastavlenii," 417–19.

74. Zybelin, *Slovo o pravil'nom vospitanii*, 12.

75. B. N. Palkin, "Gubernskaia reforma 1775 g. i organizatsiia grazhdanskoi meditsiny v Rossii," *Sovetskoe zdravookhranenie*, no. 9 (1983): 67.

76. Zybelin, *Slovo o sposobe*, 20.

77. Catherine II, *Memoirs*, 381. See also *SIRIO* 7 (1871): 86.

78. The charity lying-in hospitals, staffed by apprentice midwives and directed by physicians, had the added benefit to the state of providing a much-needed teaching site for apprentice midwives, young physicians, and medics in training, as discussed in chapter 2. In concert with these hospitals, the Medical Collegium opened permanent midwifery institutes in both cities. As discussed throughout this book, these topics deserve much more research.

79. Ransel, *Mothers of Misery*, 31–36.

80. *PSZ*, 1, vol. 16, no. 12103 (1764).

81. *MIIMVD*, 2:3:1.

82. Ransel, *Mothers of Misery*, 45–46.

83. Sussman, *Selling Mothers' Milk*, 19; Fildes, *Wet Nursing*, 144–89.

84. Sussman, *Selling Mothers' Milk*, 30, 66.

85. Ibid., 30.

86. Ibid., 85.

87. *MIIMVD*, 2:3:1. Eventually, Betskoi was forced to send many infants to the countryside. On the fosterage with peasant families, see Ransel, *Mothers of Misery*, 177–79.

88. *MIIMVD*, 2:1:3.

89. Ibid.

90. Ibid.

91. Ibid., 2:1:5.

92. Sussman, *Selling Mothers' Milk*, 25–27.

93. *MIIMVD*, 2:1:5.

94. Chistovich, *Ocherki iz istorii*, 173.

95. *MIIMVD*, 2:1:6.

96. Fildes, *Wet Nursing*, 1–67.

97. In fact, wet nursing could have a negative impact on the survival of wet nurses' own infants. Beatrice Moring has found a higher mortality rate among infants of Finnish women who worked in neighboring Saint Petersburg as wet nurses at the foundling home. See Beatrice Moring, "Motherhood, Milk, and Money: Infant Mortality in Pre-Industrial Finland," *Social History of Medicine* 11, no. 2 (1998): 177–96.

98. *MIIMVD*, 2:1:5.

99. Ibid., 2:1:6.

100. Ransel, *Mothers of Misery*, 47.

101. Maksimovich-Ambodik, *Iskusstvo povivaniia*, 1:175.

CHAPTER 4. THE CHILD'S BODY AND THE BODY POLITIC

1. Lui Sebat'en Soserot [Louis Sebastien Sauserotte], *Kratkoe ispytanie mnogikh zakosnel'nykh mnenii i zloupotreblenii do beremennykh zhenshchin, rodil'nits i novorozhdennykh mladentsov*, trans. N. M. Maksimovich-Ambodik (St. Petersburg, 1781).

2. Zhan Gulen, Ansel'm Lui Bernar Zhurden [Jean Goulin and Anselm Louis Bernard Jourdain], *Damskoi vrach v trekh chastiakh soderzhashchikh v sebe nuzhnie predokhraneniia*, trans. K. Mukovnikov (Moscow, 1793). Mukovnikov was a student in the Medical Faculty at Moscow University.

3. M. I. Gorokhovskii, Introduction to *Lechebnik ili Nastavleniia, otnositel'nyia k deiatel'noi vrachebnoi nauke*, by Anton fon Shterk [Anton von Störk], trans. M. Gorokhovskii (Moscow, 1789). Unpaginated preface.

4. Marker, *Origins of Intellectual Life*, 200, note 47.

5. S. M. Grombakh, *Russkaia meditsinskaia literatura XVIII veka* (Moscow, 1953), 34.

6. "O pervykh estestvennykh prikliucheniiakh novorozhdennogo cheloveka," *Sanktpeterburgskie vrachebnye vedomosti* 20 (1792): 152–55.

7. Kadogan, *Sredstvo*. Quoted here from the English original. Cadogan, *An Essay upon Nursing*, 25.

8. Maksimovich-Ambodik, *Iskusstvo povivaniia*, 5:80.

9. Ariès, *Centuries of Childhood*, 125.

10. See Duden's introduction for an excellent overview of the historiography up to the end of the 1990s. Duden, *The Woman beneath the Skin*. Other classics and useful entry points into the scholarship are Thomas Walter Laqueur, *Making Sex: Body and Gender from the Greeks to Freud* (Cambridge, MA: Harvard University Press, 1990); Londa Schiebinger, "Why Mammals are Called Mammals: Gender Politics in Eighteenth-Century Natural History," *American Historical Review* 98, no. 2 (April 1993): 382–411; Ilana Löwy, "Labeled Bodies: Classification of Diseases and the Medical Way of Knowing," *History of Science* 49, no. 3 (September 2011): 299–315.

11. Duden, *Woman beneath the Skin*, vii.

12. Jonathan Reinarz, "The Transformation of Medical Education in Eighteenth-Century England: International Developments and the West Midlands," *History of Education* 37, no. 4 (July 2008): 549–66; Tim Huisman, *The Finger of God: Anatomical Practice in Seventeenth-Century Leiden* (Leiden, 2009), 17–45.

13. After initial controversy and resistance, Harvey's discovery was gradually accepted by the medical community, but humoralism continued to inform prescriptions for managing health into the nineteenth century. John S. White, "William Harvey and the Primacy of the Blood," *Annals of Science* 43, no. 3 (May 1986): 239–55.

14. Zybelin, *Slovo o sposobe*, 14.

15. Ibid.

16. Maksimovich-Ambodik, *Iskusstvo povivaniia*, 5:78; Peken, *Novyi domashnii lechebnik*, 160; Kreizel', *Nastavlenie nachinaiushchim*, 114.

17. Kreizel', *Nastavlenie nachinaiushchim*, 114.

18. Zybelin, *Slovo o sposobe*, 14.

19. Maksimovich-Ambodik, *Iskusstvo povivaniia*, 5:51.

20. Ibid., 1:170.

21. Novikov, "O vospitanii i nastavlenii," 444–45.

22. Ibid., 444.

23. Ibid., 448.

24. For example, in his work toward developing a national literary language Lomonosov advocated retaining some aspects of Church Slavonic, a move he believed would help to prevent the absorption of foreign words into the Russian vernacular. Within the field of history, he fiercely attacked his colleague G. F. Mueller's support of the theory of Scandinavian origins of the Russian nation and succeeded in having Mueller's work censured as biased. Rogger, *National Consciousness*, 100–105, 203–18.

25. M. V. Lomonosov, "O sokhranenii i razmnozhenii rossiiskogo naroda," in *Polnoe sobranie sochineniia*, ed. S. I. Vavilov (Moscow, 1952), 6:384–97.

26. Rousseau, *Emile*, 42–44.

27. Maksimovich-Ambodik, *Iskusstvo povivaniia*, 5:21.

28. Ibid., 5:23.

29. Ibid.

30. Georges Louis Leclerc Buffon, *Natural History General and Particular, by the Count De Buffon*, trans. William Smellie (London, 1785). (Buffon's translator was also the first editor of the Encyclopedia Britannica and had no relationship to the physician William Smellie, who specialized in childbirth and difficult deliveries.)

31. Novikov, "O vospitanii i nastavlenii," 439.

32. Ibid.

33. Ibid., 439–40.

34. Peken, *Novyi domashnii lechebnik*, 244.

35. Grombakh, *Russkaia meditsinskaia literatura*, 201–2.

36. Alexander Radishchev, *A Journey from St. Petersburg to Moscow* in *The Literature of Eighteenth-Century Russia: An Anthology of Russian Literary Materials in the Age of Classicism and the Enlightenment from the Reign of Peter the Great, 1689–1725, to the Reign of Alexander I, 1801–1825*, ed. and trans. Harold B. Segel (New York: E. P. Dutton, 1967), 375.

37. Novikov, "O vospitanii i nastavlenii," 452.

38. Ginnie Smith, "Prescribing the Rules of Health: Self-Help and Advice in the Late Eighteenth Century," in *Patients and Practitioners: Lay Perceptions of Medicine in Pre-Industrial Society*, ed. Roy Porter (New York: Cambridge University Press, 2003), 249–82.

39. Ibid., 257.

40. Ibid., 264–65.

41. Duden, *Woman beneath the Skin*, 14; Smith, "Prescribing the Rules of Health," 280.

42. See chapter 1.

43. Peken, *Novyi domashnii lechebnik*, 17–18.

44. Ibid., 244.

45. Ibid.

46. A. G. Cross, "The Russian *Banya* in the Descriptions of Foreign and Russian Artists," *Oxford Slavonic Papers* 24 (1991): 13–38.

47. Peken, *Novyi domashnii lechebnik*, 18–21.

48. Novikov, "O vospitanii i nastavlenii," 442.

49. Maksimovich-Ambodik, *Iskusstvo povivaniia*, 5:53.

50. Ibid., 1:xx–xxv.

51. Novikov, "O vospitanii i nastavlenii," Raeff's translation, 73.

52. Maksimovich-Ambodik, *Iskusstvo povivaniia*, 5:8.

53. Bakherakht, *O neumerennosti v liubostrastii*, 32.

54. Ibid., 141–202. For more on this term in the Russian context, see Kovrigina et al., "Meditsina i zdravookhranenie," 67, note 68.

55. Ibid., 32.

56. Ibid., 3.

57. Radishchev, *Journey*, 369.

58. Ibid., 370. Italics added.

59. Maksimovich-Ambodik, *Iskusstvo povivaniia*, 5:71–75.

60. Zybelin, *Slovo o pravil'nom vospitanii*, 8.

61. Bakherakht, *O neumerennosti v liubostrastii*, 6–7. Bakherakht's interest in this topic motivated him to translate Tissot's infamous work on masturbation into Russian. Simon Andre Tissot, *Onanizm: Rassuzhdenie o bolezniakh, proizkhodiashchikh ot malakii*, trans. A. G. Bakherakht (Moscow, 1793).

62. Bakherakht, *O neumerennosti v liubostrastii*, 7.

63. Ibid., 5–6.

64. Ibid., 138–39.

65. Quoted in Bochkarev, "Vrachebnoe delo," 458.

66. Ibid., 456.

67. Although some historians in the West translate fon Ash's name as "von Asch," I transliterate his Russianized surname in order to reflect his Russian birth and national identity. Born in St. Petersburg in 1729 to a German father in service to Peter the Great, fon Ash grew up in Russia and studied medicine at Goettingen University. After receiving his medical doctorate, he returned to Russia and began a career as a physician in state service. A. Khan'kovich, "Baron Georg Tomas fon Ash," in *Nemtsy v Sankt-Peterburge (XVIII–XX veka): Biograficheskii aspekt*, ed. T. A. Schrader (St. Petersburg, 2005), 3:48–60.

68. Erasmus, *Nastavlenie*.

69. See chapter 2.

70. Bochkarev, "Vrachebnoe delo," 471.

71. See chapter 3.

72. Bochkarev, "Vrachebnoe delo," 471–72.

73. Ibid., 471–72.

74. Quoted in Slezkine, "Naturalists versus Nations," 39.

CHAPTER 5. MORAL INSTRUCTION FOR THE EMPIRE'S YOUTH

1. Novikov, "O vospitanii i nastavlenii," Raeff's translation, 69.

2. Pushkareva, *Women in Russian History*, 139–41; Evgenii Anisimov, *Zhenshchiny na rossiiskom prestole* (St. Petersburg, 1998), 335–37; Simon Dixon, *Catherine the Great* (New York: Ecco, 2009), 45–47.

3. Wolff, *Inventing Eastern Europe*, 17–88.

4. Elizabeth Dimsdale, *An English Lady at the Court of Catherine the Great*, ed. A. G. Cross (Cambridge, UK, 1989), 52–61.

5. Quoted in Wolff, *Inventing Eastern Europe*, 82.

6. Ibid., 195–234.

7. One infamous case concerned the publication of Chappe d'Auteroche's *Voyage en Sibérie*. On Catherine's response to his unflattering portrayal of Siberia, see Marcus C. Levitt, *Early Modern Russian Letters: Texts and Contexts* (Boston: Academic Studies Press, 2009), 339–57.

8. Rogger, *National Consciousness*, 253–75.

9. Marker, *Origins of Intellectual Life*, 193.

10. Hughes, *Russia*, 299–309.

11. De Madariaga, *Age of Catherine*, 488–91.

12. See Slezkine, "Naturalists versus Nations," 39.

13. Rogger, *National Consciousness*, 45–84.

14. Gleason, *Moral Idealists*, 53–85; Rogger, *National Consciousness*, 8–84.

15. E. B. Syreishchikov, *Rech' o pol'ze nravoucheniia pri vospitanii iunoshestva* (Moscow, 1783). Syreishchikov also wrote a grammar, *Kratkaia rossiiskaia grammatika*, which went through several printings between 1787 and 1796. See also Marker, *Origins of Intellectual Life*, 193.

16. Syreishchikov, *Rech'*, 5.

17. Radishchev, *Journey*, 380.

18. D. I. Fonvizin, "Primechanie izdatel'ei zhurnala," in *Sbornik materialov k izucheniiu istorii russkoi zhurnalistiki*, ed. B. P. Koz'min (Moscow, 1952), 70.

19. Kurmacheva, "Problemy obrazovaniia," 245.

20. Syreishchikov, *Rech'*, 6.

21. Kurmacheva, "Problemy obrazovaniia," 242–43.

22. N. I. Novikov, "Nravouchenie kak prakticheskoe nastavlenie," in *Izbrannye sochineniia*, ed. G. P. Makogonenko (Moscow, 1951), 399.

23. Ibid., 402; Leckey, *Patrons of the Enlightenment*, 142.

24. Kovrigina et al., "Meditsina i zdravookhranenie," 67, note 68.

25. *PSZ*, 1, vol. 16, no. 12103 (1764).

26. Galenkovskii, *Vospitanie iunoshestva v proshlom: Istoricheskii ocherk pedagogicheskikh sredstv pri vospitanii v voenno-uchebnykh zavedeniiakh* (St. Petersburg, 1904), 46–47.

27. Ibid., 54.

28. M. M. Shcherbatov, *On the Corruption of Morals in Russia*, ed. and trans. Antony Lentin (New York: Cambridge University Press, 1969), 157.

29. A. T. Bolotov, "Iz neizdannogo literaturnogo naslediia Bolotova," ed. I. Morozov and A. Kucherov, *Literaturnoe nasledtsvo* 10 (1933): 180–89.

30. Babushkina, *Istoriia russkoi detskoi literatury*, 88–91.

31. Bolotov, "Iz neizdannogo literaturnogo naslediia," 180–89.

32. Peken, *Novyi domashnii lechebnik*, 11. See also Marcus C. Levitt's discussion of what he calls "the rapprochement between 'secular' and 'religious'" in Levitt, *Early Modern Russian Letters*, 269–93.

33. Gleason, *Moral Idealists*, 79–80.

34. I draw this conclusion based on a review of the collections of eighteenth-century primers in the rare book divisions of the Russian National Library and the Russian Academy of Sciences.

35. Marker, *Origins of Intellectual Life*, 193.

36. V. O. Kliuchevskii, "Dva Vospitanii," *Russkaia Mysl'* 14, no. 3 (1893): 79–99.

37. Sumarokov, *Nastavlenie mladentsam*, 1–3.

38. *Novyi rossiiskii bukvar' s kratkimi nravoucheniiami i povestiami* (St. Petersburg, 1775), 30.

39. *Bukvar' dlia upotrebleniia rossiiskago iunoshestva* (Moscow, 1780), 22–23; A. A. Barsov, *Azbuka tserkovnaia i grazhdanskaia s kratkami primechaniiami o pravopisanii* (Moscow, 1768), 37, 36.

40. Catherine II, *Rossiiskaia azbuka dlia obucheniia iunoshestva chteniiu* (St. Petersburg, n.d.), 33–35.

41. *Rossiiskaia azbuka dlia obucheniia malen'kikh mal'chikov* (Moscow, 1795), 25–27.

42. Barsov, *Azbuka*, 29.

43. Kliuchevskii, "Dva Vospitanii," 79–99.

44. Marrese, "Poetics of Everyday Behavior," 701–39.

45. Marker, *Origins of Intellectual Life*, 192.

46. Dixon, *Catherine the Great*, 134.

47. Pavel Miliukov, "Educational Reforms," in *Catherine the Great: A Profile*, ed. Marc Raeff (New York: Hill and Wang, 1972), 93–112.

48. Franklin A. Walker, "Enlightenment and Religion in Russian Education in the Reign of Tsar Alexander I," *History of Education Quarterly* 32, no. 3 (Autumn 1992): 343–60; Elise Kimerling Wirtschafter, "Religion and Enlightenment in Eighteenth-Century Russia: Father Platon at the Court of Catherine II," *Slavonic and East European Review* 88, nos. 1–2 (January 2010): 180–203.

49. Walker, "Enlightenment and Religion," 343–44.

50. *Novyi rossiiskii bukvar'*, 33, 34–36.

51. Kurganov, *Pismovnik*, 1:1–123, 291–330; 2:212–15.

52. Babushkina, *Istoriia russkoi detskoi literatury*, 88–91.

53. Ibid.

54. Catherine II, *Zapiski pervoi chasti* (St. Petersburg, 1782).

55. Barbara Jelavich, *History of the Balkans: Eighteenth and Nineteenth Centuries* (New York: Cambridge University Press, 1983), 70–72.

56. Jelavich, *History of the Balkans*, 70–71; Kusber, "Governance, Education, and the Problems of Empire in the Age of Catherine II," in *Empire Speaks Out: Languages of Rationalization and Self-Description in the Russian Empire*, ed. Ilya Gerasimov, Jan Kusber, and Alexander Semyonov (Leiden, 2009), 81; O. P. Markova, "O proiskhozhdenii tak nazyvaemogo Grecheskogo Proekta (80-e gody XVIII v.)," *Istoriia SSSR*, no. 4 (July 1958): 52–78. On the symbolic meaning of the Crimea, see Andreas Schönle, "Garden of the Empire: Catherine's Appropriation of the Crimea," *Slavic Review* 60, no. 1 (Spring 2001): 1–23.

57. Catherine II, *Zapiski pervoi chasti*, 4–48, 80–120.

58. For example, ibid., 108, 230.

59. Kurmacheva, "Problemy obrazovaniia," 260.

60. I. I. Betskoi, excerpted in *Sbornik materialov dlia istorii prosveshcheniia v Rossii: Izvlechennykh iz Arkhiva Ministerstva narodnago prosveshcheniia*, ed. I. P. Kornilov (St. Petersburg, 1893), xxvii.

61. Rogger, *National Consciousness*, 85–125; Eric Hobsbawm, "Introduction: Inventing Tradition," in *The Invention of Tradition*, ed. Eric Hobsbawm and Terence Ranger (New York: Cambridge University Press, 1983), 1–14.

62. De Madariaga, *Age of Catherine*, 495.

63. Black, *Citizens for the Fatherland*, 130–31; Kusber, "Governance," 83–88.

64. RGIA, f. 730, op. 2, d. 1, l. 15–15 ob.

65. Ibid.

66. There is a vast literature on the topic. Two good entry points on imperialism and the problem of Russification in the nineteenth century are Miller, *The Romanov Empire*; and Don Yaroshevski, "Empire and Citizenship," in *Russia's Orient: Imperial Borderlands and Peoples*, ed. Daniel R. Brower and Edward J. Lazzerini (Bloomington: Indiana University Press, 1997), 58–79.

67. RGIA, f. 730, op. 2, d. 3, no. 36720, k. 1 (October 22, 1784).

68. Schulze, "Russification."

69. RGIA, f. 730, op. 2, d. 2, no. 36719, k. 1 (1783).

70. Tsentral'nyi gosudarstvennyi istoricheskii arkhiv Sankt-Peterburga (hereafter TsGIASPb), f. 2, op. 3, d. 4, l. 1; De Madariaga, *Age of Catherine*, 498–500; Black, *Citizens for the Fatherland*, 143.

71. Ben Ekloff, *Russian Peasant Schools: Officialdom, Village Culture, and Popular Pedagogy, 1861–1914* (Berkeley: University of California Press, 1986), 21.

72. De Madariaga, *Age of Catherine*, 500–502; Dixon, *Catherine the Great*, 135.

73. For two differing interpretations, see Max Okenfuss, "Education and Empire: School Reform in Enlightened Russia," *Jahrbücher für Geschichte Osteuropas* 27, no. 1 (1979): 51, and De Madariaga, *Age of Catherine*, 501.

74. RGIA, f. 730, op. 2, d. 1, l. 49.

75. J. L. Black offers a brief discussion. He views this handbook primarily as a "simpler version" of *On the Duties of Man and Citizen*. Black, *Citizens for the Fatherland*, 134.

76. [Theodor Iankovich de Mirievo], *Pravila dlia uchashchikhsia v narodnykh uchilishchakh, izdannyia po Vysochaishemu poveleniiu tsarstvuiushchei Imperatritsy Ekateriny Vtoryia* (St. Petersburg, 1786), 11, 12, 21.

77. See Slezkine, "Naturalists versus Nations."

78. Ia. B. Kniazhnin, "Misfortune from a Coach," in Segel, *Literature of Eighteenth-Century Russia*, 2:374–93.

79. Rogger, *National Consciousness*, 56–65; Orlando Figes, *Natasha's Dance: A Cultural History of Russia* (New York: Metropolitan Books, 2002), 51–60.

80. Gleason, *Moral Idealists*, 145.

81. Dashkova, "O smysle slova vospitanie," 15.

82. Novikov, "O vospitanii i nastavlenii," Raeff's translation, 77.

83. Peken, *Novyi domashnii lechebnik*, 120.

84. Ibid.

85. Bakherkaht, *O neumerennosti v liubostrastii*, 8.

86. Ibid., 9–11.

87. Ibid., 11.

88. Peken, *Novyi domashnii lechebnik*, 119.

89. D. I. Fonvizin, *Nedorosl'* (Hertfordshire, UK, 1965), written in 1781 and first performed in 1782.

90. Michelle Lamarche Marrese, *A Woman's Kingdom: Noblewomen and the Control of Property in Russia, 1700–1861* (Ithaca, NY: Cornell University Press, 2002), 197–99.

91. Dashkova, "O smysle slova vospitanie," 15.

92. Kurmacheva, "Problemy obrazovaniia," 244.

93. Galenkovskii, *Vospitanie iunoshestva*, 50–51.

94. Catherine II, *Memoirs*, 172–73.

95. *Novyi rossiiskii bukvar' s kratkimi nravoucheniiami i povestiami* (St. Petersburg, 1775), 30.

96. Ibid., 53–54.

97. Sumarokov, *Nastavlenie mladentsam*, 7, 9, 13; Barsov, *Azbuka*, 26.

98. I. V. Chuvashev, "Pedagogicheskie idei v russkoi khudozhestvennoi literature XVIII v.," *Sovetskaia pedagogika* 7 (1944): 51–53.

99. Dashkova, "O smysle slova vospitanie," 12–13.

100. Ibid., 13–15.

101. Galenkovskii, *Vospitanie iunoshestva*, 52–53.

102. Bakherakht, *O neumerennosti v liubostrastii*, 34.

103. Dashkova, "O smysle slova vospitanie," 16–17.

104. Radishchev, *Journey*, 380.

CHAPTER 6. THE NEW GIRLHOOD

1. I. I. Betskoi, *Ustav vospitanii dvukh sot blagorodnykh devits* (1765), reprinted in Cherepnin, *Imperatorskoe vospitatel'noe obshchestvo*, 3:31–34.

2. Lynne Vallone, *Disciplines of Virtue: Girls' Culture in the Eighteenth and Nineteenth Centuries* (New Haven, CT: Yale University Press, 1995); Deborah Simonton, "Earning and Learning: Girlhood in Pre-Industrial Europe," *Women's History Review* 13, no. 3 (September 2004): 363–86; Michèle Cohen, "'To Think, to Compare, to Combine, to Methodise': Girls' Education in Enlightenment Britain," in *Women, Gender, and Enlightenment*, ed. Sarah Knott and Barbara Taylor (New York: Palgrave Macmillan, 2005), 224–42; Jean Bloch, "Discourses of Female Education in the Writings of Eighteenth-Century French Women," in Knott and Taylor, *Women, Gender, and Enlightenment*, 243–58; Dena Goodman, "L'Ortografe des Dames: Gender and Language in the Old Regime," in Knott and Taylor, *Women, Gender, and Enlightenment*, 195–223.

3. Nadine Berenguier, "The Politics of Happy Matrimony: Cerfvol's *La Gamologie ou l'Education des Filles Destinées au Mariage*," *Studies in Eighteenth-Century Culture* 29, no. 1 (2000): 174.

4. Vivien Jones, "Advice and Enlightenment: Mary Wollstonecraft and Sex Education," in Knott and Taylor, *Women, Gender, and Enlightenment*, 140–48.

5. Fonvizin, *Nedorosl'*, 67–79.

6. Admissions took place every three years. The board meticulously filed such a document for every admitted pupil, for every admission cycle. For example, see TsGIASPb, f. 2, op. 2, d. 6, ll. 1–105 ob., passim. The board also carefully listed the familial status and property for each girl admitted. For the first admission cycle, see TsGIASPb, f. 2, op. 1, d. 720, ll. 57–60.

7. TsGIASPb, f. 2, op. 2, d. 6, l. 33, 88.

8. Marta Gutman and Ning de Coninck-Smith, "Introduction: Good to Think With—History, Space, and Modern Childhood," in Gutman and Coninck-Smith, *Designing Modern Childhoods*, 4.

9. William Craft Brumfield, *Landmarks of Russian Architecture: A Photographic Survey* (Amsterdam, 1997), 159–61. For more semiotic analysis of Russian architecture, see James Cracraft and Daniel Rowland, *Architectures of Russian Identity: 1500–Present* (Ithaca, NY: Cornell University Press, 2003).

10. Levitt, "Rapprochement," 269–93; Marker, "Faith and Secularity."

11. Gutman and Coninck-Smith, "Introduction," 5. The term "kindergarten," not coined until the 1840s, evokes this sense of a special, pleasant environment for small children. The darker side of this "islanding" of children into separate, isolated, specially designed interior spaces is explored by John R. Gillis in his epilogue to Gutman and Coninck-Smith, *Designing Modern Childhoods*, 316–30.

12. Charles Shaw Cathcart to Lord Viscount Weymouth, *SIRIO* 12 (1873): 369–70. King Gustav IV of Sweden visited Smolny in 1777. Impressed with the girls' performances and demonstrations of knowledge, he sent a congratulatory letter and a portrait to the school. One young actress also received a diamond locket from the king. TsGIASPb, f. 2, op. 2, d. 11, l. 57–57 ob.

13. Ibid., d. 11, ll. 43 ob., 49 ob–50 ob., 59–59 ob., 67 ob.–70; ibid., d. 20, l. 51–51 ob.

14. Betskoi, *Ustav vospitanii*, 31–34.

15. TsGIASPb, f. 2, op. 1, d. 227, l. 2.

16. Gutman and Coninck-Smith, "Introduction," 18.

17. Betskoi, *Ustav vospitanii*. Betskoi's new charter for the Corps of Cadets, *Novyi ustav sukhoputnago kadetskago korpusa* (1766) included explicit directions in this respect. Galenkovskii, *Vospitanie iunoshestva*, 47–55.

18. See chapters 3 and 4.

19. Gutman and Coninck-Smith, "Introduction," 18.

20. Jeremy Bentham, *Panopticon; or the Inspection-House* (1787) reprinted in *The Panopticon Writings*, ed. Miran Bozovic (London, 1995), 29–95.

21. Simon Werrett, "Potemkin and the Panopticon: Samuel Bentham and the Architecture of Absolutism in Eighteenth-Century Russia," *Journal of Bentham Studies* 2 (1999): 1–25.

22. Beautiful, color photographs of the *Smolianki* portraits can be found in *Dmitrii Grigor'evich Levitskii, 1735–1822: Katalog vremennoi vystavki Gosudarstvennogo Russkogo Muzei* (Leningrad, 1987), figures 6–10. The original paintings are owned by the Russian Museum in St. Petersburg.

23. Excerpt in I. Kornilov's introduction to *Sbornik materialov dlia istorii prosveshcheniia v Rossii: Izvlechennykh iz Arkhiva Ministerstva narodnago prosveshcheniia*, ed. I. Kornilov (St. Petersburg, 1893), 1:xxxv.

24. Raeff, *Origins of the Russian Intelligentsia*, 137–43; N. N. Aurova, "Idei prosveshcheniia v pervom kadetskom korpuse (konets XVIII–pervaia chetvert' XIX)," *Vestnik Moskovskogo Universiteta, Seriia 8: Istoriia*, no. 1 (1996): 34–42; Betskoi, *Ustav vospitanii*, 41–44.

25. Raeff, *Origins of the Russian Intelligentsia*, 138.

26. Black, *Citizens for the Fatherland*, 166; Lotman, *Besedy o Russkoi kul'ture*, 79–80; De Madariaga, *Age of Catherine*, 499.

27. Quoted in Aurova, "Idei prosveshcheniia," 36.

28. Betskoi, *Ustav vospitanii*, 42.

29. Ibid., 39.

30. See note 2. Mary Wollstonecraft, *A Vindication of the Rights of Woman, with Strictures on Political and Moral Subjects* (London, 1796), 32–258; Ruth Bloch, "Discourses of Female Education in the Writings of Eighteenth-Century French Women," in Knott and Taylor, *Women, Gender, and Enlightenment*; Dena Goodman, *The Republic of Letters: A Cultural History of the French Enlightenment* (Ithaca, NY: Cornell University Press, 1994), 90–135. On Mme Le Prince de Beaumont and Mme de Genlis, see Clarissa Campbell Orr, "Aristocratic Feminism, the Learned Governess, and the Republic of Letters," in Knott and Taylor, *Women, Gender, and Enlightenment*, 306–25.

31. Labzina, *Days of a Russian Noblewoman*, 52.

32. Carolyn Lougee, "*Noblesse*, Domesticity, and Social Reform: The Education of Girls by Fenelon and Saint-Cyr," *History of Education Quarterly* 14 (Spring 1974): 98.

33. Betskoi, *Ustav vospitanii*, 39.

34. Catherine explained as much to Voltaire in a series of exchanges. See the excerpted correspondence on the topic: "The Empress and the Philosopher: Catherine II—Voltaire Correspondence," in *Russian Women, 1698–1917: Experience and Expression; An Anthology of Sources*, ed. Robin Bisha, Jehanne M. Gheith, Christine Holden, and William G. Wagner (Bloomington: Indiana University Press, 2002), 165–68.

35. Ibid.

36. Catherine II, *Memoirs*, 85–86. Catherine reports having penned a description of herself in her teen years, which she titled "Portrait of a Fifteen-Year-Old Philosopher."

37. Betskoi, *Ustav vospitanii*, 34.

38. Ibid., 39.

39. TsGIASPb, f. 2, op. 2, d. 1, l. 9.

40. Ibid., d. 11, l. 57–57 ob.; Charles Shaw Cathcart to Lord Viscount Weymouth, *SIRIO* 12 (1873): 369–70; "Dva sobstvennoruchnyia chernovyia pisma Ekateriny II k vospitanitse Smolnago Monastyra A. Levshinoi, vposledstvii kniagine Cherkasskoi," *SIRIO* 13 (1874): 338–41.

41. I. I. Betskoi, Letter to the pupils at the Society for the Upbringing of Well-Born Maidens, reprinted in Cherepnin, *Imperatorskoe vospitatel'noe obshchestvo*, 3:102.

42. Ibid., 103.

43. Ibid.

44. Catherine II, "Catherine to Voltaire (December 15, 1770)," in *Voltaire and Catherine the Great: Selected Correspondence*, ed. and trans. A. Lentin (Cambridge, UK, 1974), 93–94.

45. TsGIASPb, f. 2, op. 3, d. 4, l. 69.

46. Ibid., l. 72.

47. Ibid., l. 73.

48. Ibid., l. 74.

49. Ibid., l. 70.

50. Ibid., l. 83.

51. Wortman, *Scenarios of Power*, 3–10.

52. A. P. Valitskaia, *Dmitrii Grigor'evich Levitskii, 1735–1822* (Leningrad, 1985), 23.

53. Vallone, *Disciplines of Virtue*, 2.

54. Quoted in A. F. Belousov, "Institutka v russkoi literature," in *Tynianovskii sbornik: Tynianovskie chteniia*, ed. M. O. Chudakova (Riga, 1990), 4:78.

55. Sally Mitchell, *The New Girl: Girls' Culture in England, 1880–1915* (New York: Columbia University Press, 1995), 3.

56. Berenguier, "Politics of Happy Matrimony," 174.

57. TsGIASPb, f. 2, op. 1, d. 316, l. 58–58 ob.

58. A. Levshina to Catherine II, *SIRIO* 13 (1874): 338–41.

59. I. I. Betskoi, *Uchrezhdenie osoblivago uchilishcha pri Voskresenskom Novodevich'em Monastyre dlia vospitaniia maloletnykh devushek* (1768), reprinted in Cherepnin, *Imperatorskoe vospitatel'noe obshchestvo*, 3:52–55.

60. TsGIASPb, f. 2, op. 1, d. 316, ll. 37, 64–69, 84–90.

61. Betskoi, *Uchrezhdenie osoblivago uchilishcha*, 52–55.

62. TsGIASPb, f. 2, op. 1, d. 227, l. 80.

63. For example, TsGIASPb, f. 2, op. 2, d. 6, l. 27.

64. Ibid., d. 11, l. 29.

65. Ibid., d. 1, l. 11; d. 16, ll. 42–44.

66. TsGIASPb, f. 2, op. 1, d. 451, ll. 1–10.

67. TsGIASPb, f. 2, op. 1, d. 227, l. 93.

68. Betskoi's personal files suggest that he gave this issue significant attention. TsGIASPb, f. 2, op. 1, d. 723, ll. 16–17.

69. Ann Stoler, "A Sentimental Education: Children on the Imperial Divide," in *Carnal Knowledge and Imperial Power: Race and the Intimate in Colonial Rule* (Berkeley: University of California Press, 2002), 112–39.

70. G. Rzhevskaia [née Alymova], "Pamiatnye zapiski Glafiry Ivanovny Rzhevskoi," *Russkii arkhiv* 1 (1871): 6.

71. TsGIASPb, f. 2, op. 2, d. 11, l. 26–26 ob.

72. Ibid., op. 3, d. 4, l. 1.

73. Ibid., d. 4, l. 57–57 ob.

74. Ibid., l. 57.

75. Robin Bisha, "The Promise of Patriarchy: Marriage in Eighteenth-Century Russia" (PhD diss., Indiana University, 1994), 34, note 22.

76. TsGIASPb, f. 2, op. 1, d. 720, ll. 3–4, 61, 81; op. 2, d. 11, l. 52 ob.

77. Ibid., op. 1, d. 720, l. 20. Over the course of the 1780s, the responsibility for disputes involving inheritable lands was shifted to local votchina departments.

78. Betskoi, *Ustav vospitanii*, 29.

79. TsGIASPb, f. 2, op. 1, d. 732, ll. 19–20.

80. Ibid.

81. TsGIASPb, f. 2, op. 2, d. 20, ll. 39–46 ob.

82. Rzhevskaia, "Pamiatnye zapiski," 4.

83. TsGIASPb, f. 2, op. 3, d. 4, l. 89 ob.

84. Ibid.

85. Rzhevskaia, "Pamiatnye zapiski," 14.

86. TsGIASPb, f. 2, op. 1, d. 316, l. 47.

87. Cherepnin, *Imperatorskoe vospitatel'noe obshchestvo*, appendix, 474.

88. E. I. Nelidova, "E. I. Nelidova," *Russkii arkhiv* 2 (1873): 2160–72.

89. I mean "patriarchy" in the feminist sense as a social construction and system that privileges older men, granting them authority over younger men, women, and children. Within this system, constructions of femininity and masculinity serve to reinforce the subordination of women and the power of men over them. See Carol Pateman, *The Sexual Contract* (Stanford, CA: Stanford University Press, 1988), 207.

90. Glagoleva, *Dream and Reality*, 20–23, 26. See the memoirs of Ekaterina Dashkova, Catherine II, and Anna Labzina for other examples of teenage marriage and early pregnancy.

91. TsGIASPb, f. 2, op. 1, d. 732, l. 35–35 ob.

92. Ibid., ll. 36–43 ob.

93. Ibid.

94. TsGIASPb, f. 2, op. 1, d. 732, l. 49–49 ob.

95. Ibid., l. 42.

96. Ibid., l. 19.

97. Ibid., l. 43 ob.

98. Ibid.

99. Ibid., l. 43.

100. Ibid.

101. The original text by Johann Ignaz von Felbiger was translated by Iankovich and given the title *O dolzhnostiakh cheloveka i grazhdanina*. Kusber, "Governance," 84. See also chapter 5.

102. From the translation of *On the Duties of Man and Citizen*, reprinted in Black, *Citizens for the Fatherland*, 204.

103. RGIA, f. 730, op. 2, d. 1, ll. 3–16.

104. For Smolny, see RGIA, f. 730, op. 2, d. 2, ll. 40–58 ob. For the Corps of Cadets, see ibid., ll. 100–105 ob.

105. TsGIASPb, f. 2, op. 1, d. 732, l. 43.

106. Ibid., l. 50.

107. Voltaire to Catherine II (March 12, 1772), in Lentin, *Voltaire and Catherine*, 131–32.

108. TsGIASPb, f. 2, op. 1, d. 732, ll. 19–20.

109. Ibid.

110. TsGIASPb, f. 2, op. 1, d. 732, ll. 19–20, 50.

111. See chapter 3.

112. RGIA, f. 730, op. 2, d. 3, no. 36720, l. 15.

113. See, for example, the character reports, all in French: TsGIASPb, f. 2, op. 2, d. 20, ll. 39–46.

114. [A. A. Barsov with N. I. Novikov?], *Karmannaia, ili Pamiatnaia knizhka dlia molodykh devits: Soderzhashchaia v sebe nastavleniia prekrasnomu polu, s pokazaniem, v chem dolzhny sostoiat' uprazhneniia ikh* (Moscow, 1784). Novikov's printing press published this work. Its authorship has not been determined definitively. J. L. Black attributes it to Anton Barsov. (See Black, *Citizens for the Fatherland*, 165.) Russian databases and union catalogs have left authorship unattributed. I reviewed two original copies of the text, one preserved at the Russian National Library and one at the Library of the Academy of Sciences. Neither copy lists an author or editor on the title page, which was not unusual for this period in Russia. Given Barsov's involvement with the other texts commissioned in conjunction with the educational reforms of the 1780s, and the wide range of his literary activities (he also compiled a text entitled *4291 Ancient Russian Proverbs*, for example), it is possible he may have been the author/editor. Novikov may have contributed to or influenced its contents.

115. [Barsov], *Karmannaia, ili Pamiatnaia knizhka*, 54–55.

116. Glagoleva, *Dream and Reality*, 25–27.

117. Labzina, *Days of a Russian Noblewoman*, 129.

118. Natal'ia Pushkareva, "Russian Noblewomen's Education in the Home as Revealed in Late Eighteenth- and Early Nineteenth-Century Memoirs," in Rosslyn, *Women and Gender*, 111–28.

119. Bisha, "The Promise of Patriarchy," 63.

120. Joe Andrew, "The Benevolent Matriarch in Elena Gan and Mar'ia Zhukova," in *Women in Russian Culture: Projections and Self-Perceptions*, ed. Rosalind Marsh (New York: Berghahn Books, 1998), 63. For a range of viewpoints on domestic ideology in the nineteenth century, see Diana Greene, "Mid-Nineteenth-Century Domestic Ideology in Russia," in Marsh, *Women in Russian Culture*, 78–97, and Barbara Alpern Engel, *Women in Russia, 1700–2000* (New York: Cambridge University Press, 2004), 35–47.

121. Sofia Khvoshchinskaia, "Reminiscences of Institute Life," in *Russia through Women's Eyes: Autobiographies from Tsarist Russia*, ed. Toby W. Clyman and Judith Vowles (New Haven, CT: Yale University Press, 1996), 87.

122. Ibid., 89.

123. Ibid., 88. See also S. A. Zakrevskaia, *Institutka: Roman v pis'makh*, *Otechestvennaia zapiski* 19, no. 12 (1841): 200–213.

124. Belousov, "Institutka v russkoi literature," 77–99.

125. Susan Stanford Friedman, "Women's Autobiographical Selves: Theory and Practice," in *The Private Self: Theory and Practice in Women's Autobiographical Writings*, ed. Shari Benstock (Chapel Hill: University of North Carolina Press, 1988), 34–62; Felicity Nussbaum, "Eighteenth-Century Women's Autobiographical Commonplaces," in Benstock, *The Private Self*, 147–72; Catriona Kelly, *A History of Russian Women's Writing: 1820–1992* (Oxford, 1994), 1–16; Toby W. Clyman and Judith Vowles, Introduction to Clyman and Vowles, *Russia through Women's Eyes*, 1–46.

126. Fonvizin, *Nedorosl'*, 118.

127. Voltaire to Catherine II (March 12, 1772), in Lentin, *Voltaire and Catherine*, 131–32.

128. Catherine II to Voltaire (April 14, 1772), in Lentin, *Voltaire and Catherine*, 135.

129. Fonvizin, *Nedorosl'*, 119.

CONCLUSION

1. For the British context, see Cody, *Birthing the Nation*, 22.

2. Anisimov, *Zhenshchiny*, 335–36.

3. *PSZ*, 1, vol. 16, no. 12103 (1764).

4. Wortman, "Russian Empress as Mother." In this essay, Wortman analyzes the empresses who followed Catherine, none of whom acted as rulers.

5. While Wortman includes many examples of Catherine's emphasis on "maternal love" for the fatherland and for her subjects, I think there is opportunity to expand upon his analyses, which tend to focus on the tropes he identifies as "Minerva" and "Legislatrix." See Wortman, *Scenarios of Power*, 110–42.

6. Zybelin, *Slovo o sposobe*, 20.

7. Quoted in Black, *Citizens for the Fatherland*, 162.

8. Thŷret, "'Blessed Is the Tsaritsa's Womb,'" 479–96; Engel, *Women in Russia*, 6–7; Wortman, "Russian Empress as Mother."

9. Kevin J. McKenna, "Empress behind the Mask: The Persona of Mme. Vsiakaia Vsiachina in Catherine the Great's Periodical Essays on Morals and Manners," *Neophilologus* 7 (1990): 1–11.

10. Bakherakht, *O neumerennosti v liubostrastii*, unpaginated preface.

11. Kreizel', *Nastavlenie nachinaiushchim*, unpaginated preface.

12. Peken, *Novyi domashnii lechebnik*, v.

13. Jürgen Habermas, "Introduction: Preliminary Demarcation of a Type of Bourgeois Public Sphere," in *The Structural Transformation of the Public Sphere: An Inquiry into a Category of Bourgeois Society* (Cambridge, MA: MIT Press, 1989), 1–26; Craig Calhoun, Introduction to *Habermas and the Public Sphere*, ed. Craig Calhoun (Cambridge, MA: MIT Press, 1996), 1–48; Keith Michael Baker, *Inventing the French Revolution: Essays on French Political Culture in the Eighteenth Century* (New York: Cambridge University Press, 1990), 168.

14. Harvey Mitchell has shown that physicians in eighteenth-century France justified their interventions in peasant villages through what he terms an "ideology of rationality and control." Peasants lacked both of these, physicians argued, requiring intervention from above to improve their habits and health. Harvey Mitchell, "Rationality and Control in French Eighteenth-Century Medical Views of the Peasantry," *Comparative Studies in Society and History* 21 (January 1979): 82–112.

15. Bruno Latour, *Science in Action: How to Follow Scientists and Engineers through Society* (Cambridge, MA: Harvard University Press, 1988), 1–20.

16. Kovrigina et al., "Meditsina i zdravookhranenie," 77; Bakherakht, "Nechto o iskusnykh," 425–26.

17. Alexander, *Bubonic Plague*, 36–37; Andreas Renner, "The Concept of the Scientific Revolution and the History of Science in Russia," in *Eighteenth-Century Russia: Society, Culture, Economy; Papers from the VII International Conference on the Study Group*

of Eighteenth-Century Russia, Wittenberg 2004, ed. Roger Bartlett and Gabriela Lehmann-Carli (Berlin, 2007), 357–72. For other national contexts, see Thomas Broman, "Rethinking Professionalization: Theory, Practice, and Professional Ideology in Eighteenth-Century German Medicine," *Journal of Modern History* 67, no. 4 (December 1995): 835–72; and Philip Rieder and Micheline Louis-Courvoisier, "Enlightened Physicians: Setting Out on an Elite Medical Career in the Second Half of the Eighteenth Century," *Bulletin of the History of Medicine* 84, no. 4 (Winter 2010): 578–606.

18. Rieder and Louis-Courvoisier, "Enlightened Physicians," 604.

19. Renner, "Concept of the Scientific Revolution," 365.

20. Wakefield, *Disordered Police State*.

21. Quoted in Valerie Kivelson, "Merciful Father, Impersonal State: Russian Autocracy in Comparative Perspective," *Modern Asian Studies* 31, no. 3 (July 1997): 657.

22. Maksimovich-Ambodik, *Iskusstvo povivaniia*, 1:ii–iii.

23. Ibid., 1:vii.

24. Angus McLaren, "A Doctor in the House: Medicine and Private Morality in France, 1800–1850," *Feminist Studies* 2, no. 2/3 (1975): 39.

25. A few examples: N. M. Maksimovich-Ambodik, "De hepate humano" (MD diss., University of Strassburg, 1775); Maksimovich-Ambodik, *Anatomiko-fiziologicheskii slovar'* (St. Petersburg, 1783); Maksimovich-Ambodik, *Emvlemy i simvoly izbrannye* (St. Petersburg, 1788); RGIA, f. 758, op. 17, d. 4.

26. Mary Louise Pratt, *Imperial Eyes: Travel Writing and Transculturation* (New York: Routledge, 1992), 6.

27. N. I. Novikov, "Retsept dlia g. Bezrassudka," in *Sbornik materialov k izucheniiu istorii russkoi zhurnalistiki*, ed. B. P. Koz'min (Moscow, 1952), 1:53–54. For a country that did not even establish a university-level medical faculty until 1763, it is remarkable that the figure of the physician entered political and cultural life. Unlike the mockery of doctors one finds in eighteenth-century literary works like *Tristram Shandy* (Dr. Slop, a man-midwife whom Sterne portrays as a quack) and *Candide* (physicians seen as greedy tricksters) or the outright hostility and rejection espoused by Rousseau, the physician as authority was confirmed by empress and public intellectuals alike in Russia.

28. Belousov, "Institutka v russkoi literature," 77–99.

29. Zakrevskaia, *Institutka*, 200–213.

30. Catherine's letter reprinted in *SIRIO* 13 (1874): 339.

31. Radishchev, *Journey*, 374.

32. Levitt, *Early Modern Russian Letters*, 281; Wirtschafter, "Religion and Enlightenment."

33. Levitt, *Early Modern Russian Letters*, 290.

34. RGIA, f. 1294, op. 1, sv. 7, dd. 5, 19.

35. RGIA, f. 758, op. 17, d. 4, ll. 12, 42–43.

Bibliography

ARCHIVES AND ABBREVIATIONS

MIIMVD   *Materialy dlia istorii Imperatorskogo Moskovskogo vospitatel'nogo doma*
PSZ   *Polnoe sobranie zakonov Rossiiskoi imperii*
RGIA   Rossiiskii gosudarstvennyi istoricheskii arkhiv (Russian State Historical Archive)
        Fond 730: Komissiia ob uchrezhdenii narodnykh uchilishche
        Fond 758: Opekunskii sovet vedomstva uchrezhdenii Imperatritsy Marii
        Fond 1294: Meditsinskii sovet pri Ministerstvo vnutrennikh del
SIRIO   *Sbornik Imperatorskogo Russkogo istoricheskogo obshchestva*
TsGIASPb   Tsentral'nyi gosudarstvennyi istoricheskii arkhiv Sankt-Peterburga (Central State Historical Archive of the City of St. Petersburg)
        Fond 2: Vospitatel'noe Obshchestvo Blagorodnykh Devits. Petersburg–Petrograd, 1764–1918.

Note: TsGIASPb is the local archive for the city of St. Petersburg and should not be confused with RGIA, the central historical archive for the imperial Russian state. Before the collapse of the Soviet Union, RGIA was known by its previous name, TsGIA. For those who recall the names of the archives during the Soviet era, this can create some confusion. When this book cites TsGIASPb, it is not a mistaken reference to the state archive but a deliberate reference to the lesser-known city archive of St. Petersburg, which at the time of publication was known officially as TsGIASPb.

PRIMARY SOURCES

Anna, Empress of Russia. "Kopiia s Ukaza v Moskvu k Doktoru Meditsiny Bliumentrostu ob otyskanii babki." In *Istoriia Meditsinyi v Rossii*, edited by V. M. Rikhter, 3:93–95. Moscow, 1814.

[Bakherakht, A. G.] "Nechto o iskusnykh i nesmyslennykh vrachakh." *Sankt-Peterburgskii vestnik* (December 1779): 425–26.

———. *O neumerennosti v liubostrastii oboikh polov*. St. Petersburg, 1779.

———. *Sobranie raznykh poleznykh lekarstv na raznyia bolezni s retseptamy*. St. Petersburg, 1779.

Barsov, A. A. *Azbuka tserkovnaia i grazhdanskaia s kratkami primechaniiami o pravopisanii*. Moscow, 1768.

[————.] *Karmannaia, ili Pamiatnaia knizhka dlia molodykh devits: Soderzhashchaia v sebe nastavleniia prekrasnomu polu, s pokazaniem, v chem dolzhny sostoiat' uprazhneniia ikh*. Moscow, 1784.

Bel'gar'd, Zh. B. [Jean-Baptiste Morvan, l'abbé de Bellegarde]. *Sovershennoe vospitanie detei*. St. Petersburg, 1747.

Bentham, Jeremy. *Panopticon; or the Inspection-House*. 1787. Reprinted in *The Panopticon Writings*, edited by Miran Bozovic, 29–95. London, 1995.

Betskoi, I. I. *Kratkoe nastavlenie, vybrannoe iz luchshikh Avtorov s nekotorymi fizicheskimi primechaniami o vospitanii detei ot rozhdeniia ikh do iunoshestva*. 1766. Reprinted in *Russkaia pedagogika v glavneishikh ee predstaviteliakh*, edited by M. I. Demkov, 12:56–76. Moscow, 1898.

————. "Pis'ma Ivana Ivanovicha Betskogo k vospitannitsam Vospitatel'nago Obshchestva blagorodnykh devits." 1770. Reprinted in *Imperatorskoe vospitatel'noe obshchestvo blagorodnykh devits: Istoricheskii ocherk, 1764–1914*, edited by N. P. Cherepnin, 3:102–3. St. Petersburg, 1914.

————. *Uchrezhdenie osoblivago uchilishcha pri Voskresenskom Novodevich'em Monastyre dlia vospitaniia maloletnykh devushek*. 1768. Reprinted in *Imperatorskoe vospitatel'noe obshchestvo blagorodnykh devits: Istoricheskii ocherk, 1764–1914*, edited by N. P. Cherepnin, 3:52–55. St. Petersburg, 1914.

————. *Ustav vospitanii dvukh sot blagorodnykh devits*. 1765. Reprinted in *Imperatorskoe vospitatel'noe obshchestvo blagorodnykh devits: Istoricheskii ocherk, 1764–1914*, edited by N. P. Cherepnin, 3:31–34. St. Petersburg, 1914.

Bliumentrost', L. L. "Izvestitel'noe donesenie Imperatritse Anne Ioannovne ot Doktora Bliumentrosta ob iskusstve babki." In *Istoriia Meditsinyi v Rossii*, edited by V. M. Rikhter, 3:95–97. Moscow, 1814.

Bolotov, A. T. *Detskaia filosofiia, ili nravouchitel'nye razgovory mezhdu odnoiu gospozheiu i eia det'mi sochinennye dlia pospeshestvovaniia istinnoi pol'ze molodykh liudei*. Moscow, 1776.

————. "Iz neizdannogo literaturnogo naslediia Bolotova." Edited by I. Morozov and A. Kucherov. *Literaturnoe nasledtsvo* 10 (1933): 180–89.

Bud'e de Vil'mer, P. [Pierre Boudier de Villemert]. *Drug zhenshchin, ili iskrennee nastavlenie dlia povedeniia prekrasnogo pola*. Moscow, 1765.

Buffon, Georges Louis Leclerc. *Natural History General and Particular, by the Count De Buffon*. Translated by William Smellie. London, 1785.

Bukvar' dlia upotrebleniia rossiiskago iunoshestva. Moscow, 1780.

Cadogan, William. *An Essay upon Nursing, and the Management of Children from Their Birth to Three Years of Age. By a Physician in a Letter to One of the Governors of the Foundling Hospital. Published by Order of the General Committee*. London, 1773.

———— [Vil'gel'm Kadogan]. *Sredstvo kakim obrazom bez povrezhdeniia zdorov'ia detei vospityvat' s nachala ikh rozhdeniia do okonchaniia tret'iago goda ikh vozrasta*. Moscow, 1789.

Cathcart, Charles Shaw. Lord Cathcart to Lord Viscount Weymouth. *SIRIO* 12 (1873): 369–70.

Catherine II. *Documents of Catherine the Great: The Correspondence with Voltaire and the Instruction of 1767, in the English text of 1768.* Edited by William F. Reddaway. New York: Cambridge University Press, 1931.

———. "Dva sobstvennoruchnyia chernovyia pisma Ekateriny II k vospitannitse Smolnago Monastyra A. Levshinoi, vposledstvii kniagine Cherkasskoi." *SIRIO* 13 (1874): 338–41.

———. "The Empress and the Philosopher: Catherine II—Voltaire Correspondence." In *Russian Women, 1698–1917: Experience and Expression; An Anthology of Sources,* edited by Robin Bisha, Jehanne M. Gheith, Christine Holden, and William G. Wagner, 165–68. Bloomington: Indiana University Press, 2002.

———. *Instruktsiia Kniaziu Nikolaiu Ivanovichu Saltykovu pri naznachenii ego k vospitaniiu Velikikh Kniazei.* 1784. Reprinted as *O vospitanii i obrazovanii vnukov.* St. Petersburg, 1994.

———. *Izbrannye sochineniia.* St. Petersburg, 1894.

———. *The Memoirs of Catherine the Great.* Edited by Dominique Maroger. Translated by Moura Budberg. New York: Macmillan, 1961.

———. *Nakaz Eia Imperatorskago Velichestva Ekateriny Vtoryia Samoderzhitsy Vserossiiskiia dannyi Komissii o Sochinenii Proekta Novago Ulozheniia.* 1767. Reprint, St. Petersburg, 1893.

———. *Rossiiskaia azbuka dlia obucheniia iunoshestva chteniiu.* St. Petersburg, n.d.

———. *Zapiski pervoi chasti.* St. Petersburg, 1782.

Cherepnin, N. P., ed. *Imperatorskoe vospitatel'noe obshchestvo blagorodnykh devits: Istoricheskii ocherk, 1764–1914.* St. Petersburg, 1914.

Coxe, William. *Travels into Poland, Russia, Sweden, and Denmark: Interspersed with Historical Relations and Political Inquiries.* 1785. Reprint, New York: Arno Press, 1971.

Dashkova, Ekaterina. *The Memoirs of Princess Dashkova.* Translated by Kiril Fitzlyon. Durham, NC: Duke University Press, 1995.

———. "O smysle slova vospitanie." *Sobesednik liubitelei rossiiskogo slova* 2 (1783): 12–28.

Diderot, Denis. "Encyclopedia." Excerpt reprinted in *The Enlightenment,* edited by Dena Goodman and Kathleen Anne Wellman, 14–20. Boston: Houghton Mifflin, 2004.

Dimsdale, Elizabeth. *An English Lady at the Court of Catherine the Great.* Edited by A. G. Cross. Cambridge, UK, 1989.

Dmitrii. "Mudrye sovety roditel'iam." In *Russkaia pedagogika v glavneishikh eia predstaviteliakh,* edited by M. I. Demkov, 12:45–46. Moscow, 1898.

———. "O dolge materei." In *Russkaia pedagogika v glavneishikh eia predstaviteliakh,* edited by M. I. Demkov, 12:46–47. Moscow, 1898.

Drashuvov, V., ed. *Materialy dlia istorii Imperatorskago moskovskago vospitatel'nago doma.* Moscow, 1863–68.

Erasmus, I. F. *Nastavlenie kak kazhdomu cheloveku voobshche v razsuzhdenie diety, a osoblivo zhenshchinam v beremennosti, v rodakh i posle rodov sebia soderzhat' nadlezhit.* Moscow, 1762.

[Felbiger, Johann Ignaz.] *O dolzhnostiakh cheloveka i grazhdanina; Kniga, k chteniiu opre-delennaia v narodnykh gorodskikh uchilishchakh.* Translated by Theodor Iankovich de Mirievo. St. Petersburg, 1783.

Fonvizin, D. I. *Nedorosl'.* Hertfordshire, UK, 1965.

———. "Primechanie izdatel'ei zhurnala." Reprinted in *Sbornik materialov k izucheniiu istorii russkoi zhurnalistiki,* edited by B. P. Koz'min, 1:70. Moscow, 1952.

Gorn, Iogan van der [Johan von Hoorn]. *Povival'naia babka ili Dostovernoe nastavlenie chrez voprosy i otvety.* Translated by I. Pagenkampf. Moscow, 1764.

Gorokhovskii, M. Introduction to *Lechebnik ili Nastavleniia, otnositel'nyia k deiatel'noi vrachebnoi nauke,* by A. fon Shterk [Anton von Störck]. Translated by M. Gorokhovskii. Moscow, 1789.

Gulen, Zhan, and Ansel'm Lui Bernar Zhurden. [Jean Goulin and Anselm Louis Bernard Jourdain]. *Damskoi vrach v trekh chastiakh, soderzhashchikh v sebe nuzhnie pre-dokhraneniia.* Translated by K. Mukovnikov. Moscow, 1793.

[Iankovich De Mirievo, Theodor]. *Pravila dlia uchashchikhsia v narodnykh uchilishchakh, izdannyia po Vysochaishemu poveleniiu tsarstvuiushchei Imperatritsy Ekateriny Vtoryia.* St. Petersburg, 1786.

Iunosti chestnoe zertsalo ili pokazanie k zhiteiskomu obkhozhdeniiu. Sobrannoe ot raznykh avtorov. St. Petersburg, 1717.

Khvoshchinskaia, Sofia. "Reminiscences of Institute Life." In *Russia through Women's Eyes: Autobiographies from Tsarist Russia,* edited by Toby W. Clyman and Judith Vowles, 76–108. New Haven, CT: Yale University Press, 1996.

Kniazhnin, Ia. B. "Misfortune from a Coach." In *The Literature of Eighteenth-Century Russia: An Anthology of Russian Literary Materials of the Age of Classicism and the Enlightenment from the Reign of Peter the Great, 1689–1725, to the Reign of Alexander I, 1801–1825,* edited and translated by Harold B. Segel, 2:374–93. New York: E. P. Dutton, 1967.

Kolesov, V. V., and V. V. Rozhdestvenskaia, eds. *Domostroi.* St. Petersburg, 1994.

Kondoidi, P. Z. Documents Related to Midwifery Reform. 1754–57. Reprinted in Ia. Chistovich, *Ocherki iz istorii russkikh meditsinskikh uchrezhdenii XVIII stoletiia,* 137–55. St. Petersburg, 1870.

Kornilov, I. P., ed. *Sbornik materialov dlia istorii prosveshcheniia v Rossii: Izvlechennykh iz Arkhiva Ministerstva narodnago prosveshcheniia.* Vol. 1. St. Petersburg, 1893.

Koz'min, E. P., and V. D. Koz'mina, eds. *Sbornik materialov k izuchenii istorii russkoi zhurnalistiki.* Moscow, 1952.

Kreizel', I. *Nastavlenie nachinaiushchim uprazhniat'sia v povival'nom iskusstve, sostiashchee v dvukh chastiakh.* Moscow, 1792.

Kurganov, N. G. *Pismovnik* [sic] *soderzhashchii v sebe nauku rossiiskago iazyka so mnogim prisovokupleniem raznogo uchebnago i poleznago veshchesloviia.* St. Petersburg, 1769.

Labzina, Anna. *Days of a Russian Noblewoman: The Memories of Anna Labzina, 1758–1821.* Edited and translated by Gary Marker and Rachel May. DeKalb: Northern Illinois University Press, 2001.

Lokk, Dzh. [John Locke]. *O vospitanii detei.* Moscow, 1759.

Lomonosov, M. V. "O sokhranenii i razmnozhenii rossiiskogo naroda." In *Polnoe sobranie sochineniia*, edited by S. I. Vavilov, 6:384–97. Moscow, 1952.

Maksimovich-Ambodik, N. M. *Anatomiko-fiziologicheskii slovar'*. St. Petersburg, 1783.

———. "De hepate humano." MD diss., University of Strassburg, 1775.

———. *Emvlemy i simvoly izbrannye*. St. Petersburg, 1788.

———. *Iskusstvo povivaniia ili nauka o babich'em dele: Na piat' chastei razdelennaia i mnogimi risunkami snabdennaia*. St. Petersburg, 1784–86.

Nelidova, E. I. "E. I. Nelidova." *Russkii arkhiv* 2 (1873): 2160–72.

Novikov, N. I. *Detskoe chtenie dlia serdtsa i razuma*. Moscow, 1785–89.

———. *Izbrannye sochineniia*. Edited by G. P. Makogonenko. Moscow, 1951.

———. "Retsept dlia g. Bezrassudka." In *Sbornik materialov k izucheniiu istorii russkoi zhurnalistiki*, edited by B. P. Koz'min, 1:53–54. Moscow, 1952.

Novyi rossiiskii bukvar' s kratkimi nravoucheniiami i povestiami. St. Petersburg, 1775.

"O pervykh estestvennykh prikliucheniiakh novorozhdennogo cheloveka." *Sankt-peterburgskie vrachebnye vedomosti* 20 (1792): 152–55.

Peken, Kh. *Domashnii lechebnik*. Moscow, 1765.

Peken, M. Kh. *Novyi domashnii lechebnik*. Moscow, 1796.

Plavil'shchikov, P. A. "Teatr." *Zritel': Ezhemesiachnoe izdanie* 2 (June 1792): 121–45.

Polnoe sobranie zakonov Rossiiskoi Imperii, poveleniem Gosudaria Imperatora Nikolaia Pav-lovicha sostavlennoe, sobranie pervoe s 1649 po 12 Dekabria 1925 goda, 1-aia seriia. St. Petersburg, 1830.

Pouncy, Carolyn Johnston, ed. and trans. *The Domostroi: Rules for Russian Households in the Time of Ivan the Terrible*. Ithaca, NY: Cornell University Press, 1994.

Radishchev, Alexander. "Beseda o tom, chto est' syn otechestva." *Beseduiushchii grazh-danin: Ezhemesiachnoe izdanie* 3 (1789): 308–24.

———. *A Journey from St. Petersburg to Moscow*. In *The Literature of Eighteenth-Century Russia: An Anthology of Russian Literary Materials in the Age of Classicism and the Enlightenment from the Reign of Peter the Great, 1689–1725, to the Reign of Alexander I, 1801–1825*, edited and translated by Harold B. Segel, 1:352–92. New York: E. P. Dut-ton, 1967.

Rikhter, V. M., ed. *Istoriia meditsiny v Rossii*. Moscow, 1814.

Rossiiskaia azbuka dlia obucheniia malen'kikh mal'chikov. Moscow, 1795.

Rost, Kh. *Derevenskoi vrachebnik, ili legkoi sposob pol'zovat'sia nedostatochnym liudiam ot vsiakikh boleznei prostymi ili domashnimi veshchami, ne imeia nadobnosti v lekarstvakh aptekarskikh*. Moscow, 1793.

Rousseau, Jean-Jacques. *Emile; or, On Education*. Translated by Allan Bloom. New York: Basic Books, 1979.

Rzhevskaia [née Alymova], G. "Pamiatnye zapiski Glafiry Ivanovny Rzhevskoi." *Russkii arkhiv* 9, no. 1 (1871): 1–52.

Shcherbatov, M. M. *On the Corruption of Morals in Russia*. Edited and translated by Antony Lentin. New York: Cambridge University Press, 1969.

Smellie, William. *A Set of Anatomical Tables with Explanations, and an Abridgement of the Practice of Midwifery; With a View to Illustrate a Treatise on that Subject, and a Collec-tion of Cases*. Edinburgh, 1780.

Soserot, Lui Sebat'en. [Sauserotte, Louis Sebastien]. *Kratkoe ispytanie mnogikh zakos-nel'nykh mnenii i zloupotreblenii do beremennykh zhenshchin, rodil'nits i novorozhden-nykh mladentsov.* Translated by N. M. Maksimovich-Ambodik. St. Petersburg, 1781.

Sumarokov, A. P. *Nastavlenie mladentsam: Moral', istoriia i geografiia.* St. Petersburg, 1774.

Syreishchikov, E. B. *Rech' o pol'ze nravoucheniia pri vospitanii iunoshestva.* Moscow, 1783.

Thomas, Antoine-Léonard. "Essay on the Character, Morals, and Mind of Women across the Centuries (1772)." In *The Enlightenment,* edited by Dena Goodman and Kathleen Wellman, 162–65. Boston: Houghton Mifflin, 2004.

Tissot, Simon Andre. *Onanizm: Rassuzhdenie o bolezniakh, proizkhodiashchikh ot malakii.* Translated by A. G. Bakherakht. Moscow, 1793.

Voltaire [François-Marie Arouet] and Catherine II, Empress of Russia. *Voltaire and Catherine the Great: Selected Correspondence.* Edited and translated by A. Lentin. Cambridge, UK, 1974.

Wollstonecraft, Mary. *A Vindication of the Rights of Woman, with Strictures on Political and Moral Subjects.* London, 1796.

———. "A Vindication of the Rights of Woman." Excerpt in *The Enlightenment,* edited by Dena Goodman and Kathleen Wellman, 173–78. Boston: Houghton Mifflin, 2004.

Zakrevskaia, S. A. *Institutka: Roman v pis'makh. Otechestvennaia zapiski* 19, no. 12 (1841): 200–307.

Zybelin, S. G. *Slovo o pravil'nom vospitanii s mladenchestva.* Moscow, 1775.

———. *Slovo o sposobe, kak predupredit' mozhno ne malovazhnuiu mezhdu prochimi med-lennago umnozheniia naroda.* Moscow, 1780.

SECONDARY SOURCES

Aldis, Janet. *Madame Geoffrin: Her Salon and Her Times, 1750–1777.* New York: J. P. Put-nam's Sons, 1905.

Aleksandrova, N. V. "Spetsifiki vospitaniia i obrazovaniia rossiiskago dvorianstva v poslednei chetverti XVIII veka." *Vestnik Cheliabinskogo Universiteta* 1, no. 1 (1998): 26–30.

Alexander, John T. *Bubonic Plague in Early Modern Russia: Public Health and Urban Dis-aster.* Baltimore: Johns Hopkins University Press, 1980.

———. *Catherine the Great: Life and Legend.* New York: Oxford University Press, 1989.

Andrew, Joe. "The Benevolent Matriarch in Elena Gan and Mar'ia Zhukova." In *Women and Russian Culture: Projections and Self-Perceptions,* edited by Rosalind Marsh, 60–77. New York: Berghahn Books, 1998.

Anisimov, Evgenii. "Petr I: Rozhdenie imperii." *Voprosy istorii,* no. 7 (1989): 3–20.

———. *Zhenshchiny na rossiiskom prestole.* St. Petersburg, 1998.

Ariès, Philippe. *Centuries of Childhood: A Social History of Family Life.* New York: Alfred A. Knopf, 1962.

Armstrong, David. "Bodies of Knowledge/Knowledge of Bodies." In *Reassessing Fou-cault: Power, Medicine, and the Body,* edited by Colin Jones and Roy Porter, 17–27. New York: Routledge, 1994.

Aurova, N. N. "Idei prosveshcheniia v pervom kadetskom korpuse (konets XVIII–pervaia chetvert' XIX)." *Vestnik Moskovskogo Universiteta, Seriia 8: Istoriia*, no. 1 (1996): 34–42.

Babushkina, A. P. *Istoriia russkoi detskoi literatury*. Moscow, 1948.

Baker, Keith Michael. *Inventing the French Revolution: Essays on French Political Culture in the Eighteenth Century*. New York: Cambridge University Press, 1990.

Banks, Amanda Carson. *Birth Chairs, Midwives, and Medicine*. Jackson: University Press of Mississippi, 1999.

Barran, Thomas. *Russia Reads Rousseau, 1762–1825*. Evanston, IL: Northwestern University Press, 2002.

Belousov, A. F. "Institutka v russkoi literature." *Tynianovskii sbornik: Tynianovskie chteniia*, edited by M. O. Chudakova, 4:77–99. Riga, 1990.

Berdyshev, A. P. *Andrei Timofeevich Bolotov: Vydaiushchiisia deiatel' nauki i kul'tury, 1738–1833*. Moscow, 1988.

Berenguier, Nadine. "The Politics of Happy Matrimony: Cerfvol's *La Gamologie ou l'Education des Filles Destinées au Mariage*." *Studies in Eighteenth-Century Culture* 29, no. 1 (2000): 173–200.

Berezina, V. G., and A. V. Zapadov. *Istoriia russkoi zhurnalistiki XVIII–XIX vekov*. Moscow, 1973.

Bisha, Robin. "The Promise of Patriarchy: Marriage in Eighteenth-Century Russia." PhD diss., Indiana University, 1994.

Bisha, Robin, Jehanne M. Gheith, Christine Holden, and William G. Wagner, eds. *Russian Women, 1698–1917: Experience and Expression; An Anthology of Sources*. Bloomington: Indiana University Press, 2002.

Black, J. L. *Citizens for the Fatherland: Education, Educators, and Pedagogical Ideals in Eighteenth-Century Russia*. Boulder, CO: East European Quarterly, 1979.

Bloch, Jean. "Discourses of Female Education in the Writings of Eighteenth-Century French Women." In *Women, Gender, and the Enlightenment*, edited by Sarah Knott and Barbara Taylor, 243–58. New York: Palgrave Macmillan, 2005.

Bloch, Ruth. "American Feminine Ideals in Transition: The Rise of Moral Motherhood, 1785–1815." *Feminist Studies* 4, no. 2 (June 1978): 100–26.

Block, Gisela. "Racism and Sexism in Nazi Germany: Motherhood, Compulsory Sterilization, and the State." In *When Biology Became Destiny: Women in Weimar and Nazi Germany*, edited by Renate Bridenthal, Atina Grossmann, and Marion A. Kaplan, 271–96. New York: Monthly Review Press, 1984.

Blum, Carol. *Strength in Numbers: Population, Reproduction, and Power in Eighteenth-Century France*. Baltimore: Johns Hopkins University Press, 2002.

Blyakher, L. J. *History of Embryology in Russia from the Middle of the Eighteenth Century to the Middle of the Nineteenth Century*. Washington, DC: Smithsonian Institution, 1982.

Bochkarev, V. N. "Vrachebnoe delo i narodnoe prizrenie v Rossii XVIII veka: Po materialam Zakonodatel'noi Komissii 1767 goda." In *Sbornik statei v chest' Matveia Kuz'micha Liubavskago*, 442–89. Petrograd, 1917.

Bonner, Thomas Neville. *Becoming a Physician: Medical Education in Britain, France, Germany, and the United States, 1750–1945*. New York: Oxford University Press, 1995.

Boucé, Paul-Gabriel. "Imagination, Pregnant Women, and Monsters in Eighteenth-Century England and France." In *Sexual Underworlds of the Enlightenment*, edited by G. R. Rousseau and Roy Porter, 86–100. Chapel Hill: University of North Carolina Press, 1988.

Broman, Thomas. "Rethinking Professionalization: Theory, Practice, and Professional Ideology in Eighteenth-Century German Medicine." *Journal of Modern History* 67, no. 4 (December 1995): 835–72.

Brower, Daniel R., and Edward J. Lazzerini, eds. *Russia's Orient: Imperial Borderlands and Peoples, 1700–1917*. Bloomington: Indiana University Press, 1997.

Brumfield, William Craft. *Landmarks of Russian Architecture: A Photographic Survey*. Amsterdam, 1997.

Calhoun, Craig. Introduction to *Habermas and the Public Sphere*, edited by Craig Calhoun, 1–48. Cambridge, MA: MIT Press, 1996.

Calvert, Karin Lee Fishbeck. *Children in the House: The Material Culture of Early Childhood, 1600–1900*. Boston: Northeastern University Press, 1992.

Campbell, Linda. "Wet-Nurses in Early Modern England: Some Evidence from the Townshend Archive." *Medical History* 33 (July 1989): 360–70.

Cherepnin, N. P. *Imperatorskoe vospitatel'noe obshchestvo blagorodnykh devits: Istoricheskii ocherk, 1764–1914*. St. Petersburg, 1914.

Chernyaeva, Natalia. "Childcare Manuals and Construction of Motherhood in Russia, 1890–1990." PhD diss., University of Iowa, 2009.

Chistovich, Ia. *Ocherki iz istorii russkikh meditsinskikh uchrezhdenii XVIII stoletiia*. St. Petersburg, 1870.

Chuvashev, I. V. "Pedagogicheskie idei v russkoi khudozhestvennoi literature XVIII v." *Sovetskaia pedagogika* 7 (1944): 47–53.

Clements, Barbara Evans, Rebecca Friedman, and Dan Healey, eds. *Russian Masculinities in History and Culture*. New York: Palgrave, 2002.

Clyman, Toby W., and Judith Vowles. Introduction to *Russia through Women's Eyes: Autobiographies from Tsarist Russia*, edited by Toby W. Clyman and Judith Vowles. New Haven, CT: Yale University Press, 1996.

Cody, Lisa Forman. *Birthing the Nation: Sex, Science, and the Conception of Eighteenth-Century Britons*. New York: Oxford University Press, 2005.

Cohen, Michèle. "'To Think, to Compare, to Combine, to Methodise': Girls' Education in Enlightenment Britain." In *Women, Gender, and Enlightenment*, edited by Sarah Knott and Barbara Taylor, 224–42. New York: Palgrave Macmillan, 2005.

Costlow, Jane T., Stephanie Sandler, and Judith Vowles, eds. *Sexuality and the Body in Russian Culture*. Stanford, CA: Stanford University Press, 1993.

Cracraft, James, and Daniel Rowland. *Architectures of Russian Identity: 1500–Present*. Ithaca, NY: Cornell University Press, 2003.

Cross, A. G. "The Russian *Banya* in the Descriptions of Foreign and Russian Artists." *Oxford Slavonic Papers* 24 (1991): 13–38.

Curran, Andrew. "The Faces of Eighteenth-Century Monstrosity." *Eighteenth-Century Life* 21 (May 1997): 1–3.

Davidoff, Leonore, and Catherine Hall. *Family Fortunes: Men and Women of the English Middle Class, 1780–1850.* Chicago: University of Chicago Press, 1987.

Dekker, Rudolf. *Childhood, Memory, and Autobiography in Holland.* London, 2000.

De Madariaga, Isabel. *Russia in the Age of Catherine the Great.* New Haven, CT: Yale University Press, 1981.

Dixon, Simon. *Catherine the Great.* New York: Ecco, 2009.

Dlugach, R. V. "Deti i knigi, 1770–1860." In *Materialy po istorii russkoi detskoi literatury, 1750–1855,* edited by A. K. Pokrovskaia and N. V. Chekhov, 1:265–301. Moscow, 1927.

Dmitrii Grigor'evich Levitskii, 1735–1822: Katalog vremennoi vystavki Gosudarstvennogo Russkogo Muzei. Leningrad, 1987.

Donegan, Jane B. *Women and Men Midwives: Medicine, Morality, and Misogyny in Early America.* Westport, CT: Greenwood Press, 1978.

Douthwaite, Julia V. *The Wild Girl, Natural Man, and the Monster: Dangerous Experiments in the Age of Enlightenment.* Chicago: University of Chicago Press, 2002.

Downs, Laura Lee. *Childhood in the Promised Land: Working-Class Movements and the Colonies de Vacances in France, 1880–1960.* Durham, NC: Duke University Press, 2002.

Drashuvov, V., ed. *Materialy dlia istorii Imperatorskago Moskovskago Vospitatel'nago Doma.* Moscow, 1863–68.

Duden, Barbara. *The Woman beneath the Skin: A Doctor's Patients in Eighteenth-Century Germany.* Cambridge, MA: Harvard University Press, 1998.

Dukes, Paul. *Catherine the Great and the Russian Nobility: A Study Based on the Materials of the Legislative Commission of 1767.* Cambridge, MA: Harvard University Press, 1967.

Ekloff, Ben. *Russian Peasant Schools: Officialdom, Village Culture, and Popular Pedagogy, 1861–1914.* Berkeley: University of California Press, 1986.

Elias, Norbert. *The Civilizing Process: The History of Manners.* Translated by Edmund Jephcott. New York: Urizen Books, 1978.

Engel, Barbara Alpern. *Women in Russia, 1700–2000.* New York: Cambridge University Press, 2004.

Engelstein, Laura. *The Keys to Happiness: Sex and the Search for Modernity in Fin-de-Siècle Russia.* Ithaca, NY: Cornell University Press, 1992.

Epp, George K. *The Educational Policies of Catherine II: The Era of Enlightenment in Russia.* New York: Peter Lang, 1984.

Farrow, Lee. *Between Clan and Crown: The Struggle to Define Noble Property Rights in Imperial Russia.* Newark, DE: University of Delaware Press, 2004.

Figes, Orlando. *Natasha's Dance: A Cultural History of Russia.* New York: Metropolitan Books, 2002.

Fildes, Valerie. *Wet Nursing: A History from Antiquity to the Present.* London, 1988.

Filippini, Nadia. "The Church, the State, and Childbirth: The Midwife in Italy during the Eighteenth Century." In *The Art of Midwifery: Early Modern Midwives in Europe,* edited by Hilary Marland, 153–75. New York: Routledge, 1993.

Findlen, Paula. "Women on the Verge of Science: Aristocratic Women and Knowledge in Early Eighteenth-Century Italy." In *Women, Gender, and Enlightenment*, edited by Sarah Knott and Barbara Taylor, 265–87. New York: Palgrave Macmillan,2005.

Foucault, Michel. "Governmentality." In *The Foucault Effect: Studies in Governmentality*, edited by Graham Burchell, Colin Gordon, and Peter Miller, 87–104. Chicago: University of Chicago Press, 1991.

Frieden, Nancy Mandelker. "Child Care: Medical Reform in a Traditionalist Culture." In *The Family in Imperial Russia: New Lines of Historical Research*, edited by David Ransel, 236–59. Urbana: University of Illinois Press, 1978.

———. *Russian Physicians in an Era of Reform and Revolution, 1856–1905*. Princeton, NJ: Princeton University Press, 1981.

Friedman, Rebecca. *Masculinity, Autocracy, and the Russian University, 1804–1863*. New York: Palgrave Macmillan, 2005.

Friedman, Susan Stanford. "Women's Autobiographical Selves: Theory and Practice." In *The Private Self: Theory and Practice in Women's Autobiographical Writings*, edited by Shari Benstock, 34–62. Chapel Hill: University of North Carolina Press, 1988.

Furdell, Elizabeth Lane. *Publishing and Medicine in Early Modern England*. Rochester, NY: University of Rochester Press, 2002.

Galenkovskii, P. A. *Vospitanie iunoshestva v proshlom: Istoricheskii ocherk pedagogicheskikh sredstv pri vospitanii v voenno-uchebnykh zavedeniiakh*. St. Petersburg, 1904.

Gelbart, Nina Rattner. *The King's Midwife: A History and Mystery of Madame du Coudray*. Berkeley: University of California Press, 1998.

Gerasimov, Ilya, Sergey Glebov, Jan Kusber, Marina Mogilner, and Alexander Semyonov. "New Imperial History and the Challenges of Empire." In *Empire Speaks Out: Languages of Rationalization and Self-Description in the Russian Empire*, edited by Ilya Gerasimov, Jan Kusber, and Alexander Semyonov, 3–32. Leiden, 2009.

Geyer-Kordesch, Johanna. "German Medical Education in the Eighteenth Century: Prussian Context and Its Influence." In *William Hunter and the Eighteenth-Century Medical World*, edited by W. F. Bynum and Roy Porter, 177–205. New York: Cambridge University Press, 1985.

Gillis, John R. "Epilogue." In *Designing Modern Childhoods: History, Space, and the Material Culture of Children*, edited by Marta Gutman and Ning de Coninck-Smith, 316–30. New Brunswick, NJ: Rutgers University Press, 2008.

Glagoleva, Olga E. *Dream and Reality of Russian Provincial Young Ladies, 1700–1850*. Pittsburgh, PA: Center for Russian and Eastern European Studies, University of Pittsburgh, 2000.

Gleason, Walter. *Moral Idealists, Bureaucracy, and Catherine the Great*. New Brunswick, NJ: Rutgers University Press, 1981.

Goodman, Dena. "Enlightenment Salons: The Convergence of Female and Philosophic Ambitions." In *The Enlightenment*, edited by Dena Goodman and Kathleen Wellman, 96–105. Boston: Houghton Mifflin, 2004.

———. "L'Ortografe des Dames: Gender and Language in the Old Regime." In *Women, Gender, and Enlightenment*, edited by Sarah Knott and Barbara Taylor, 195–223. New York: Palgrave Macmillan, 2005.

———. *The Republic of Letters: A Cultural History of the French Enlightenment*. Ithaca, NY: Cornell University Press, 1994.

Goodman, Dena, and Kathleen Anne Wellman, eds. *The Enlightenment*. Boston, MA: Houghton Mifflin, 2004.

Gorshkov, Boris. *Russia's Factory Children: State, Society, and Law, 1800–1917*. Pittsburgh, PA: University of Pittsburgh Press, 2009.

Goscilo, Helena. "Cosmetics—or Dying to Overcome Nature in an Age of Art and Artifice." In *Women and Gender in Eighteenth-Century Russia*, edited by Wendy Rosslyn, 73–104. Burlington, VT: Ashgate, 2003.

Green, Monica H. "Gendering the History of Women's Healthcare." *Gender and History* 20, no. 3 (November 2008): 487–518.

Greene, Diana. "Mid-Nineteenth-Century Domestic Ideology in Russia." In *Women and Russian Culture: Projections and Self-Perceptions*, edited by Rosalind Marsh, 78–97. New York: Berghahn Books, 1998.

Griffiths, David M. "Eighteenth-Century Perceptions of Backwardness: Projects for the Creation of a Third Estate in Catherinian Russia." *Canadian-American Slavic Studies* 13, no. 4 (Winter 1979): 452–72.

Grombakh, S. M. *Russkaia meditsinskaia literatura XVIII veka*. Moscow, 1953.

Grossmann, Atina. "Feminist Debates about Women and National Socialism." *Gender and History* 3 (Autumn 1991): 350–58.

Grundy, Isobel. "Sarah Stone: Enlightenment Midwife." In *Medicine in the Enlightenment*, edited by Roy Porter, 128–44. Amsterdam, 1995.

Gutman, Marta, and Ning de Coninck-Smith, eds. *Designing Modern Childhoods: History, Space, and the Material Culture of Children*. New Brunswick, NJ: Rutgers University Press, 2008.

Habermas, Jürgen. *The Structural Transformation of the Public Sphere: An Inquiry into a Category of Bourgeois Society*. Cambridge, MA: MIT Press, 1989.

Hamlin, David. "The Structures of Toy Consumption: Bourgeois Domesticity and Demand for Toys in Nineteenth-Century Germany." *Journal of Social History* 36, no. 4 (2003): 857–69.

Harley, David. "Provincial Midwives in England: Lancashire and Cheshire, 1660–1760." In *The Art of Midwifery: Early Modern Midwives in Europe*, edited by Hilary Marland, 27–48. New York: Routledge, 1993.

Heathorn, Stephen. *For Home, Country, and Race: Constructing Gender, Class, and Englishness in the Elementary School, 1880–1914*. Toronto: University of Toronto Press, 2000.

Hecht, Jacqueline. "From 'Be Fruitful and Multiply' to Family Planning: The Enlightenment Transition." *Eighteenth-Century Studies* 32, no. 4 (1999): 536–51.

Hesse, Carla. "Introduction: Women Intellectuals in the Enlightened Republic of Letters." In *Women, Gender, and Enlightenment*, edited by Sarah Knott and Barbara Fisher, 259–64. New York: Palgrave Macmillan, 2005.

Heywood, Colin. "*Centuries of Childhood*: An Anniversary—and an Epitaph?" *Journal of the History of Childhood and Youth* 3, no. 3 (2010): 343–65.

Hobsbawm, Eric, and T. O. Ranger. *The Invention of Tradition*. New York: Cambridge University Press, 1983.

Hubbs, Joanna. *Mother Russia: The Feminine Myth in Russian Culture*. Bloomington: Indiana University Press, 1988.

Hughes, Lindsey. *Russia in the Age of Peter the Great*. New Haven, CT: Yale University Press, 1998.

Huisman, Tim. *The Finger of God: Anatomical Practice in Seventeenth-Century Leiden*. Leiden, 2009.

Hunt, Lynn, ed. *Eroticism and the Body Politic*. Baltimore: Johns Hopkins University Press, 1991.

———. *The Family Romance of the French Revolution*. Berkeley: University of California Press, 1992.

Jackson, Mark. "Developing Medical Expertise: Medical Practitioners and the Suspected Murders of New-Born Children." In *Medicine in the Enlightenment*, edited by Roy Porter, 145–65. Amsterdam, 1995.

Jacobus, Mary, Evelyn Fox Keller, and Sally Shuttleworth, eds. *Body/Politics: Women and the Discourses of Science*. New York: Routledge, 1990.

Jelavich, Barbara. *History of the Balkans: Eighteenth and Nineteenth Centuries*. New York: Cambridge University Press, 1983.

Jennings, Jeremy. "The Debate about Luxury in Eighteenth- and Nineteenth-Century French Political Thought." *Journal of the History of Ideas* 68, no. 1 (January 2007): 79–105.

Jones, Vivien. "Advice and Enlightenment: Mary Wollstonecraft and Sex Education." In *Women, Gender, and Enlightenment*, edited by Sarah Knott and Barbara Taylor, 140–55. New York: Palgrave Macmillan, 2005.

———. "The Death of Mary Wollstonecraft." *Journal for Eighteenth-Century Studies* 20, no. 2 (September 1997): 187–205.

Jordanova, Ludmilla. *Nature Displayed: Gender, Science, and Medicine, 1760–1820*. London, 1999.

Kaiser, Daniel H. "The Poor and Disabled in Early Eighteenth-Century Russian Towns." *Journal of Social History* 32, no. 1 (Autumn 1998): 125–55.

Keller, Eve. *Generating Bodies and Gendered Selves: The Rhetoric of Reproduction in Early Modern England*. Seattle: University of Washington Press, 2006.

Kelly, Catriona. *Children's World: Growing Up in Russia, 1890–1991*. New Haven, CT: Yale University Press, 2007.

———. *A History of Russian Women's Writing: 1820–1992*. Oxford, 1994.

———. *Refining Russia: Advice Literature, Polite Culture, and Gender from Catherine to Yeltsin*. Oxford, 2001.

Kerber, Linda. *Women of the Republic: Intellect and Ideology in Revolutionary America*. Chapel Hill: University of North Carolina Press, 1980.

Khan'kovich, A. "Baron Georg Tomas fon Ash." In *Nemtsy v Sankt-Peterburge (XVIII–XX veka): Biograf4cheskii aspekt*, edited by T. A. Schrader, 3:48–60. St. Petersburg, 2005.

Khodnev, A. I. *Istoriia Imperatorskago Vol'nogo Ekonomicheskago Obshchestva s 1765 do 1865 goda.* St. Petersburg, 1865.

King, Helen. *Midwifery, Obstetrics and the Rise of Gynaecology: The Uses of a Sixteenth-Century Compendium.* Aldershot, UK, 2007.

King, Margaret L. "Concepts of Childhood: What We Know and Where We Might Go." *Renaissance Quarterly* 60, no. 2 (Summer 2007): 371–407.

Kirschenbaum, Lisa A. *Small Comrades: Revolutionizing Childhood in Soviet Russia, 1917–1932.* New York: RoutledgeFalmer, 2001.

Kivelson, Valerie. "Merciful Father, Impersonal State: Russian Autocracy in Comparative Perspective." *Modern Asian Studies* 31, no. 3 (July 1997): 635–63.

Kliuchevskii, V. O. "Dva Vospitanii." *Russkaia Mysl'* 14, no. 3 (1893): 79–99.

———. "Two Childhoods." Translated by Max Okenfuss. *History of Education Quarterly* 17 (Winter 1977): 417–47.

Knott, Sarah, and Barbara Taylor, eds. *Women, Gender, and Enlightenment.* New York: Palgrave Macmillan, 2005.

Kopanev, N. A. "Rasprostranenie frantsuzskoi knigi v Moskve v seredine XVIII veka." In *Frantsuzskaia kniga v Rossii XVIII veka: Ocherki istorii,* edited by S. P. Luppov, 59–173. Leningrad, 1986.

Kovrigina, V. A., E. K. Sysoeva, and D. N. Shanskii. "Meditsina i zdravookhranenie." In *Ocherki russkoi kultury XVIII veka,* edited by B. A. Rybakov, 3:50–84. Moscow, 1988.

Kurmacheva, M. D. "Problemy obrazovaniia v ulozhennoi komissii 1767 g." In *Dvorianstvo i krepostnoi stroi Rossii XVI–XVIII vv: Sbornik statei, posviashchennyi pamiati Alekseia Andreevicha Novosel'skogo,* edited by N. I. Pavlenko, 240–64. Moscow, 1975.

Kusber, Jan. "Governance, Education, and the Problems of Empire in the Age of Catherine II." In *Empire Speaks Out: Languages of Rationalization and Self-Description in the Russian Empire,* edited by Ilya Gerasimov, Jan Kusber, and Alexander Semyonov, 59–88. Leiden, 2009.

———. "Individual, Subject, and Empire: Toward a Discourse on Upbringing, Education, and Schooling in the Time of Catherine II." *Ab Imperio,* no. 2 (2008): 125–56.

Laqueur, Thomas Walter. *Making Sex: Body and Gender from the Greeks to Freud.* Cambridge, MA: Harvard University Press, 1990.

Latour, Bruno. *Science in Action: How to Follow Scientists and Engineers through Society.* Cambridge, MA: Harvard University Press, 1988.

Lavrovskii, N. A. *O pedagogicheskom znachenii sochinenii Ekateriny Velikoi.* Kharkov, 1856.

Leckey, Colum. *Patrons of the Enlightenment: The Free Economic Society in Eighteenth-Century Russia.* Newark, DE: University of Delaware Press, 2011.

Levin, Eve. "Childbirth in Pre-Petrine Russia: Canon Law and Popular Traditions." In *Russia's Women: Accommodation, Resistance, Transformation,* edited by Barbara Evans Clements, Barbara Alpern Engel, and Christine D. Worobec, 44–59. Berkeley: University of California Press, 1991.

———. *Sex and Society in the World of the Orthodox Slavs, 900–1700.* Ithaca, NY: Cornell University Press, 1989.

Levitt, Marcus C. *Early Modern Russian Letters: Texts and Contexts.* Boston: Academic Studies Press, 2009.

Likhacheva, E. *Materialy dlia istorii zhenskogo obrazovanii v Rossii (1086–1796).* St. Petersburg, 1890.

Lindemann, Mary. "Professionals? Sisters? Rivals? Midwives in Braunschweig, 1750–1800." In *The Art of Midwifery: Early Modern Midwives in Europe,* edited by Hilary Marland, 176–91. New York: Routledge, 1993.

Lindenmeyr, Adele. "Public Life, Private Virtues: Women in Russian Charity, 1762–1914." *Signs: Journal of Women in Culture and Society* 18, no. 3 (1993): 562–91.

Lotman, Iurii. *Besedy o russkoi ku'lture: Byt' i traditsii russkogo dvorianstva (XVIII–nachalo XIX veka).* St. Petersburg, 1994.

———. "The Poetics of Everyday Behavior in Russian Eighteenth-Century Culture." In *The Semiotics of Russian Culture,* edited by Iurii Lotman and B. A. Uspenskii, 239–56. Ann Arbor: Department of Slavic Languages and Literatures, University of Michigan, 1984.

Lougee, Carolyn. "*Noblesse,* Domesticity, and Social Reform: The Education of Girls by Fenelon and Saint-Cyr." *History of Education Quarterly* 14 (Spring 1974): 87–113.

Löwy, Ilana. "Labeled Bodies: Classification of Diseases and the Medical Way of Knowing." *History of Science* 49, no. 3 (September 2011): 299–315.

Maikov, P. M. *Ivan Ivanovich Betskoi: Opyt' ego biografii.* St. Petersburg, 1904.

Maklakova, I. P. "Reformy obrazovaniia vtoroi poloviny XVIII veka." In *Otechestvennaia istoriia: Liudi, sobytiia, mysl',* edited by A. A. Sevast'ianova, 95–106. Riazan', 1998.

Makogonenko, G. P. *Nikolai Novikov i russkoe prosveshchenie XVIII veka.* Moscow, 1951.

Marker, Gary. "Faith and Secularity in Eighteenth-Century Russian Literacy, 1700–1775." In *Christianity and the Eastern Slavs.* Vol. 2 of *Russian Culture in Modern Times,* edited by Robert P. Hughes and Irina Paperno, 3–24. Berkeley: University of California Press, 1994.

———. "God of Our Mothers: Reflections on Lay Female Spirituality in Late Eighteenth- and Early Nineteenth-Century Russia." In *Orthodox Russia: Belief and Practice under the Tsars,* edited by Valerie Kivelson and Robert H. Greene, 193–210. University Park: Pennsylvania State University Press, 2003.

———. *Publishing, Printing, and the Origins of Intellectual Life in Russia, 1700–1800.* Princeton, NJ: Princeton University Press, 1985.

Markova, O. P. "O proiskhozhdenii tak nazyvaemogo Grecheskogo Proekta (80-e gody XVIII v.)." *Istoriia SSSR,* no. 4 (July 1958): 52–78.

Marland, Hilary, ed. *The Art of Midwifery: Early Modern Midwives in Europe.* New York: Routledge, 1993.

———. "The '*Burgurlijke*' Midwife: The *Stadsvroedvrouw* of Eighteenth-Century Holland." In *The Art of Midwifery: Early Modern Midwives in Europe,* edited by Hilary Marland, 193–213. New York: Routledge, 1993.

Marrese, Michelle Lamarche. "'The Poetics of Everyday Behavior' Revisited: Lotman, Gender, and the Evolution of Russian Noble Identity." *Kritika: Explorations in Russian and Eurasian History* 11, no. 4 (Fall 2010): 701–39.

———. *A Woman's Kingdom: Noblewomen and the Control of Property in Russia, 1700–1861*. Ithaca, NY: Cornell University Press, 2002.

Maynes, Mary Jo, Birgitte Soland, and Christina Benninghaus, eds. *Secret Gardens, Satanic Mills: Placing Girls in European History, 1750–1960*. Bloomington: Indiana University Press, 2004.

McCleary, Cindy. *The Satirical Gaze: Prints of Women in Late Eighteenth-Century England*. New York: Oxford University Press, 2004.

McKenna, Kevin J. "Empress behind the Mask: The Persona of Mme. Vsiakaia Vsiachina in Catherine the Great's Periodical Essays on Morals and Manners." *Neophilologus* 7 (1990): 1–11.

McLaren, Angus. "A Doctor in the House: Medicine and Private Morality in France, 1800–1850." *Feminist Studies* 2, no. 2/3 (1975): 39–54.

McTavish, Liane. *Childbirth and the Display of Authority in Early Modern France*. Burlington, VT: Ashgate, 2005.

Meckel, Richard Alan. "Childhood and the Historians: A Review Essay." *Journal of Family History* 9 (Winter 1984): 415–24.

Merchant, Carolyn. *The Death of Nature: Women, Ecology, and the Scientific Revolution*. San Francisco: Harper & Row, 1980.

Miliukov, Pavel. "Educational Reforms." In *Catherine the Great: A Profile*, edited by Marc Raeff, 93–112. New York: Hill and Wang, 1972.

Miller, Alexei. *The Romanov Empire and Nationalism: Essays in the Methodology of Historical Research*. Translated by Serguei Dobrynin. Budapest, 2008.

Mitchell, Harvey. "Rationality and Control in French Eighteenth-Century Medical Views of the Peasantry." *Comparative Studies in Society and History* 21 (January 1979): 82–112.

Mitchell, Sally. *The New Girl: Girls' Culture in England, 1880–1915*. New York: Columbia University Press, 1995.

Moring, Beatrice. "Motherhood, Milk, and Money: Infant Mortality in Pre-Industrial Finland." *Social History of Medicine* 11, no. 2 (1998): 177–96.

Müller, Anja. *Fashioning Childhood in the Eighteenth Century: Age and Identity*. Burlington, VT: Ashgate, 2006.

Newlin, Thomas. *The Voice in the Garden: Andrei Bolotov and the Anxieties of Russian Pastoral, 1738–1833*. Evanston, IL: Northwestern University Press, 2001.

Nikitin, Aleksandr. *Kratkii obzor sostoianiia meditsiny v Rossii v tsarstvovanie Imperatritsy Ekateriny II*. St. Petersburg, 1855.

Nussbaum, Felicity. "Eighteenth-Century Women's Autobiographical Commonplaces." In *The Private Self: Theory and Practice in Women's Autobiographical Writings*, edited by Shari Benstock, 147–72. Chapel Hill: University of North Carolina Press, 1988.

Okenfuss, Max J. *The Discovery of Childhood in Russia: The Evidence of the Slavic Primer*. Newtonville, MA: Oriental Research Partners, 1980.

———. "Education and Empire: School Reform in Enlightened Russia." *Jahrbücher für Geschichte Osteuropas* 27, no. 1 (1979): 41–68.

Orr, Clarissa Campbell. "Aristocratic Feminism, the Learned Governess, and the Republic of Letters." In *Women, Gender, and Enlightenment*, edited by Sarah Knott and Barbara Taylor, 306–25. New York: Palgrave Macmillan, 2005.

Ortiz, Teresa. "From Hegemony to Subordination: Midwives in Early Modern Spain." In *The Art of Midwifery: Early Modern Midwives in Europe*, edited by Hilary Marland, 95–114. New York: Routledge, 1993.

Palkin, B. N. "Gubernskaia reforma 1775 g. i organizatsiia grazhdanskoi meditsiny v Rossii." *Sovetskoe zdravookhranenie*, no. 9 (1983): 66–70.

———. *K istorii russkoi meditsiny XVIII veka*. Alma-Ata, 1953.

Pateman, Carol. *The Sexual Contract*. Stanford, CA: Stanford University Press, 1988.

Peruga, Mónica Bolufer. "Introduction: Gender and the Reasoning Mind." In *Women, Gender, and Enlightenment*, edited by Sarah Knott and Barbara Taylor, 189–94. New York: Palgrave Macmillan, 2005.

Petrov, B. D. *Ocherki istorii otechestvennoi meditsiny*. Moscow, 1962.

Pokrovskaia, A. K., and N. V. Chekhov, eds. *Materialy po istorii russkoi detskoi literatury, 1750–1855*. Moscow, 1927.

Popiel, Jennifer. "'Education Is but Habit': Childhood, Individuality, and Self-Control in France, 1762–1833." PhD diss., University of Pennsylvania, 2000.

———. "Making Mothers: The Advice Genre and the Domestic Ideal, 1760–1830." *Journal of Family History* 29, no. 4 (October 2004): 339–50.

Porter, Roy. *The Greatest Benefit to Mankind: A Medical History of Humanity*. New York: W. W. Norton, 1997.

———. "A Touch of Danger: The Man-Midwife as Sexual Predator." In *Sexual Underworlds of the Enlightenment*, edited by G. R. Rousseau and Roy Porter, 206–24. Chapel Hill: University of North Carolina Press, 1988.

Poska, Allyson M. "Babies on Board: Women, Children, and Imperial Policy in the Spanish Empire." *Gender and History* 22, no. 2 (August 2010): 269–83.

Pouncy, Carolyn Johnston, ed. and trans. Introduction to *The Domostroi: Rules for Russian Households in the Time of Ivan the Terrible*, 1–54. Ithaca, NY: Cornell University Press, 1994.

Pratt, Mary Louise. *Imperial Eyes: Travel Writing and Transculturation*. New York: Routledge, 1992.

Pushkareva, Natal'ia. *Chastnaia zhizn' russkoi zhenshchiny: Nevesta, zhena, liubovnitsa*. Moscow, 1997.

———. "Materinstvo i materinskoe vospitanie v rossiiskikh sem'iakh XVIII–nachala XIX v." *Rasy i narody* 25 (1998): 104–24.

———. "Russian Noblewomen's Education in the Home as Revealed in Late Eighteenth- and Early Nineteenth-Century Memoirs." In *Women and Gender in Eighteenth-Century Russia*, edited by Wendy Rosslyn, 111–28. Burlington, VT: Ashgate, 2003.

———. *Women in Russian History: From the Tenth to the Twentieth Century*. Translated and edited by Eve Levin. Armonk, NY: M. E. Sharpe, 1997.

Raeff, Marc. "The Emergence of the Russian European: Russia as a Full Partner of Europe." In *Russia Engages the World, 1453–1825*, edited by Cynthia Hyla Whittaker,

Edward Kasinec, and Robert H. Davis, 118–37. Cambridge, MA: Harvard University Press, 2003.

———. "Imperial Policies of Catherine II." In *Major Problems in the History of Imperial Russia*, edited by James Cracraft, 234–43. Lexington, MA: D. C. Heath, 1993.

———. *Origins of the Russian Intelligentsia: The Eighteenth-Century Nobility*. New York: Harcourt, Brace, and World, 1966.

———, ed. *Russian Intellectual History: An Anthology*. New York: Harcourt, Brace, and World, 1966.

———. "The Well-Ordered Police State and the Development of Modernity in Seventeenth- and Eighteenth-Century Europe: An Attempt at a Comparative Approach." *American Historical Review* 80 (December 1975): 1221–43.

Ramer, Samuel C. "Childbirth and Culture: Midwifery in the Nineteenth-Century Russian Countryside." In *The Family in Imperial Russia: New Lines of Historical Research*, edited by David L. Ransel, 218–35. Urbana: University of Illinois Press, 1978.

———. "Who Was the Russian Feldsher?" *Bulletin of the History of Medicine* 50, no. 2 (1976): 213–25.

Ransel, David L., ed. *The Family in Imperial Russia: New Lines of Historical Research*. Urbana: University of Illinois Press, 1978.

———. *Mothers of Misery: Child Abandonment in Russia*. Princeton, NJ: Princeton University Press, 1988.

Reinarz, Jonathan. "The Transformation of Medical Education in Eighteenth-Century England: International Developments and the West Midlands." *History of Education* 37, no. 4 (July 2008): 549–66.

Reinier, Jacqueline S. "Rearing the Republican Child: Attitudes and Practices in Post-Revolutionary Philadelphia." *William and Mary Quarterly* 39 (January 1982): 150–63.

Rendall, Jane. "'Women That Would Plague Me with Rational Conversation': Aspiring Women and Scottish Whigs, c. 1790–1830." In *Women, Gender, and Enlightenment*, edited by Sarah Knott and Barbara Taylor, 326–48. New York: Palgrave Macmillan, 2005.

Renner, Andreas. "The Concept of the Scientific Revolution and the History of Science in Russia." In *Eighteenth-Century Russia: Society, Culture, Economy; Papers from the VII International Conference on the Study Group of Eighteenth-Century Russia, Wittenberg 2004*, edited by Roger Bartlett and Gabriela Lehmann-Carli, 357–72. Berlin, 2007.

Rieder, Philip, and Micheline Louis-Courvoisier. "Enlightened Physicians: Setting Out on an Elite Medical Career in the Second Half of the Eighteenth Century." *Bulletin of the History of Medicine* 84, no. 4 (Winter 2010): 578–606.

Rogger, Hans. *National Consciousness in Eighteenth-Century Russia*. Cambridge, MA: Harvard University Press, 1960.

Rosslyn, Wendy, ed. *Women and Gender in Eighteenth-Century Russia*. Burlington, VT: Ashgate, 2003.

Rosslyn, Wendy, and Alessandra Tosi, eds. *Women in Russian Culture and Society, 1700–1825*. Basingstoke, UK, 2007.

Salmon, Marylynn. "The Cultural Significance of Breastfeeding and Infant Care in Early Modern England and America." *Journal of Social History* 28 (Winter 1994): 247–60.

Schiebinger, Londa. *Nature's Body: Gender in the Making of Modern Science.* Boston: Beacon Press, 1993.

———. "Why Mammals are Called Mammals: Gender Politics in Eighteenth-Century Natural History." *American Historical Review* 98, no. 2 (April 1993): 382–411.

Schönle, Andreas. "Garden of the Empire: Catherine's Appropriation of the Crimea." *Slavic Review* 60, no. 1 (Spring 2001): 1–23.

———. "The Scare of the Self: Sentimentalism, Privacy, and Private Life in Russian Culture, 1780–1820." *Slavic Review* 57, no. 4 (Winter 1998): 723–46.

Schrader, Abby M. "Unruly Felons and Civilizing Wives: Cultivating Marriage in the Siberian Exile System, 1822–1860." *Slavic Review* 66, no. 2 (Summer 2007): 230–56.

Schulte, Regina, ed. *The Body of the Queen: Gender and Rule in the Courtly World, 1500–2000.* New York: Berghahn Books, 2006.

Schulze, Ludmilla. "The Russification of the St. Petersburg Academy of Sciences and Arts in the Eighteenth Century." *British Journal for the History of Science* 18, no. 60 (November 1985): 305–35.

Scott, Joan Wallach. *Gender and the Politics of History.* New York: Columbia University Press, 1988.

Sewell, Jane Eliot. *Cesarean Section: A Brief History.* Washington, DC: The American College of Obstetricians and Gynecologists, 1993.

Shorter, Edward. "The Management of Normal Deliveries and the Generation of William Hunter." In *William Hunter and the Eighteenth-Century Medical World*, edited by W. F. Bynum and Roy Porter, 371–84. New York: Cambridge University Press, 1985.

Simonton, Deborah. "Earning and Learning: Girlhood in Pre-Industrial Europe." *Women's History Review* 13, no. 3 (September 2004): 363–86.

Slezkine, Yuri. "Naturalists versus Nations: Eighteenth-Century Russian Scholars Confront Ethnic Diversity." In *Russia's Orient: Imperial Borderlands and Peoples, 1700–1917*, edited by Daniel R. Brower and Edward J. Lazzerini, 27–57. Bloomington: Indiana University Press, 1997.

Smith, Douglas. "Freemasonry and the Public in Eighteenth-Century Russia." In *Imperial Russia: New Histories for the Empire*, edited by Jane Burbank and David L. Ransel, 281–304. Bloomington: Indiana University Press, 1998.

———. *Working the Rough Stone: Freemasonry and Society in Eighteenth-Century Russia.* DeKalb: Northern Illinois University Press, 1999.

Smith, Ginnie. "Prescribing the Rules of Health: Self-Help and Advice in the Late Eighteenth Century." In *Patients and Practitioners: Lay Perceptions of Medicine in Pre-Industrial Society*, edited by Roy Porter, 249–82. New York: Cambridge University Press, 2003.

Sorokin, Iu. S., ed. *Slovar' Russkogo iazyka XVIII veka.* 4th ed. Leningrad, 1988.

Staniukovich, T. V. *Kunstkamera Peterburgskoi Akademii Nauk.* St. Petersburg, 1953.

Steinbrügge, Leiselotte. "The Moral Sex." In *The Enlightenment*, edited by Dena Goodman and Kathleen Wellman, 178–83. Boston: Houghton Mifflin, 2004.

Stoler, Ann. "A Sentimental Education: Children on the Imperial Divide." In *Carnal
Knowledge and Imperial Power: Race and the Intimate in Colonial Rule*, 112–39. Berkeley: University of California Press, 2002.

Sussman, George D. *Selling Mothers' Milk: The Wet-Nursing Business in France, 1715–
1914*. Urbana: University of Illinois Press, 1982.

Svodnyi katalog russkoi knigi grazhdanskoi pechati XVIII veka, 1725–1800. 5 vols. Moscow,
1962–67.

Terrall, Mary. "Metaphysics, Mathematics, and the Gendering of Science in Eighteenth-
Century France." In *The Enlightenment*, edited by Dena Goodman and Kathleen
Wellman, 138–45. Boston: Houghton Mifflin, 2004.

Theré, Christine. "Women and Birth Control in Eighteenth-Century France." *Eighteenth-
Century Studies* 32, no. 4 (1999): 552–64.

Thŷret, Isolde. *Between God and Tsar: Religious Symbolism and the Royal Women of Muscovite Russia*. DeKalb: Northern Illinois University Press, 2001.

———. "'Blessed Is the Tsaritsa's Womb': The Myth of Miraculous Birth and Royal
Motherhood in Muscovite Russia." *Russian Review* 53, no. 4 (1994): 479–96.

Tovrov, Jessica. *The Russian Noble Family: Structure and Change*. New York: Garland,
1987.

Valitskaia, A. P. *Dmitrii Grigor'evich Levitskii, 1735–1822*. Leningrad, 1985.

Vallone, Lynne. *Disciplines of Virtue: Girls' Culture in the Eighteenth and Nineteenth Centuries*. New Haven, CT: Yale University Press, 1995.

Voegelin, Eric. *From Enlightenment to Revolution*. Durham, NC: Duke University Press,
1975.

Vucinich, Alexander. *Science in Russian Culture: A History to 1860*. Stanford, CA: Stanford University Press, 1963.

Wagner, Peter. "The Discourse on Sex—or Sex as Discourse: Eighteenth-Century
Medical and Paramedical Erotica." In *Sexual Underworlds of the Enlightenment*,
edited by G. S. Rousseau and Roy Porter, 46–68. Chapel Hill: University of North
Carolina Press, 1988.

Wakefield, Andre. *The Disordered Police State: German Cameralism as Science and Practice*. Chicago: University of Chicago Press, 2009.

Walicki, Andrzej. *A History of Russian Thought from the Enlightenment to Marxism*.
Translated by Hilda Andrews-Rusiecka. Stanford, CA: Stanford University Press,
1979.

Walker, Franklin A. "Enlightenment and Religion in Russian Education in the Reign
of Tsar Alexander I." *History of Education Quarterly* 32, no. 3 (Autumn 1992): 343–60.

Waters, Elizabeth. "The Modernization of Russian Motherhood, 1917–1937." *Soviet
Studies* 44, no. 1 (1992): 123–35.

Werrett, Simon. "Potemkin and the Panopticon: Samuel Bentham and the Architecture of Absolutism in Eighteenth-Century Russia." *Journal of Bentham Studies* 2
(1999): 1–25.

White, John S. "William Harvey and the Primacy of the Blood." *Annals of Science* 43, no. 3 (May 1986): 239–55.

Whittaker, Cynthia Hyla. "The Idea of Autocracy among Eighteenth-Century Historians." *Russian Review* 55 (April 1996): 149–71.

Wiesner, Merry E. "The Midwives of South Germany and the Public/Private Dichotomy." In *The Art of Midwifery: Early Modern Midwives in Europe*, edited by Hilary Marland, 77–78. New York: Routledge, 1993.

Wilson, Adrian. "Participant or Patient? Seventeenth-Century Childbirth from the Mother's Point of View." In *Patients and Practitioners: Lay Perceptions of Medicine in Pre-Industrial Society*, edited by Roy Porter, 129–44. New York: Cambridge University Press, 1985.

———. "William Hunter and the Varieties of Man-Midwifery." In *William Hunter and the Eighteenth-Century Medical World*, edited by W. F. Bynum and Roy Porter, 343–70. New York: Cambridge University Press, 1985.

Wirtschafter, Elise Kimerling. *The Play of Ideas in Russian Enlightenment Theater.* DeKalb: Northern Illinois University Press, 2003.

———. "Religion and Enlightenment in Eighteenth-Century Russia: Father Platon at the Court of Catherine II." *Slavonic and East European Review* 88, nos. 1–2 (January 2010): 180–203.

———. "Thoughts on the Enlightenment and Enlightenment in Russia." *Journal of Modern Russian History and Historiography* 2, no. 2 (January 2009): 1–26.

Wolff, Larry. *Inventing Eastern Europe: The Map of Civilization on the Mind of the Enlightenment.* Stanford, CA: Stanford University Press, 1994.

Wortman, Richard. "The Russian Empress as Mother." In *The Family in Imperial Russia: New Lines of Historical Research*, edited by David L. Ransel, 60–74. Urbana: University of Illinois Press, 1978.

———. *Scenarios of Power: Myth and Ceremony in Russian Monarchy.* Princeton, NJ: Princeton University Press, 1995.

Yarmolinsky, Avrahm. *Road to Revolution: A Century of Russian Radicalism.* Princeton, NJ: Princeton University Press, 1986.

Yaroshevski, Don. "Empire and Citizenship." In *Russia's Orient: Imperial Borderlands and Peoples*, edited by Daniel R. Brower and Edward J. Lazzerini, 58–79. Bloomington: Indiana University Press, 1997.

Young, John Harley. *Cæsarean Section: The History and Development of the Operation from Earliest Times.* London, 1944.

Index

Note: *Page numbers in italics indicate figures.*

Academy of Arts, 96, 98–99

Academy of Sciences: "commercial consciousness" emerging at, 15; director of (*see* Dashkova, Ekaterina); establishment of, 96; fetal development studied at, 30; need for Russian academics at, 109; training for academics in, 33. *See also* medical bureaucracy; Medical Collegium

accoucheurs: appointments as, in Russia, 45–46, 154; in France, 27, 32; in gender hierarchy, 149; on lessening girls' modesty, 139; manual translated by, 47. *See also* man-midwifery; midwifery tools

advice literature: changing attitudes toward child development in, 14–15; on child rearing for nobility then for other parents, 22–23; conduct manuals, 14–15, 110–11, 139–40; home health manuals, 16, 18, 76; household manuals, 14, 56; legitimacy constructed in, 147–48; men addressed in, 76–77; paradox in advice for girls, 118–19; surge in child rearing topics, 16, 18; wet nurses referenced in, 56; women as subject and audience for, 76. *See also* reading public; reformers

akusherstvo, translation of, 28–29. *See also* accoucheurs; man-midwifery

alcohol, 80, 82, 111

Alembert, Jean le Rond d', 29

Alexander, John T., 7, 149

Alexander I, 103

alphabets, 16, 102, 103, 104

Alymova, Glafira, 133, 134, 135

anatomical theater, 47, 78

anatomy: circulatory system concept, 79, 176n13; female modesty and, 36, 50, 118–19, 130, 137–39; illustrations in manuals, 53; midwifery training in, 49–50; as necessary training, 30, 36

animals: degeneration thesis on, 83; infant feeding by, 66–67; infant milk from, 72, 74

Anna of Russia, 30–31

Ariès, Philippe, 4

The Art of Midwifery or the Science of Midwives' Affairs (Maksimovich-Ambodik): access to, 50; birthing beds illustrated, 52; on breast-feeding, 57–58; frontispiece and title page, 19, 53; goal in writing, 18; midwifery tools illustrated, 51; various bindings of, 171n120

Ash, Georg fon, 20, 90–91, 153, 178n67